MURTHA, WAR FIGHTER

Fighting for the Soul of America

Brad Clemenson and Jim Penna

outskirtspress
DENVER, COLORADO

The opinions expressed in this manuscript are solely the opinions of the author and do not represent the opinions or thoughts of the publisher. The author has represented and warranted full ownership and/or legal right to publish all the materials in this book.

Murtha, War Fighter
Fighting for the Soul of America
All Rights Reserved.
Copyright © 2012 Brad Clemenson and Jim Penna
v3.0

Cover Photo © 2012 Edward Mitchell. All rights reserved - used with permission.
Back cover photo taken by Marine Corps public affairs officer and thus in the public domain.
Most interior images are used by permission of Joyce Murtha, including photos of him in his youth, photos taken by military personnel are in the public domain. The John F. Kennedy Presidential Library and Museum, Boston, owns the Profile in Courage Award photo of Congressman Murtha, Caroline Kennedy and Edward Kennedy, May 22, 2008. Col. John Huygya, USMC-Ret., owns the photo of Congressman Murtha fly fishing, Jan. 1, 2008.

This book may not be reproduced, transmitted, or stored in whole or in part by any means, including graphic, electronic, or mechanical without the express written consent of the publisher except in the case of brief quotations embodied in critical articles and reviews.

Outskirts Press, Inc.
http://www.outskirtspress.com

ISBN: 978-1-4327-8699-1

Library of Congress Control Number: 2012902575

Outskirts Press and the "OP" logo are trademarks belonging to Outskirts Press, Inc.

PRINTED IN THE UNITED STATES OF AMERICA

This book is dedicated to the War Fighters – the brave men and women who have served and sacrificed so much for our country.

"Those that fail to learn from history are doomed to repeat it."
Winston Churchill

"To announce that there must be no criticism of the president, or that we are to stand by the President, right or wrong, is not only unpatriotic and servile, but is morally treasonable to the American public. Nothing but the truth should be spoken about him or anyone else. But it is even more important to tell the truth, pleasant or unpleasant, about him more than anyone else."
Theodore Roosevelt
Editorial in the Kansas City Star
May 7, 1918
A quote hung in Murtha's office

"The statutes don't make government work. They're nice statutes but they don't do anything. They guide you, but they're just there. It's the living people that make democracy and our government work."
Chris Matthews
Speaking about Jack Murtha

Table of Contents

About the Authors VII
Acknowledgements VIII

Preface:
Blood and Treasure X

Chapter 1
Character and Courage 1

Chapter 2
Almost Wild 10

Chapter 3
Whole New Ball Game 23

Chapter 4
Street Corner Guys 35

Chapter 5
Hawk 47

Chapter 6
The Warrior, Not the War 58

Chapter 7
Looks Like Rain 69

Chapter 8
9/11 79

Chapter 9
"Energize, Iraqatize and Internationalize" 91

Chapter 10
Rebuked and Ignored 101

Chapter 11
Political Payback 112

Chapter 12
Darby Rules of Engagement 127

Chapter 13
Troops, Torture and Twisted Words..135

Chapter 14
Mothers and Mission Accomplished..147

Chapter 15
November 17, 2005 160

Chapter 16
"Cowards Cut and Run"..170

Chapter 17
Mavericks, Renegades and Troublemakers...............................182

Chapter 18
Bush Bashing without the Bush 194

Chapter 19
In Cold Blood 204

Chapter 20
Swift Boaters and Basement Tapes...219

Chapter 21
Bringin' Down the House...230

Chapter 22
Civility and Results..241

Chapter 23
Race and Rock Ridge...255

Chapter 24
The Soul of America 267

About the Authors

Brad Clemenson first met Congressman Jack Murtha as a news reporter for the *Johnstown Tribune-Democrat*, where he worked for ten years. Clemenson then earned a masters degree in journalism with a focus on government at American University in Washington, DC. He became a Washington correspondent for Newhouse Newspapers. In 1990, Clemenson accepted a position as Murtha's communications director and was promoted to Murtha's district director in 2003. In 2007, he accepted a position with the Pennsylvania Environmental Council, where he coordinates the Laurel Highlands Conservation Landscape Initiative and Lift Johnstown. Clemenson has a bachelor's degree from Bucknell University, Lewisburg, Pennsylvania.

Jim Penna was a broadcaster and journalist in Johnstown and Pittsburgh, Pennsylvania, for over two decades. In 1999, he joined the news team at the FOX affiliate in the Altoona/Johnstown/State College market and, within a year, became news director. With his length of service, location within the 12th Congressional District represented by Murtha, and his specialization in government and politics, Penna interviewed Jack Murtha one-on-one more often than any other print or broadcast journalist. The two men spoke often about issues after the camera was off as well. Since 2010, Penna has served as district director to Congressman Mark Critz, Murtha's successor in Congress. Penna has a bachelor's degree in communications from Indiana University of Pennsylvania.

Acknowledgements

The first version of this book was written solely by Jim Penna and was finished literally just days before the death of Congressman John P. Murtha. Penna sought advice and suggestions from a number of people, including Brad Clemenson, who had worked for Murtha for 17 years. After talking with prospective publishers, Penna concluded that a lot more background was needed to articulate who Jack Murtha was and place the man more broadly within the times. In subsequent conversations, Clemenson agreed to fill in the missing information and flesh out the story. Ultimately, after three major re-writes had added substantial additional information and thoroughly re-worked the material, the co-authors agreed that Mr. Clemenson's name should appear first among the co-authors. Significant content in this book comes directly from their personal experiences working directly with Murtha and with others involved with Murtha's office and campaigns.

The book would not have happened without the help of many people.

Joyce Murtha, widow of Congressman Murtha, was enormously helpful in providing insights and information for this book, and in verifying, clarifying, and providing context for lots of information provided from other sources, including interviews with other people. Nobody knew Jack Murtha nearly as well as Joyce Murtha, and she was tremendously generous with her time in providing may clarifications and comments in reading two drafts of the book. She even corrected some information in Mr. Murtha's official biography.

Several members of Murtha's "Team," as he called his closest advisors, were also enormously helpful. They include David H. Morrison, who served as staff director for the Defense Appropriations Subcommittee; Gabrielle Carruth, who was Murtha's associate staff for Defense Appropriations; Charles T. Horner III, a veteran who was an Army appropriations liaison, special assistant to the undersecretary of defense comptroller, and Defense Appropriations staff assistant for Murtha; Danel R. Cunningham, a retired Army officer who was an Army budget liaison officer for congressional appropriations committees; and John G. Plashal, who served in the Marine Corps and Peace Corps, worked on the House Appropriations staff, and helped write Murtha's book, *From Vietnam to 9/11: On the Front Lines of National Security*.

Several former members of Murtha's congressional staff provided many insights and recollections. They include Col. John A. Hugya, U.S. Marine Corps, Ret., who knew Murtha from their days in the Marine Corps and served as Murtha's chief of staff; Cindy Abram; Patrick Alwine, Matthew Mazonkey, and Mary Kay Voyko.

Outside of the Murtha staff, we want to thank Chris Matthews of *Hardball*; House Minority Leader and former Speaker Nancy Pelosi; Congressmen Mike Doyle, Bob Brady, and Carol Shea-Porter, for their interviews; and Edward Mitchell of Edward Mitchell Communications, who was a Murtha campaign consultant for many campaigns; and the many other people who were interviewed for and/or quoted in this book.

Invaluable editing assistance was provided by Robin Strachan and Leslie Lehman-Clemenson. Additional editing assistance was provided by Hannah Clemenson. Graphic design assistance with the cover was provided by Kimberly Williams.

Finally, this book would not have been possible without the support of our wives, Leslie Lehman-Clemenson and Elizabeth Bolton Penna.

Preface:

Blood and Treasure

The patriotic, brassy crescendos of the local high school band stirred up the crowd of more than two hundred people who crammed into the big lobby of Highlands Hospital in the small city of Connellsville, Pennsylvania, to honor a local war hero.

On a cold January day in 2005, the crowd was so big that a speaker was set up outside for the people who spilled out around the front of the building and onto the grass.

Every branch of the service was represented, along with the American Legion, Veterans of Foreign Wars, and Vietnam Veterans of America. Veterans representing every war of the past century were there, including a man in his nineties.

Every dignitary in Fayette County and several from beyond were there to pay tribute, including the state senator, county commissioners, the mayor, and the adjutant from the local American Legion Post.

Congressman Jack Murtha was also there — not only to pay tribute, but also to present a Purple Heart to Salvador "Sam" Ross Jr., who had come home to Connellsville blind and without a foot that he had lost in Iraq.

Connellsville is a proud but humble community that has seen better days. The Pittsburgh coal seam was the most valuable mineral resource in U.S. history, centered on Connellsville, and conveniently located just an hour from the massive steel mills of Pittsburgh, which bought coke produced from coal by the trainload. The collapse of steel and coal in the 1970s and 1980s produced an exodus of people and economic challenges for those who remained.

Sam Ross was in many respects typical of the area. He was patriotic, had limited opportunities for work in Fayette County, and did what many people from low and moderate incomes did in struggling communities across the country: he enlisted in the Army.

A combat engineer with the 82nd Airborne Division, Ross was disposing of munitions near Baghdad, Iraq, on May 18, 2003. He was cradling a mine in a sand-filled shovel when something went wrong and the mine exploded.

"I remember seeing a black hole. The pain was so excruciating, my body just went numb," Ross told the local *Connellsville Daily Courier*.

He was blown into the air. Shards of metal and wire cut into his leg. Shrapnel blew off the right side of his eye, detaching his retina and damaging his optic nerve. He was given seventy-two hours to live and spent more than a month in a coma at Walter Reed Army Hospital, where he had more than a dozen surgeries, including amputation of the leg below the knee. He had some perception of light in his left eye, but otherwise was blind.

He was angry and bitter, and Jack Murtha tried to help.

Murtha was the first combat veteran of the Vietnam War to be elected to Congress. At the time, he had been in Congress for thirty-one years and was ranking member of the Defense Appropriations Subcommittee. He was a behind-the-scenes advisor to every Defense Secretary and, indeed, every president — both Republican and Democrat – since then-President Gerald R. Ford sent him to lead a congressional delegation to Vietnam in 1975. He had championed every military conflict during his tenure and garnered decisive votes from fellow Democrats on numerous occasions, including supporting the resolution for the 1991 Middle East War.

Murtha met Ross on one of his almost weekly visits to the

military hospitals of Walter Reed and Bethesda. As a constituent from Pennsylvania's 12th Congressional District, Murtha presented Ross with the Purple Heart while he was still in Walter Reed, and had arranged for the presentation to be repeated publicly back home to support and encourage Ross.

Murtha routinely used real examples of the difficulties that veterans faced to make his point about the sacrifices of the men and women in uniform and on several occasions spoke publicly about Ross.

"They did everything they could do for him in Walter Reed. And then he went home and his father was in jail," Murtha said. "His mother had not seen him. There was no one at home and he was by himself."

Murtha arranged an appointment for Ross to be assessed at Johns Hopkins Medical Center in hopes that at least some of Ross's vision might be restored. The effort failed, but that was not what angered Murtha.

"They started sending bills; collection agencies sent him bills! Imagine! He is by himself in his own home and a collection agency from Johns Hopkins sends him bills!" Murtha fumed, angry not only because of the bills, but also because they had been sent to a blind man who could not read the bills himself.

"Obviously we straightened it out, but that is the kind of thing that happens when you forget about the veteran," he fumed.

The bills were easy to straighten out, but the torment and loneliness of Sam Ross presented a far more difficult problem. Ross and other mangled war fighters tormented Jack Murtha, who wanted so much to give these heroes a better life. But with Ross having no father, mother, or other close family or friends around to help, there was only so much that Murtha could do.

Scheduling a big public celebration with the high school band, gifts, accolades from local dignitaries and the past national commander of the American Legion, and Murtha's pinning of the Purple Heart in public certainly helped Ross in the short-term. He told local media that he was going through some tough times, but added, "Members of the community make it easier."

Murtha recalled the inspiration of his great grandmother, saying, "We are put on this earth to make a difference," suggesting that Sam Ross had lived to stay on this earth for a purpose.

As Murtha pinned the Purple Heart on Ross, the crowd bellowed out "God Bless America," and the occasion truly was a celebration.

The *Pittsburgh Tribune-Review* covered the event. Their headline on January 14, 2005, said, "Murtha: Iraq can't be abandoned." Murtha rapped the administration for the faulty intelligence predicting Saddam Hussein would unleash chemical or biological weapons when U.S. troops crossed a line going into Baghdad, and for repeatedly changing their rationale to justify the war. But bottom-line, he concluded, "You can't just abandon it."

Sunni leaders wanted Iraq's first democratic elections to be postponed later that month, but Murtha said the election would not quell the unrest, and the election would heighten tensions in the short-term.

"We can't win militarily. You have to win politically," he said.

Through most of 2005, Murtha did what he had almost always done throughout his career: kept a very low profile nationally.

In late August that year, he made his third inspection trip to Iraq to see first-hand how things were going. He held no press conference upon returning, but at the request of House Minority Leader Nancy Pelosi, agreed to address the Iraq Working Group, an ad hoc group of about thirty House Democrats on September 7.

Almost two weeks later, on September 20, 2005, *The Hill* Washington weekly ran a headline, "Murtha cools further on Iraq strategy." Murtha's only comment was, "I'm not ready to talk about it yet. I was thinking I would have a press conference after they (the

Iraqis) complete the constitution."

The article quoted members of Congress who had heard him speak. They said Murtha had said the situation could not be resolved with American troops — that the troops should be withdrawn after the constitution was done on October 15 because, if the United States did not withdraw, the Iraqis would never stand up for themselves. That was about the total sum and substance of the article.

Then, as the Iraqis took up the constitution, violence escalated. Deaths of U.S. troops soared. In December 2004, a year-and-a-half into the conflict, 1,300 had died. By October 2005, 2,000 men and women had made the ultimate sacrifice in this barren, far-away land.

Meanwhile, Murtha got bad news about Sam Ross. Ross would disappear at times, and searchers usually would find him in the woods by himself. He turned to drink and, despite his blindness, often started fights when he was drunk. He was arrested for assault on a police officer who had been summoned to a bar where Ross was out of control.

Murtha was clearly touched by Ross and wanted desperately to help make his life more bearable, maybe even inspire Ross in turn to become an inspiration for other seriously wounded Iraqi veterans. Michelle Cunningham, head of Highlands Hospital, had been working with Murtha to make arrangements for Ross to talk to other seriously wounded Iraqi veterans in hopes that he might inspire and encourage them. Ross was doing better, at least for a short while, she said.

But the blinded veteran was largely blinded by rage to the helping hands that were extended. Every time Murtha got bad news about Ross's latest escapades, the sadness and frustration was obvious on his face.

And Ross was one of the hundreds of wounded soldiers, sailors, airmen, and Marines who Murtha met on his routine visits to the military hospitals.

Eventually, Ross went to state prison. By 2010, he had been

released from prison, but inquiries by community leaders could not determine what had become of him. Apparently he was no longer living in Fayette County.

Murtha's closest advisors, staff, and family agree that, as Murtha became convinced that we had lost the hearts and minds of the Iraqis, his experiences with the wounded were a primary factor that led him in November 2005 to call for redeploying our troops from Iraq, which brought an instant onslaught of attacks.

Murtha was intense about almost everything he did. He was passionate when he focused on trying to help the lives of the men and women who proudly wore the uniform of their country. He was deeply and personally affected by every wounded veteran and family member he met and could not help, while finding great personal reward with each one whose life he had made a little better.

Joyce Murtha, Murtha's widow, said he insisted on visiting the troops almost weekly, even though each visit took a heavy toll.

"That was tough on him. I could always tell when he'd been to Walter Reed or Bethesda Medical Center that day. He'd spend a lot of time talking to the families," Joyce Murtha said. She paraphrased the Congressman: "They'd always want to get home as soon as possible, but they can't realize how tough it'll be when they get out. I tell them, don't leave; stay here as long as you can before you have to leave."

Murtha's staff understood why he was impacted by the visits.

Gabrielle Carruth, Murtha's staff associate to the Defense Appropriations Subcommittee for five years, said they typically would see troops who had been out of major trauma and recovering for more than thirty days. One day, they let Murtha and his aide into the intensive care unit to visit a Marine at Bethesda Naval Hospital.

"His family was by his side, he was in a coma, his wife was stroking his arm, and his children were around him. He was unrecognizable because the shrapnel had really torn him apart and the kids were crying uncontrollably," Carruth said, describing the scene with the mother, the wife, and the three children as "just heart wrenching."

"I think we both came out of that emotionally wounded. The war impacts real people, whole families," she said, noting that Murtha was highly concerned about the impact on families, not just the impact on the military.

Murtha would become antsy if he went even a week without visiting the wounded, although those visits took such a toll, draining him emotionally and physically.

Those who accompanied him when he went with other members of Congress said they were repeatedly amazed at how well he connected with the wounded, especially in comparison to other members. Other members seemed to be uneasy around people with such horrific physical trauma.

But Murtha would look these mangled warriors right in the eye and bark, "What the hell happened to you?" Then he would listen carefully to their stories and repeatedly ask, "What do you need? What can we do? What aren't we doing? When did your loved ones find out about it? Could that process have been better?"

"The empathy that he routinely showed is just so different. He just had a way of getting them to open up to him. They wanted to tell their stories and he knew how important it was to listen. It was mutually cleansing," Carruth said.

Cindy Abram, Murtha's communications director for three years based in Johnstown, Pennsylvania, accompanied Murtha only once on a visit to Bethesda, but it was a day she will never forget.

"The only thing I know for sure: he was just profoundly affected by his visits to the hospitals and information he got from those wounded troops," she said. When he barked direct, imperative questions, she said, "I was amazed by the way they responded to him. That was *the* most emotional work day I ever put in."

Abram recalled a lieutenant who had been there for some time, saying. "He was in pretty good shape, sitting on the edge of the bed cross-legged. I can still see him sitting there. He knew the name (Murtha) and you could see the respect."

Another young Marine, who was not as familiar with Murtha, was lying on the bed with his girlfriend.

"You could almost see him (the Marine) change during the interview. He continued to sit there. Mr. Murtha asked him questions. I don't want to say he was disrespectful at first, but as he realized that the Congressman was here to get his views on things, at first he wasn't impressed at all, but he became very respectful."

Murtha asked a lot of questions, "and he wanted to hear the answers," she said.

That day Murtha also visited a Marine who was less than twenty-four hours out of intensive care. His injuries were horrific, and he was bandaged almost from head to foot. There was a priest in the room but nobody else. Abram described what happened:

"We didn't stay long because speaking was a struggle for him. But before we left, Mr. Murtha looked at him, touched his arm gently, told him how much he and the rest of the country appreciated his sacrifice, and told him to call if he needed anything at all.

"When Mr. Murtha turned to leave, there was a look on his face that I'd never seen before and never saw again. It seemed to be a mixture of sympathy and anger and sadness and determination and God knows what else. He (Murtha) had recovered — at least on the surface — by the time we reached the next room, but I'll never forget that look," she said.

"Maybe ten minutes later, we were leaving the hospital and had just gotten off an elevator with our escorts from the hospital when the other elevator stopped, and the parents of that young Hispanic Marine got off. They spoke with heavy accents, but they made it clear how much the Congressman's visit meant to them. The father stood off to the side, smiling broadly, but the woman was so emotional, she was absolutely bubbling with excitement. The mother was half crying, half laughing, and nearly bouncing with excitement. She was a tiny woman, but she stood on her tiptoes to reach up to hug him, and he bent over nearly double to hug her back. There was so much raw emotion flowing from both of them that I had to choke back tears. Then the Congressman put one hand on each on their shoulders and thanked them not only for their son's sacrifice, but for theirs as well. It was unforgettable," she said, adding, "Oh my God, that this man could have so much effect on an immigrant couple whose son is so badly wounded."

Murtha would talk to the Marines, and then talk to the families separately. "Do you need anything? Are you getting everything you need? Can I do anything for you?" she quoted him, adding, "That was absolutely my most unforgettable work day ever — and I worked for thirty-five years. That day I saw a side of him that other people don't see. There was something far more important to him than politics, and it's the troops."

Murtha used his position as ranking member of the Defense Appropriations Subcommittee to advance several programs and technologies that would help these wounded warriors.

He literally raised hell with military leaders and the Veterans Administration when he realized that thousands of returning war veterans were suffering from what he called "battle fatigue," more commonly known as delayed-stress syndrome or post-traumatic stress disorder.

He learned about it largely from talking with families, such as a constituent whose son tried to kill himself and ended up in jail for armed bank robbery.

In a House floor speech, he emphasized the need to address stress disorders and recalled visiting a mental health ward with Congressman Bill Young, a Florida Republican and chair of the Defense Appropriations Subcommittee. Young shared Murtha's concern that 50,000 returning troops would have stress disorders, but would not get Purple Hearts.

"We don't get any recognition at all. We get shunned aside as if we were cowards," Murtha quoted them.

Murtha directed funding and pushed the military and VA to establish routine protocols to reach out to veterans after they had returned from war to make sure they were coping, and to reach out to the family and friends of the veterans so that others could recognize the problem and try to get help.

Traumatic brain injury or TBI was another huge problem. Even before the Iraq War, in February 2003, Murtha was honored by the Brain Injury Association of America for funding he directed to improve the chances of recovery for these victims. As the war wore on, he became highly concerned. By 2006, there were estimates that 150,000 military personnel had some level of brain injury, and in 2008, the RAND Corporation put the number at 320,000.

IEDs are made with plastic explosives and butane or gasoline inserted into 155-millimeter shells. They can destroy a Humvee and create a shock wave of air traveling 1,600 feet per second. Such intense reverberations can literally cause the human brain to swell to the point that people are comatose, but the large majority of brain injuries from the war produce symptoms such as personality changes that are often difficult to distinguish from stress disorders.

Murtha was instrumental in creating a network of sixteen Defense and Veterans Brain Injury Centers, including one in Johnstown, to try to help the most serious cases.

He also directed funding into developing a nerve block that stops pain — even the pain of having a limb completely blown off. The pain block is a major help in reducing the shock that sets in after traumatic injuries and now is commonly used in hospitals during surgery.

Arguably there was no one in Congress or elsewhere who was more committed to helping our military and veterans.

David Morrison, staff director for the defense subcommittee at the time, said Murtha's experiences in fighting for the wounded warriors was one of three factors that eventually drove him to come out against the Iraq war.

"In the beginning, he was not really convinced that Iraq posed a direct threat to U.S. national security, which he always considered essential in any decision to go to war. He defaulted to the administration in the absence of a very strong reason not to," Morrison said.

Second, Morrison said Murtha had developed the clear sense that leaders in the administration "had no idea what they were doing" and, worse yet, they were hiding information and perhaps even lying to him. Based on his visits to Iraq, Morrison said, it became clear to Murtha that the whole rationale for going to war was "a falsehood, bankrupt."

The war was being executed poorly. Major problems recurred with spare parts, personnel, and equipment being worn out from over-deployment. Secretary of Defense Donald Rumsfeld was talking about reducing the number of troops while Murtha was saying that more troops were needed to gain control within the limited time before we would lose the hearts and minds of the Iraqi and American people. Rumsfeld and Cheney were incommunicative, even arrogant, and it became clear to Murtha that they were "not only unable to run the war but, in fact, were hiding important information," Morrison said.

The third factor was Murtha's personal experiences working with the wounded.

Ultimately, Morrison said, Murtha came to view the war as "a waste of blood and treasure."

Congressman Mike Doyle, a Democrat from a district adjacent to Murtha's, centered in Pittsburgh, had been mentored by Murtha and came to be known as "a Murtha lieutenant." Doyle typically hung around Murtha in "the Pennsylvania corner" — the back, side corner of the House floor where Murtha could be found by other members who wanted his advice or help, and where any member coming to vote might be politely collared and convinced to come over and hear what was on Murtha's mind.

"He was growing dissatisfied with how the war was going, and he felt that we were losing the battle for the hearts and minds of the Iraqi people, which he always felt was central," Doyle said. "Every time we would do something, there was collateral damage (to civilians). It was like one step forward, two steps back. It was becoming increasingly clear to him, I believe, that some of what he had been told by the Bush administration wasn't true regarding weapons of mass destruction and so on, and I think you could see it starting to eat away at him."

Doyle continued, "The other factor was, Jack would spend a lot of time quietly visiting soldiers who had come home, and a lot of them, because of the IEDs, had terrible burns, or they were in a lot of pain. The flack jackets kept them alive, but they lost limbs and eyes and ears. And I think that started to really get to him, too."

Murtha looked at the whole picture of how the war was being conducted and "went from being affected by it to being angry."

Then one day, Jack Murtha was in a funk.

"I remember one day, him sitting in the chair, and he was in a particularly foul mood," Doyle recalled. "I finally said 'What's gotten up your craw that you're so miserable today?' And he said, 'Those f***ers lied to me!' I said, 'Who lied to you' and he said, 'God damn it, the administration lied to me,' and I laughed because I was never a big George Bush fan, and I said, 'Gee, there's a news flash, Jack. The administration lied to you.' He said, 'No, you don't understand.' He said, 'I'm gonna do something about this,' and I said, 'What are you gonna do,' and he said, 'I'm gonna shake this whole place up.'"

Throughout his thirty-one years in Congress, Murtha had always worked behind the scenes, not out in front of the media. But the next day, this decorated Vietnam veteran and respected expert on military issues went before the national cameras and proclaimed, "The war in Iraq is not going as advertised. It is a flawed policy wrapped in illusion.... Our military has done everything that has been asked of them. The U.S. cannot accomplish anything further in Iraq militarily. It is time to bring them home."

Republicans immediately lashed out at Murtha. One called him a coward on the House floor, and the phrase "cut and run" was bantered around everywhere. But as a decorated Vietnam war veteran and lifelong champion for the war fighter, Murtha stood up to the political onslaught as he took on a mission he had never taken on before: the war fighter became a fighter against a war.

Chapter 1

Character and Courage

The world shook on November 17, 2005, when a little-known Congressman from Pennsylvania came before the national media to declare, "The war in Iraq is not going as advertised. It is a flawed policy wrapped in illusion."

The wrath of the right wing was immediately unleashed on Jack Murtha when, after two years of war, this behind-the-scenes leader on military issues said it was time to move U.S. troops out of Iraq. He was instantly a hero and a villain, a flash-point around whom debate and elections turned.

Congressman John P. Murtha was one tough son of a bitch. This is a blunt description, but whoever first coined the colorful phrase had to be talking about a man much like Jack Murtha.

Murtha was tough because he had to be tough — physically, mentally, and emotionally. Murtha's abusive father was reckless and out of control, venting on the family for reasons that had nothing to do with the alcoholism that controlled him. Young Jack Murtha grew strong and fought back against his father. He modeled himself on a straight-laced, button-down grandfather and drew inspiration from a great-grandmother who had told him as a four-year-old, "You're put on this earth to make a difference."

He became a star athlete in high school and college, then quit college to join the Marine Corps during the Korean War, although the war ended before he got to Korea. At age thirty-three, he received medals for his service as a volunteer in Vietnam. Murtha could not be physically intimidated. He towered above most of the crowd at six feet, four inches tall, an imposing frame matched by a personality that could consume any room, either through his persona as a Marine drill instructor or his infectious laugh. People close to him knew when he was about to jab someone in fun because he telegraphed his intentions with the gleam in his eyes.

Murtha could not be pushed around politically, either, because long before "winning the hearts and minds" had become a catchy phrase for those with limited understanding of war, Jack Murtha had learned those lessons. He had learned those lessons both in the mud and jungles of Vietnam and from the boos he got while speaking in support of the war shortly after returning from Vietnam in 1967. By then, even in conservative rural Pennsylvania, some people were beginning to speak out against an increasingly unpopular war that used as many soldiers as a president wanted to use, thanks to the draft system.

Over his career, Murtha applied that knowledge in assessing political realities both at home and abroad, and he had an incredibly shrewd political perception to judge the mood of his district or the nation, and to inject that perception into the discussion in Washington.

Murtha was not a perfect man. He was frequently described as "gruff" — a very fitting description given the way he could jump on people, even his closest friends. He often would shoot from the hip and say things that created a stir, yet he almost never second-guessed himself or retracted a statement — not even when he claimed Marines in Haditha had killed innocent civilians "in cold blood."

In his youth, his father was gone for many years, and abused the family when he was home, so Murtha had every excuse in the world for not achieving in life; yet he did achieve. He became the kind of man that every steel worker and coal miner who helped build the region wanted in a son. He was a special blend of common, yet extraordinary.

Within Congress, Murtha became well-respected, although he was different in one uncommon way: Jack Murtha rarely spoke unless he had something big to say.

He constantly reached out to members of the other party and pushed for Congress to work in a bipartisan manner to address the issues. He mentored many young members, freely offering advice about "voting their home districts" and always keeping their word.

He became a respected expert on military and foreign affairs and a behind-the-scenes master of the political game, maneuvering inside Congress for the votes to get committee chairmanships or leadership posts for his allies.

But he was not known outside of the Capitol because he always preferred to work behind the scenes in Washington, and he was not known outside his district because the only headlines he pursued were for the folks at home in local newspapers and television.

That all changed on November 17, 2005. Congressman John P. Murtha was about to speak out before the national media. This time, when he was done, the world changed.

Calling the war in Iraq "a flawed policy wrapped in illusion," Jack Murtha abandoned the role of behind-the-scenes shepherd of foreign policy and took on President George W. Bush and the attack machine of Karl Rove, deputy White House chief of staff, who was incredibly effective at silencing all doubters and marginalizing all critics as unpatriotic for not supporting the war, for not being tough on terrorists.

As a life-long hawk and relentless champion of the war fighter, no one in Congress had more credibility than Jack Murtha when it came to military issues. Murtha was among the very few who could speak out against the war while making it clear that he was not speaking against the warrior. He was the only one who could take America beyond the "false patriotism" that was turning the world's beacon of freedom into a debate-free nation.

As the first combat veteran of Vietnam elected to Congress in 1974, Murtha's counsel had been sought by every president of either party throughout his thirty-six years in Congress, starting in 1975, when he was part of the first congressional delegation to visit Vietnam after that war. Every president, that is, except George W. Bush.

Murtha never needed to talk to the world. Why talk to the world when he could have so much more impact simply by talking directly to the president?

As Congress prepared to consider a resolution to support the war in Iraq in 2003, Murtha had serious reservations and told his colleagues in Congress that he had not been convinced that Saddam Hussein — as nasty as the man was — presented a direct threat to the United States that would justify our going to war.

Just days before that vote, Murtha had a conversation that changed his mind. That conversation was with Vice President Dick Cheney. Murtha and Cheney were close from the years when Cheney was defense secretary and Murtha was the House Defense Appropriations Subcommittee chairman. While Murtha never publicly blamed Cheney for having misled him, his lingering anger about how he had been misled leading up to this vote was clearly a factor in his coming out two years later to call for moving U.S. troops out of Iraq.

In explaining his vote at the time, Murtha said that he had always respected the power of presidents as "commander in chief" on international issues and held out some hope that Saddam Hussein, when faced by a country united to go to war against him, might still back down.

If Murtha felt betrayed by taking Cheney's word in voting for the Iraq War, he never said so, not even to his closest associates. He would say such things as "we used to be good friends" or "he's changed," but it was not in Murtha's character to go after the man. Not even privately.

Many Democrats in Congress looked up to Murtha on defense issues, so when he voted for the war, he carried many votes with him.

But from the onset of the conflict, Murtha saw problems. In the initial invasion, the troops with the best equipment to handle chemical weapons got stuck in Turkey because the administration failed to understand the concerns that Turkish leaders had about being the launch pad for war against their neighbor. Murtha soon went to Iraq and was stunned and angry about the critical shortages of equipment that were costing lives and limbs. War advocates said the Iraqis would welcome us with flowers in the streets and would pay for the war with oil revenues — neither of which happened. Then the mission was repeatedly redefined and rationalized as the administration admitted Iraq did not have weapons of mass destruction, and claims that Hussein had been harboring terrorists proved to be false.

Murtha soon recognized that both sides in a civil war were now targeting U.S. troops, and the conflict needed a diplomatic rather than a military solution. He then tried repeatedly to be heard by the White House, defense secretary, and others who controlled or might influence Bush on national policy.

He was simply cut off, rebuked, and ignored.

Murtha was livid when his letter to the president was answered almost seven months later — not by the president or even the defense secretary, but by a Pentagon official several pegs down from the top, an official Murtha insisted on calling "a staffer." People close to him saw the crust blow off the retired Marine colonel.

Yet it would take another twenty months before Murtha went public with his call to redeploy the troops from Iraq. Twenty months in which he constantly visited the soldiers with horrific wounds — lost limbs, lost sight, lost minds, and lost bodily functions caused by traumatic brain injuries. Twenty months in which he agonized over the fact that the nation's leaders had no exit strategy, no plan for getting out. Twenty months during which the hearts and minds of the Iraqis had been lost through Abu Ghraib and Haditha, and both sides in a civil war had now turned on U.S. troops. Twenty months in which every day more men and women were killed or wounded with still no exit plan.

Who was this man who had both the courage and credibility to take the barrage of epithets, hate, and anger?

John Patrick Murtha Jr. died on February 8, 2010, at age seventy-seven from complications from gall bladder surgery. He wanted to be remembered for his love of family and the military, which he saw as his extended family. He wanted to be remembered for helping to advance medicine. Diabetes, heart disease, and cancer were all wars for Murtha, but few people outside of his district knew of his passion for reducing suffering and finding cures for various diseases. He wanted to be known for rebuilding the economy of a region devastated by the collapse of the steel and coal industries. Yet outside the region, more people likely associated him with "earmarking" and "pork barrel." They cannot appreciate how committed he was to creating jobs and how he connected with the common man.

Murtha was intensely under the microscope from the moment he called for the redeployment of American forces in Iraq on that November day. Although he is a fulcrum on which history turned, there are things that few people know about him, things that define him and define this chapter in American history.

Murtha possessed a humility exceeded by no elected official of his time because he had the heaviest of political trump cards and never played that card.

Months before the terrorist attacks of September 11, 2001, and even before George W. Bush had been sworn in as president of the United States, Murtha warned Bush and Cheney that the most serious threat to national security was the use of domestic airlines as weapons against us. Yet not only did he never say "I told you so," he never spoke of the discussion publicly after 9/11.

That warning demonstrates two things: First, that Jack Murtha was not a media hound as his political enemies claimed when he dared to challenge the silence that had been imposed on the American political system. If he had wanted attention, this warning would have gotten him plenty of spotlight. Second, to demonstrate that while most people were oblivious to such a threat before 9/11, Jack Murtha had a deep understanding of defense and national security issues that virtually nobody could match.

Murtha's pivotal role in the war in Iraq and in enabling the Democrats to take control of both Congress and the White House over the next three years was clearly historic, but there is a critical lesson to be learned from this chapter of history.

Political leaders opposed to the war remained silent because they feared being painted as unpatriotic if they went public with that opinion. Others supported the war, but felt it was being mishandled. These leaders were also silent out of fear — fear of being banished from their political party for not being a part of the team, or fear that they would be defeated politically if they left themselves open to being labeled as "unpatriotic."

So often, debate in Washington, and indeed across our nation, is stifled by the political process of Republicans and Democrats vying for power. At this time, debate in Washington was being stifled by fear. Any member of Congress who criticized the war was instantly branded as a liberal coward who was soft on terrorism, and then targeted in their next re-election campaign. Except in the most liberal districts, they all became afraid to speak out.

Only Jack Murtha, as a lifelong hawk, military man, bipartisan champion of the war fighter, and respected senior member of Congress, could jump-start the engine of debate and conversation. People had come to believe that our nation's freedom of speech and open debate on such matters was a sign of weakness to our enemies when, in fact, it is a sign of our strength as a free nation.

No one else could have gotten the nation's leaders and the people back to being able to talk openly about the direction of the nation. Less than a year after Murtha spoke out, the Democrats regained control of Congress. Two years later, they won the White House and increased their majorities in the House and Senate. While the economic collapse of 2008 was a major factor in the 2008 election, the widely accepted view that President Bush had bungled the war and run down the economy with the wasteful war spending was also a big factor.

That view would have been far less common without Jack Murtha.

Murtha was not a left-wing liberal, as his distracters tried to claim. He was not a coward, as he was called on the House floor by one Republican Congresswoman, who learned quickly that his years of respect trumped such venomous rhetoric.

Murtha was an intensely private man who had avoided the sort of head-on public confrontation he faced in calling for redeployment. While many tried to label him as "cut and run," the fact is, this Pennsylvania Congressman spent his lifetime fighting for the troops, and in the case of Iraq, had labored for years to convince the White House that many more troops were needed in Iraq. He first called for a troop surge in Iraq just months after the war began — and years before the White House would come up with the very same idea. But by the time the White House was ready to surge, the hearts and minds of the Iraqi people had long been lost.

Murtha's ability to speak out against the war was built on years of working for his people in Southwestern Pennsylvania, earning their trust and loyalty; years of becoming an expert on the military; years of earning respect from fellow lawmakers with his mentoring and advice. All that would be needed in this pivotal moment in history.

This book offers some insights into an American patriot, into how a man from such humble beginnings became so pivotal at this moment in history. It is not intended to be his entire life's story. This is a snapshot of the man and the time, a time when the American political system was frozen, not in the gridlock of policy disagreements that so often grips the process, but frozen in fear.

Jack Murtha was the only American with the credentials, wisdom, and courage to challenge not only a war, but also the deafening silence borne of political fear. The life of this courageous patriot should be a beacon and a lasting reminder that politics can stifle debate, undermine our democracy, and perhaps worst of all, cost America deeply in blood and treasure.

Chapter 2

Almost Wild

Four boys, one mother, one cabin, one stream, no bathtub, no father, but lots of wild West Virginia woods, lush and full mountain forests, full with birds and wildlife, full of deep hollows and places where people could get lost or lonesome.

That's where Jack Murtha and his three brothers spent their summers as kids: alone with their mother and grandmother in a cabin. They grew up "almost wild" each summer, according to brother Robert "Kit" Murtha.

The family struggled to get by as the marriage of the mother and father was an on-again, off-again proposition. Murtha's father was alternately abusive or gone.

John Patrick Murtha Jr. was born in New Martinsburg, West Virginia, in 1932, the first of four sons conceived by his father and Mary Edna (Ray) Murtha. The first three brothers were born in three years and in three separate towns as their mother and father were married, divorced, and remarried "a couple or three times," according to Kit Murtha. When the fourth son was born in 1937, their father left again and stayed away through World War II.

"I'm gonna tell you something: Dad was an alcoholic, a mean son of a bitch. So, you know, Mother left, and he did a lot of things that she wouldn't accept. Mother did a good job with grandfather's help," Kit said.

And the kids?

While Jack as the oldest was more responsible, typical of first-born children, in the summers as a group, "We were almost wild," Kit said.

"We were just normal old boys. I am sure we were trouble for Mother. We had a church right beside us. We played ball in their lot and broke windows; we did those kinds of things. Grandfather had a cabin out in the woods of West Virginia. Mother would take the four of us out to that cabin and we would stay out there all summer. We bathed in the creek in the summer and went to school in September," Kit said, adding with just a touch of sarcasm, "I guess they got us out of town because we were kind of ornery."

Four or five cabins sat along a stream on the edge of the woods. Usually nobody else was around — just the four boys, their mother and grandmother, and on weekends, usually their grandfather.

"I have to say that was a great time. We went out in that camp. It had no lights; it had kerosene; didn't have any electricity. We had an ice box; the guy delivered ice. It was good now that I look back on it. We had an outhouse and the water through a well up on the hill. We had to go up and get it. It taught us something. We turned out all right. We were all good Marines. We were all good people, but we had that problem," Kit said, referring to their dad.

"Jack had fond memories of their summers in the woods," his widow, Joyce, said. "His mother was a nature enthusiast, knew all the birds, animals, and plants, and taught the boys on long hikes through the hills and woods."

As a grown man, Murtha loved to garden, fish, and watch birds. He was almost obsessed with finding a way to keep the squirrels from getting into the bird feeder in his back yard, which faced woods behind his suburban Johnstown home. He championed many conservation initiatives, obtaining funds to restore the Stonycreek

River, Indian Creek and other streams badly polluted by abandoned mine drainage, and to preserve abandoned railroad corridors as trails, such as the Great Allegheny Passage.

He had a love for nature born in the carefree solitude of the mountains of West Virginia, and fed by his mother. Freedom to run, freedom to climb, freedom to swim, but perhaps also a freedom from the intense emotions that are anything but liberating to a family dealing with abuse.

Peace would come to the family during and after World War II, when his father served in the military and stayed away until 1947, two years after the war.

When his father and mother again reunited, a showdown followed in which a teenaged John Patrick Murtha Jr. demonstrated a flash of his willingness to take a stand. He may still have been the Senior's son, but by this time he made it clear he was no longer a boy.

"The second world war came along and he (Father) went to the Army, spent his time down in Panama and then he came back about 1947," Kit said. "He wasn't very nice or congenial. When you think about it, in those days men thought they owned women, and they did those types of things. When the old man and Mother went back to Pennsylvania, Jack was about fifteen, sixteen. The old man started drinking and doing things he shouldn't do. And one day he started picking on Jack and was going to do something with him, and Jack threw a bucket at him and cut his head. He (Dad) needed stitches. He scared the hell out of us until we were a little bit older."

By then, Jack Murtha Jr. had grown tall and strong. The family moved to Mount Pleasant, Pennsylvania, where they struggled financially because Grandfather Ray was not there to take care of their bills, and Murtha's father got back to heavy drinking. But Murtha played football and starred on the basketball team. He was enterprising, rising early to deliver newspapers and pumping gas in a service station to earn money.

The influence of his grandfather, Charles S. Ray, was clearly showing in the young Jack Murtha. Ray had a remarkably strong influence on Murtha's life.

"He was the father figure in Jack's formative years," Joyce Murtha said. "He supported the family, built a house next door exactly like his, and was a community leader. Before going to Paden City, West Virginia, to run the family-owned Pottery, which employed eight hundred people, Ray was superintendent of schools in Saltsburg, Pennsylvania. He was also president of the bank in Paden City.

While times were tough during the Great Depression, Grandfather Ray managed to keep the Paden City Pottery in business, and gave his son-in-law, Murtha's father, a job there. Even after his father left, the family did better than many others across the nation, at that time, because Ray took care of them. Not only did he keep his four growing grandsons fed, he even built that second house for them.

"He set a wonderful example for Jack to follow," Joyce said. "Jack got his love of reading from his grandfather and his mother. Grandfather Ray never came down to breakfast without wearing a three-piece suit, and Jack was always careful to dress well. Grandfather taught him to always pay his bills and to be financially responsible."

Murtha's great grandparents also were an influence. Although his great-grandfather, Abraham Tidball Bell, died before Murtha was born, Murtha often spoke about Bell. Bell was bivouacked in the U.S. Capitol toward the end of the Civil War, and Murtha kept his letters, a diary, and cap. Bell lost an arm while serving as a missionary to native Americans after the Civil War and then became a Presbyterian minister in Blairsville, Pennsylvania. Bell's grandfather fought in the Revolutionary War — a tradition of service that continued through Murtha's generation, when he and his three brothers all served in the military.

Murtha's great grandmother, Mary Bell, lived to be ninety-six, by which time the six-year-old Murtha had embedded in his mind a phrase of hers that he variously recited as "one person can make a difference" or "you're put on this earth to make a difference."

That influence was not always obvious. When Murtha graduated from Ramsey High School in 1950, his brother Kit said he was more into sports and girls than school — rather ordinary.

Enter Grandfather Ray again. Ray paid the tuition for Murtha to go to Kiskiminetas Springs School, a preparatory school, for some remedial academics.

"Kiski Prep really taught him to study," said Joyce. "The headmaster at Kiski Prep was someone he really respected a lot. He said after Kiski, he knew how to get an education."

The next year, Murtha enrolled in Washington and Jefferson College in the City of Washington in Southwestern Pennsylvania. As a freshman, he became a star on the football team, which had only twenty-nine players because many young men were in the military during the Korean War. Although Murtha caught the winning touchdown in a big game that year, he was struck by the fact that another young man who would have been on that football team had just been killed in action in Korea.

In an interview for the Veterans History Project, conducted by California University of Pennsylvania, Murtha recalled, "During the winter time, I stood up there and looked down at the red light which was on the corner. I was at Hayes Hall, which was a hall right on the corner in the center of the campus. I thought, 'This is not the place I should be. I have no business being here when other people are in the Korean War.' It was the height of the Korean War. I decided right then that I would enlist. I enlisted and my mother was unhappy. She wanted me to finish college. Of course, obviously the Korean War was going on, and she did not like that. But the point was, I felt that it was my duty."

Although his mother and grandfather were furious, the often rather ordinary Jack Murtha was about to do something extraordinary.

Murtha was no ordinary Marine — not that there is any such thing as an "ordinary" Marine — but this Marine truly stood out.

Upon completing basic training, he was awarded the American Spirit Honor Medal, which is given to less than one in 10,000 new recruits. "Gung ho" was not enough to win this award — obsessively gung ho, fit, and ambitious as hell would be the minimal requirements for such an award.

Throughout his life, he told people that he was most proud of that award — and this is a Marine who earned sixteen medals, including the Bronze Star with Combat "V", two purple hearts, the Vietnamese Cross of Gallantry, and, when he retired from the Marine Corps with thirty-seven years of service, the Navy Distinguished Service Medal, which was presented to him personally by the Marine Corps Commandant.

After finishing boot camp, Murtha quickly became a drill instructor, and years later, everyone who knew him well — his employees, his aides in Congress, his fellow Congressmen, even the colonels and generals who had to deal with him — knew that he could turn on a dime and be in their face with his drill-instructor persona.

That persona is where Murtha earned the reputation as a tough son of a bitch. That persona helped him earn the reputation as "gruff."

Drill-instructor Murtha was not content with the life of an enlisted man. He passed a four-year college equivalency test and was offered enrollment in the U.S. Naval Academy, but declined in favor of the Officer Training Course, according to his book, written with John Plashal, *From Vietnam to 9/11 — On the Front Lines of National Security*.

The enlisted-man drill instructor soon was Lieutenant Murtha, clamoring to go to Korea. When he finally got his orders to ship out, the war ended.

Stationed at Camp Lejeune, North Carolina, he was mentored by "a crusty career Marine, Major Wilson," who instilled in him the credo, "Pay attention to details," he wrote in his book. That credo was something he lived by and instilled in others whom he mentored throughout his career.

Something else happened while at Camp Lejeune that shaped Murtha's life. He had a fender-bender. He stopped by an insurance office to file a claim, but was directed to another office by the attractive young woman behind the desk. He started to leave, hesitated, hesitated some more, came back, and asked the young woman for a date.

Joyce Bell said "no," that she did not date Marines, but Murtha pressed, "Never?"

She conceded that she had dated a couple Marines whom she knew through church.

So he asked, "If I came by and talked to you every day this week, would you feel like you knew me and go out?"

She brightened, smiled, and said, "Maybe."

At the end of the week, after coming or at least calling every day — he had duty assignments two days — he showed up and asked to drive her home. She agreed, introduced him to her parents and they went out on their first date, a movie, *Gone With the Wind*.

Joyce had been planning to move to the Virginia suburbs of Washington, D.C., with a girlfriend, and by chance, about the same time she moved, Murtha was transferred to the Marine base at Quantico, Virginia. They continued to see each other, and Joyce said they occasionally drove into nearby Washington and past the Capitol, where Murtha would say, "We'll be back here some day."

Jack Murtha and Joyce Bell got married in 1955 in Alexandria, Virginia, shortly after he went off active duty. By then, he was attending the University of Pennsylvania in Philadelphia and working at Scott Paper Company, and Joyce moved into his third-floor apartment near campus.

Penn was expensive, so Murtha transferred to the University of

Pittsburgh and they moved to Irwin, Pennsylvania, where he could work in his dad's Sunoco station on the evening shift. In December 1956, their daughter, Donna, was born. Murtha would rise at four a.m. to study, head off to school, and then work three to eleven p.m. at the gas station. In early 1958, they had twin sons, John and Patrick.

"He dropped out of school when I became pregnant with the boys. I was furious with him," Joyce recalled. "I told him he had ruined our life. He promised me he would go back as soon as we could afford it."

About that time, the demons of Murtha's father brought a curious twist of fate, which brought the family to a place they had never seen before, the small, steel city of Johnstown, Pennsylvania.

While Murtha had his differences with his father over the years, he still had a love and respect for the man and tried where he could to help. Murtha had seen a new system in Philadelphia in which a car could be washed in just a minute. Murtha researched the potential business, and which towns and cities had a dirty environment, the right population, and the necessary weather conditions for such a business. He presented his father with the idea of starting a "Minute Car Wash" in Johnstown, where the huge complex of Bethlehem Steel Corporation included blast furnaces and coke ovens.

In 1956, Murtha's dad started the business according to Murtha's plan. But by 1958, as the booze had again wrecked his father's ability to function, and the business was teetering financially, Jack Murtha took over management of his father's car wash.

The frugal, task-oriented Murtha soon had paid off the debts of both the business and the father, and Murtha became the owner of the car wash.

By 1959, Murtha was taking on new responsibilities as commanding officer of the 34th Rifle Company of the Marine Corps Reserves.

But while most ordinary people would feel overwhelmed by

raising three small kids, running a small business, and commanding a Marine Corps Reserve unit, Murtha thirsted for more. He thirsted for knowledge.

He began taking classes at the University of Pittsburgh at Johnstown and, after two years, transferred to the Pitt main campus more than an hour away in Pittsburgh. In 1962, he finished his degree in economics, and the next year took graduate-level courses in economics and political science at Indiana University of Pennsylvania, about forty minutes from his home in Johnstown.

Throughout his life, Murtha was an obsesive reader. He had taken courses in speed reading and, through his years in Congress, prided himself in reading a book a week. He did not read light novels. He consumed history books and accounts of life and times in Russia, the Balkans, Southeast Asia, wherever there was global conflict.

"Jack read an incredible number of books about war, whether it be the Revolutionary War, the Civil War, World War I, World War II, Korea," said Joyce. "He read every book he could find on Lincoln, such as *Team of Rivals* by Doris Kearns Goodwin; Teddy Roosevelt, a particular favorite; Churchill — most books he wrote and books about him, such as *The Last Lion* by William Manchester; all of (David) McCullough's books — he especially liked *Truman*. He re-read the classics from time to time."

At the time of his death, Murtha was reading two books: *Americans in Paris: Life and Death Under the Nazi Occupation* by Charles Glass, and *Imperial Cruise* by James Bradley, which explored the era when President Roosevelt believed that American power, extending from the annexation of Hawaii in 1898, would spread across Asia, just as it had across North America.

His fascination with history was evident throughout his life. For much of his career, he served on the Interior Appropriations Subcommittee along with Defense. He worked to fund many National Park Service sites, including Gettysburg National Battlefield and the

Presidio in San Francisco. In his district, major improvements were made at three National Park sites, including Fort Necessity National Battlefield, and several historic sites and museums were refurbished or developed, including the Johnstown Flood Museum and the Jimmy Steward Museum in Indiana, Pennsylvania.

Surprisingly, Murtha did not read all that much at the car wash. When business was slow, he would play chess or paint pictures. He also made an extraordinary friend.

At the age of eight, young Danny Perkins started to shine shoes in Downtown Johnstown, seeking customers in Central Park, on street corners, even in bars to augment his ten-cent allowance. "I made eighty-five cents. I thought I was rich," Perkins recalled.

One day, he walked home past the car wash and was amazed to see the long line of cars. Perkins thought it was nirvana; the car wash would bring the customers to him. So he approached one of the workers and asked for permission to shine shoes there.

"He said I need to ask the owner. He pointed to this tall, lean-and-mean structure. It was Jack. I went up to him and said, 'Can I shine shoes here?' He looked me up and down," Perkins hesitated in recounting the story, his head rolling up and down as intense eyes sized up the small, black child who was brazen enough to make such a request.

"'Yea, you can shine shoes here. But if you stop any cars, I'm going to have to ask you to leave,'" Perkins continued. "I thought well, it takes me three minutes to shine a pair of shoes. I agreed, and I walked away. And then I saw the sign — 'Minute Car Wash' — and I thought, 'I have a problem here.'"

Perkins came up with a solution: he got a buddy to shine one shoe while Perkins shined the other. Murtha was impressed with the kid's ingenuity. Perkins kept coming back and was ambitious and inquisitive. When business was slow, he would walk around to see how things worked. If the foreman was not around and something needed to be done, he just did it.

Murtha soon had this young, black teenager running the business in a town that was about ninety-five percent white.

"He told me, 'When customers come in, try to greet them, find out their name, go up and ask them, 'How are you doing, Mr. Schrott?' They'll like that.' So I just started doing that. 'Good morning, Mr. Schrott. Good morning, Mr. Krebs.' The first time I did that, 'Good afternoon, Mr. Schrott' — 'How'd you know my name?' They were genuinely impressed."

It was the politics of business and the precursor to the politics of politics: know the customers' names. And while many regular mill workers came in, Murtha also got to know the city's movers and shakers — people like Dick Schrott, the general manager of WJAC, the local television station, and Walter Krebs, publisher of the *Tribune-Democrat*, the local newspaper.

Murtha also employed up to a hundred people in his car wash, which had a chain that pulled the cars through while workers did the scrubbing, cleaned the tires, and emptied the ash trays. Murtha was often called "a man of the people." About half of his workers, at any given time, were on parole.

"He was a D.I.," Perkins said, referring to Murtha's past as a drill instructor. "And every time he would discipline somebody, that D.I. training would come back, so his style was a lot more radical than mine. However I did adopt some of that, and the guys tolerated it. They took that from a kid, and these were some tough characters who were on parole."

Perkins was given authority to call out extra workers and to send home or "cut" workers depending on the pace of business.

"One time he said, 'Daniel, I'm going to bring a couple guys out here and want you to put them to work. Watch them closely and make sure they're on the ball.' I put them to work. I had to correct the one guy a couple of times. The one guy wasn't working too well, so I told him he couldn't work any more. I sent him home. It turns out they were his (Murtha's) sons. I remember when I told him to go home, he went inside and told his father that I had cut him off. He (Murtha) said, 'Sit over there. Be quiet.'"

Tough son of a bitch or tough love, either way, Murtha was tough, even with his own kids.

Murtha later started to include Perkins and Perkins' best friend, Kelly Washington, when he took his two sons on outdoor adventures. They went camping, canoeing, whitewater rafting, and rock climbing.

Perkins described how Murtha would hike the boys into the woods and provide instruction. "The first thing you got to do is find a location," he quoted his mentor, describing how to check the ground for flatness, rockiness, and other factors.

"In the Marine Corps, we were often on patrols, four-person patrols," he quoted Murtha. "The first person looks ahead, the second person looks to the right, the third person looks to the left. Where's the fourth guy look? Kelly?"

Kelly guessed, "'Backwards?' 'No.' 'Straight ahead?' 'No — Daniel, what do you think?'" Perkins hesitated and said, "'Up?' 'Yes!'"

"We would do these kinds of things. There would be a didactic. He would talk about what they would eat, things we had to be careful of. They were all instructional in design and then we would put up our tent. He'd tell us stories about being out in the woods, the coldest he ever was, what do you do in case something happens," Perkins recalled.

Meanwhile, the war in Vietnam was heating up. Murtha wanted to go there.

Gung ho Murtha typically volunteered for the most vigorous challenges. He went to jungle warfare school in Panama and guerilla warfare school at Camp Pendleton, California. He was promoted to major.

About that time, then-President Lyndon B. Johnson increased U.S.

troop strength from 125,000 to 230,000 and ordered U.S. troops to engage in direct combat.

"Jack was running the car wash and wanted to go to Vietnam. He worked very hard so they would send him to Vietnam. He went to all these training things, survival schools, and they weren't going to send him because he had three children," brother Kit recalls, noting that Murtha pushed the issue far up the chain of command. "He said, 'Hey, you spent all this money getting me trained and now you aren't going to send me down there?' So they sent him to Vietnam."

Chapter 3

Whole New Ball Game

A company of four hundred and fifty Marines was outside of its Tactical Area of Responsibility south of De Nang and the Song Ke Long River in South Vietnam. Someone in Major Jack Murtha's company spotted a radio.

"I said, 'Hold fast, don't do anything. You see a radio, it's going to be North Vietnamese,'" Murtha said. "Well, we had very little artillery down there with them. We had four deuce mortars and eighty-one -millimeter mortars. We didn't have heavy stuff. It was overcast, so we could not get air (support) in."

The Marines went after this radio, went beyond the range of the artillery, got trapped, and took a heavy beating. "The whole regimental command structure went down. We reinforced them with two more battalions (but) lost a lot of people that particular incident," he said.

Failure to follow training by going beyond the range of air support was one lesson, but Murtha was just getting to the part of the story that, nearly four decades later, shaped how he reacted to reports of innocent people being killed in Iraq. He recalled the incident in a 2006 interview for the Veterans Oral History Project, a Library of Congress program that encouraged people to record interviews with veterans talking about their war experiences, saying:

"... usually there was this thing called a body count. So the commanding officers said, 'You don't have a big enough body count,' because I was the guy who was supposed to report the body count of the enemy. I said, 'We have always reported actually what we found. We didn't report anything else.' He said, 'You have to report a higher body count because if you don't, they'll blame me for taking this beating.' I said, 'Well I'm just telling you, Colonel, that there's not that many.'

"We had an argument and I wouldn't give in," Murtha continued. "We reported actually what we saw and there may have been a lot more casualties, but we didn't see them. They relieved the colonel (of duty) and he knew they would because they felt he had lost that particular series of battles. But that's the way the war went."

On numerous other occasions, Murtha told people he had been threatened that if he did not report more Viet Cong casualties, he would be charged with insubordination, or otherwise have his military career destroyed. The gruff Maj. Murtha refused to lie then, and years later, the gruff Congressman Murtha knew from experience that, under the command structure of the mission-minded military, some people see no substitute for success — even if that means lying or covering up the facts.

As a Marine regiment intelligence officer, Murtha learned lessons in Vietnam — lessons about training and intelligence, having a clear and achievable goal, and winning hearts and minds, both in the country at war and back home. In Congress, he would draw on these lessons during discussion or debate on various conflicts. But the pressure he got to report a higher body count became forefront in his mind when, almost forty years later, he heard an account of Marines killing innocent women and children in Haditha, Iraq, while the official news release indicated that these people had been killed by an improvised explosive device or IED.

Murtha told another story in that interview with another profound lesson: "I remember one incident where the colonel said to me, 'The battalion commander just called and he said he's got thirty-five or forty people that have just been killed by the VC (Viet Cong).' He said, 'There is something wrong here. They brought them in and it doesn't sound right. Go down and see what the situation is.' So I went down with the second battalion to look at these people, and they had been burned.

"I said right away this is napalm. These guys weren't killed by the VC. The VC were very careful who they killed, anyway, because they knew — they killed people that didn't agree with them (but) they were much more careful about it" with innocent civilians, Murtha said.

He recalled his conversation with the Vietnamese: "'Take these (bodies) back to your village. We'll pay you, as we always did, for the people we killed. We apologized for it, 'We're sorry. It was a mistake.'"

The situation almost got worse. "The battalion commander came back and he had called *Time* magazine and told them to come in, (that) the VC had killed some people. So he was trying to counter this. He was trying to run his own public relations thing. Well, it turns out that a few months later, I asked the company commander who was in charge of that sector what happened and he said napalm hit these guys and killed them. So I was right, and if *Time* magazine had come and seen this...."

"So there are two wars that go on all the time. There is the war for the hearts and minds of the people. We'd lost the hearts and minds of the people in Vietnam because of the way we operated. We've lost the hearts and minds of the people in Iraq because of the way we operated in Iraq. So we have this combination. You have to do it (the military action) very quickly. One of the things some generals are complaining about today in Iraq is that we didn't have enough troops initially when we went in, in order to make the transition to peace," Murtha said in the 2006 interview.

"This is the reason that I have been so adamant about the only answer we have is to redeploy. I recognize in looking at the carnage in the public relations battle, we've lost it. We have no alternative now but to redeploy our forces and let the Iraqis handle this themselves."

Murtha often pointed out that in Fallujah, Marines pushed 150,000 Iraqis out of their homes during the battle to avoid killing too many innocent civilians, but many of their homes were damaged or destroyed, and keeping the insurgents from returning was much tougher than forcing them out. Sometimes, military victories can be won with overwhelming force that results in loss of hearts and minds, and this was a prime example to Murtha.

Accidental killings, destroying civilians' homes, and other collateral damage always brings a heavy price, Murtha explained. "Now the other thing in Vietnam and Iraq that hurts us: When you do a military operation, you kill a lot of people. You do it to protect Americans, and I adhere to that because you use artillery, you use air. You want to suppress the enemy so that you can go in with the least amount of Americans killed. Well, you make enemies with the Iraqis or the Vietnamese, whichever one you're talking about. Every time we went into a village, we had to use superior fire power. We, in many cases, killed civilians, and there was a public relations battle going on all the time."

Murtha's body count story relates to the PR campaign at home, and his napalm story relates to the PR campaign on the war front. He clearly understood from his experiences in Vietnam that military campaigns are about winning battles, but wars often are won or lost by the PR campaigns about hearts and minds.

He also knew that the PR is not about what the media reports. If American soldiers killed innocent people, whether in Vietnam or Iraq, the locals knew what happened. No level of lying or sophisticated public relations could hide such gruesome facts. And if American military personnel were allowed to systematically lie about numbers of casualties or how civilians had died and similar things, then America would have no credibility, and no amount of PR could change that.

Vietnam had changed Jack Murtha. He had learned, he had grown, and he had become even tougher through his experience. And after Vietnam, with one goal met, the ambitious Murtha soon was pursuing his next ambition: political office.

John P. Saylor was elected to Congress thirteen times in the hills of Western Pennsylvania from 1949 to 1972. Pennsylvania had been in the forefront in creating the national conservation movement and, by the mid-1900s, planting and protecting forests was a pillar of Republican politics. Saylor made a name for himself as a conservationist, advocating for the National Wilderness Act, the National Wild and Scenic Rivers Act, and other legislation. Serving a very rural district with only one city, Johnstown, Saylor had no major challenges for re-election. But he had a bit of a surprise in 1968 when a politically unknown owner of a car wash ran for the Democratic nomination.

Murtha was always interested in politics and occasionally said things that gave people hints that he wanted to run for office. But those closest to him saw a different Murtha when he returned from Vietnam in 1968.

Murtha wasted no time in announcing his challenge to Saylor and he immediately went to work.

"He was a very, very hard worker. We'd start campaigning at six a.m. at the mill gates or start at five a.m. when he wanted to drive to the mines," recalled Mary Kay Voytko, who started working for Murtha at Minute Car Wash in 1967 and worked for his congressional office for thirty-six years.

Murtha received virtually no support from organizations because he was considered such a long-shot. He ran a shoestring campaign the likes of which would never work today. He had no paid staff and did almost no advertising. His campaign literature was hand-typed brochures run off on an old mimiograph machine at the car wash. His buttons were hand-painted by a Mr. Fisher, who lived two doors from the car wash and had gotten to know Murtha by playing chess with him on rainy days, Voytko said, describing Murtha as "young, personable, a real go-getter."

He made a very strong impression on people, but ultimately, lost by a wide margin — not as wide as some Saylor opponents, but disappointing nonetheless.

As fate would have it, a few months later, the state Representative from Johnstown, Edward W. McNally, died in office, and Murtha was asked if he wanted the nomination to run for the seat in a special election.

At first, he said no; he did not want to work on the state level. Then he decided he would run, and later said it was the best decision he ever made because he learned how the system worked and learned the protocol in legislative bodies, according to his widow, Joyce.

This time, with no incumbent, Murtha had the active support of several groups, including the International Ladies Garment Workers Union, which brought out a small army of volunteers and had members in every small town across the district.

Murtha ran against Republican T.T. "Teddy" Metzgar, who was well known as a member of the Pennsylvania Fish Commission. Local odds-makers figured Metzgar was the favorite against the relative newcomer, a car-wash owner who was not a native.

Murtha surprised many in winning.

"I think even John Torquato was surprised," Voytko said of the Democratic Party Chairman at the time.

Murtha was re-elected in 1970 and 1972, and the next year another untimely death spelled opportunity.

In October 1973, Congressman Saylor died during heart surgery in Houston, Texas.

Joyce Murtha said the timing was peculiar. Five years had passed since Murtha had challenged Saylor, but he had made a strong enough impression that in October 1973, he was invited to speak at a dinner in Clarion County, which was part of the Congressional District where he had campaigned in 1968. The Murthas drove from Johnstown on the rough roads and Joyce recalled the long drive back, when Jack said he wanted to run for Congress again.

"I told him, 'Not now. Just give me a couple of years until the kids are out of school,'" Joyce recalled.

Jack Murtha said okay.

Early the next morning, about five a.m., the Murthas' phone rang. He was told that Saylor had died. "We had gotten back late the night before from Clarion and when the call came, Jack turned to me and said, 'I know what we decided last night, Joyce, but it is now or never.' I agreed with him."

Daniel Perkins was working at the car wash when a customer told him about Saylor's fate. He went to the office to tell Murtha. "I remember him just sort of staring off into space. I said, 'This kind of creates a whole new ball game.'

"'That's right Daniel, this is a whole new ball game,'" Murtha told him.

Murtha was selected by local Democratic Party leaders as the nominee in a special election to fill Saylor's unexpired term. An extremely tough campaign followed, with Murtha the underdog taking on Saylor's long-term chief of staff, Harry Fox, in a race that drew national attention because of the impeachment proceedings and eventual resignation of President Richard Nixon, stemming from the Watergate scandal.

Murtha avoided the national spotlight, telling media that Nixon was irrelevant: the election was all about local issues.

Before he died, Murtha was having staff write down his reflections of various occasions. In a reflection of his 1974 campaign, Murtha said, "Across America, the Watergate scandal was shaking the nation and it was becoming clear that the energy crisis was becoming a major national concern. The national press covered our race because of the implications that the outcome might have for the upcoming November congressional elections. I was more concerned about the local issues, and largely avoided the national press. At the time, many Democratic politicians openly expressed their views that the President was guilty, but I was careful not to say too much."

Then-Vice-President Gerald Ford campaigned for Fox, while Murtha had campaign rallies around the district with Senators Walter Mondale, Edmund Muskie, Henry "Scoop" Jackson, and Joseph Biden, as well as then-Governor Milton Shapp.

Murtha campaigned as he had in 1968, enlisting volunteers and cruising around the sprawling rural district in a bus emblazoned with "Murtha's the Man." This time, he received huge support from unions, which were increasingly important in Pennsylvania's Appalachian mountains pocked with coal mines and steel mills in Johnstown and the Allegheny Valley north of Pittsburgh. With layoffs common during economic downturns, women flocked to jobs in the sewing factories in every little town for that second paycheck that kept the kids fed and the mortgage paid when the mills and the mines had layoffs. Those mills, mines, and garment factories were all unionized.

Murtha also put together student volunteers at every college, encouraging hundreds of young people to register and vote. The AFL-CIO helped recruit a Penn State University linebacker to coordinate the efforts on campuses. Indiana County was typically a strong Republican area, but a big turnout at Indiana University of Pennsylvania cut deeply into the Republican margin there and was a key to the ultimate outcome.

"The entire election cost less than $100,000 and, in the end, it came down to which candidate was best able to get out the vote," Murtha recalled. "Throughout the whole campaign, the only day I took off was Christmas. On the day of the election, the energy crisis had advanced to the point that there were fuel shortages and long lines at the pump. Our campaign actually had gas stations set aside gas for our campaign workers, who were driving people to and from the polls.

"The evening of the election, as the votes were coming in, it was obvious that it was going to be a very close call," Murtha said. "Finally, the Democratic chairman, John Torquato, said to me, 'You've lost the election. Come down to the courthouse and concede.' The only precincts left to count were the traditionally Republican areas of Westmont, a Johnstown suburb. I went down to the courthouse with my wife, Joyce; my mother; and my children, who were all crying and upset about my loss. While we were on our way to the court house, Nunzio Medile and Sam Kaminsky went around and got the numbers of the votes from Westmont, and we found out we had won by 350 votes. That figure would shrink to 230 when the total of 120,000 votes that were cast came in."

Fox demanded a re-count, which whittled down Murtha's official, final margin to a mere 122 votes.

Years later, talking to school kids, at political rallies or other events, Murtha often recalled that margin when he told people that one vote can make a difference; that their vote, in particular, had enabled him to go to Washington to fight to keep America strong and build our economy back home.

Murtha had a stunning ability to recall names and faces. People he met in his 1974 campaign would bump into him twenty or thirty years later and be greeted by name without hesitation.

Kit Murtha said his brother could pigeon-hole any seemingly random bit of information and years later pull it out as if it were fresh. Kit Murtha said his brother had family slots, political slots, military slots, slots for all sorts of issues – tons of information that he retained and could pull out of those pigeon holes on a heartbeat years later.

One characteristic perhaps helped Murtha with his amazing

recall. He essentially had no social life. He was an extraordinarily private man.

He had very few means of release or escape. He worked in his garden a lot and loved roses. He hung a bird feeder in the back yard, although he got infuriated when squirrels got into the bird food, so perhaps it was not that much of a release. He loved to fly fish, although many years he got on the streams only once or twice. And he played a lot of golf. He was especially good with his short game and putting, at one time getting his handicap down to about ten.

Political and community events where he interacted with constituents were by and large the extent of his social life.

He never spoke of his father, and from very early in his political career, identified himself as John P. Murtha, not John P. Murtha Jr., as if he never wanted to invite inquiries into his family history. Or perhaps, from the moment that bucket cracked his father's skull, Murtha had decided to be defined by his own deeds, not the actions of a father tortured by alcohol.

That addiction explains another fairly unique characteristic of Murtha, especially compared with most people involved in politics: he resolutely avoided alcohol.

"He told me once that, for all he knew, he already was an alcoholic but just didn't know it, and he didn't want to start drinking and find out for sure," said John Hugya, who knew Murtha from his Marine Corps days and later was Murtha's Chief of Staff.

Most Murtha staffers never once had seen their boss take a sip of alcohol at the countless dinners, picnics, rallies, and other events he attended. Hugya, who knew Murtha for fifty-one years, recalls one exception from their Marine Corps years. After an extremely rigorous, night-into-day training maneuver on a very hot day, the exercise ended with no water at hand. But another Marine had stashed a few bottles of beer. Everyone was so parched that they virtually chugged their beers, whereas Murtha, after a brief hesitation, took one, too.

Murtha sipped his and never quite finished it.

Another exception came years later, when Murtha cut a ribbon on an equipment upgrade at Latrobe Brewing Company, which made Rolling Rock Beer in the heart of his district. When the program ended, company executives proposed a toast and broke out bottles of beer in front of a crowd of rank-and-file union workers. Murtha downed his like one of the boys, although he declined the offer of a second. Those bottles, by the way, were seven-ounce ponies.

Murtha's relationship with his father had a profound effect on him in another way. The tough old Marine drill instructor often described as "gruff" had a sincere interest in stopping domestic abuse.

From time to time, he quietly visited the Alice Paul House in Indiana and the Women's Help Center in Johnstown, two domestic-violence shelters, and spoke at their fundraisers.

Murtha also took a strong interest in abuse in military families. He insisted over the years that the military needed to impress on personnel that spouse abuse was simply not acceptable. He would tell the generals that he understood that they were training the soldiers to react instantly and kill the enemy. But he was insistent that they also needed to instill the need for self-control at home.

Susan Shahade, executive director of the Women's Help Center, said Murtha took an interest in the center not long after it had opened in the early 1980s.

While many people saw the gruff Marine colonel, Shahade said, "What I saw was a lamb, gentle and kind – and from his eyes to his handshake. Although I know the giant of the man, he was endearing. Just gentle, approachable."

Shahade said he never talked about his father or suggested he knew anything about domestic abuse from his family life.

Lenore Patton, who ran the Alice Paul House, said Murtha was among the first elected officials to recognize the critical need for such shelters. "This was the beginning of the domestic violence movement, and Jack was way ahead of his time," she said.

Patton told Murtha about the causes of domestic violence, what can be done about it, and how big the problem was. So when military leaders told Murtha, "No, no, that's not happening, he recognized that it was," she said.

"He was empathic and caring," she said, but acknowledged, "I saw the other side of him, too."

That "other side" was Murtha's political side.

"I'd be lobbying him for some liberal cause and he looked at me and said, 'You're the most liberal people in the most liberal part of my district. If I voted like you wanted, I'd never get elected."

Indiana, like most college towns, attracted some intellectuals and free thinkers who were proud to be branded as liberal, whereas Murtha realized that folks across the broader area were relatively conservative, at least on social issues.

"We were very liberal, and although he didn't agree with us most of the time, he'd listen to me," Patton recalled. Sometimes he would move a little in her direction. Occasionally she could convince him. But he was always "approachable," she said.

Patton was among Murtha's first supporters, working in his 1974 campaign and then running his Indiana office for a while.

Years later, Patton occasionally received a package, usually containing a book on women's issues and a hand-written note. Jack Murtha never forgot the people who worked for him, especially not those who were among "the originals," the people who backed his first successful congressional campaign.

Chapter 4

Street Corner Guys

The floor of the United States House of Representatives is a massive stage where history has often been made. But far more often, the action there is not all that dramatic.

In one such moment, Congress's newest member, John Patrick Murtha, sat quietly off to the side watching what went on.

Wilbur Mills, a creator of Medicare and one of the most powerful members of Congress, approached Murtha.

"What are you doing sitting here?" Mills asked.

"I'm trying to learn my way around here," Murtha replied.

Having won by the narrowest of margins in the special election in February, 1974, Murtha was sworn into office by himself, not with a class of others who had been elected at the same time. Murtha did something highly unusual: he declined to take committee assignments right away and chose instead to sit on the House floor to learn about the procedures and "the players."

Wilbur Mills was one such "player" in the 1960s and 1970s, not only because he was chairman of the tax-writing House Ways and Means Committee but also because he made a habit of studying IRS tax codes, and knew them inside and out.

Although Mills resigned as chairman just months after this because of problems with alcohol and a stripper, he told Murtha to do two things, which Murtha took to heart.

"Keep your word and study an issue; study one particular issue, because you'll have no impact otherwise," Murtha recalled Mills telling him in an interview with Robert V. Remini, professor emeritus in history from the University of Oklahoma, for the book, *The House: The History of the House of Representatives*.

"If you get up and speak all the time, you'll have no impact," Mills said. And if you become an expert in one subject, other members will seek your advice.

At that time, Murtha's good friend, Daniel Perkins, had graduated from the University of Pittsburgh and become a Marine Lieutenant stationed in Quantico, Virginia, not far from Washington. Perkins drove up to visit his mentor each week.

Perkins said he vividly recalled a conversation early in Murtha's ascent to power. Murtha turned over a napkin and listed members of his committees, noting their seniority and ages. "He said this guy is a senior guy and he's not going anywhere…. But this guy, there'll probably be a slot (when he retires) so I probably can get up to defense,'" Perkins recalled.

"That's where he wanted to be. He said, 'I think I can get up to defense pretty quickly.' He had plotted this out and I remember him telling me how much time it would take, and some of it was pretty accurate. But he knew what he wanted; he knew exactly what he wanted to be."

In November, eight months after Murtha's first election, ninety new Democrats were elected, and in 1976, seventy-five more came in. Murtha shot up in seniority, which at the time meant a lot more than today in getting committee assignments and having impact. He soon got on the House Defense Appropriations Subcommittee, which would become a major source of his influence in Washington.

Murtha pursued a two-pronged approach to power. With his experience in Vietnam and his seat on Defense Appropriations, he could become the guy who would be sought out by many other members of Congress to understand military and foreign affairs.

But Murtha had a mentor who showed him the way to broader power and influence.

Thomas P. "Tip" O'Neill was a lot like Murtha. Both were Irish Catholics, congenial, from working-class districts, and understood intuitively that "all politics is local." That phrase was O'Neill's mantra, and Murtha recognized in his special election campaign that the national angst over President Nixon's Watergate scandal would not be enough to carry him to victory. He worked a grass-roots campaign based on the local issues.

By the time Tip O'Neill became speaker of the House in 1977, he and Murtha already had a very strong relationship. Although O'Neill was quite liberal, reflective of his roots in Boston, Massachusetts, he knew that winning the big legislative battles in Congress would require coalitions among Democrats with a wide variety of perspectives, both politically and geographically.

Chris Matthews, host of the show *Hardball* on MSNBC, was O'Neill's administrative assistant from 1981 to 1987, when O'Neill retired.

"He (Murtha) was always around, and he was close to the speaker, one of our close, close, close confidants and really a warm friend of Tip," Matthews recalled. "Tip was a politician and Tip could be a politician, but he got a certain smile when he was around Murtha, almost totally in heaven when in his company. He loved being in the company of Murtha, and I think it's one of the reasons every time he took a trip somewhere, he took Murtha with him.

"And I felt so comfortable with Murtha," Matthews continued, noting that his grandfather, Charlie Shields, was from Murtha's district in Latrobe, Pennsylvania, and loved to talk about state and national politics with Matthews when Matthews was growing up in Philadelphia. "I loved my grandpop and I loved Murtha the same way

– he reminded me of my grandpop even though he wasn't that much older than me. He had that old neighborhood feel and Tip liked those guys. 'He's a street corner guy like me,' Tip would say. They'd all gone to college but didn't have airs, didn't act like campus-type guys. And Tip's friends were like that, like (Dan) Rostenkowski (of Illinois) and Sylvio Conte (of Massachusetts). They were all like that – they were middle-middle-middle socially. There was a real comfort factor."

When O'Neill did something that Murtha liked, Murtha would tell him, "Ten strikes, Mr. Speaker, ten strikes," referring to bowling, Matthews recalled.

Murtha soon became a whip for O'Neill, pressing colleagues to vote the "right" way and counting votes. He constantly observed action on the House floor, hanging out in the far right corner, which became known as "the Pennsylvania corner."

Perched out of the way, he could corner his Pennsylvania colleagues. He built voting blocks among those from neighboring states that shared geographic issues, such as concern for the struggling steel industry. Leaders who needed votes on a controversial issue soon came to understand that Murtha could deliver those votes, but he had demands on other issues.

From that broadening political base, Murtha began to forge broader coalitions. On defense issues, he would reach out to conservative Southern Democrats. When Murtha wanted to make a deal, perched in his Pennsylvania corner, he could watch members come and go on the floor and seize the opportunity to reach out to particular members who could make or break the vote on a crucial issue.

Mentored by O'Neill, Murtha almost certainly would have become the majority whip and, eventually, speaker, but he was named as an unindicted co-conspirator in an undercover investigation by the Federal Bureau of Investigation called Abscam in 1980. He was recorded on video tape telling FBI agents posing as representatives of an Arab sheik that he did not want a $50,000 bribe, although he said he might consider it later. He pressed to have the Arabs invest in business development in his district.

Although charges were never filed and the House Ethics Committee voted to take no action against Murtha, Abscam was brought up by many political opponents over the years. The issue found little traction because Murtha had a counter that played well at home: he was just trying to create jobs in a district that was losing steel and coal jobs by the thousands.

John Hugya, Murtha's long-time chief of staff, explained where Murtha's head was when undercover agents offered Murtha a drawer full of cash to do something that actually was legal: to help people become U.S. citizens. Murtha did not want the cash for himself. He wanted the Arabs to create a legal business-investment account to finance local companies to rebuild the local economy and create jobs.

"This was not long after the (1977 Johnstown) flood and unemployment was twenty-four percent in Johnstown. Most people have no idea what that looks like. It was awful. Those are the kind of numbers you saw in the Great Depression, and Mr. Murtha was very anxious to find a way to solve the problem," Hugya explained.

"I can recall a bunch of us going over to Altoona for dinner the one night and during the meal, Mr. Murtha talking about these Arabs who wanted him to help out with bringing some friends or relatives into the country legally. He talked about how they were going to set up this bank account that people could come and borrow money. He was pretty open about it and was excited about what it could mean."

Not long after that, Abscam went public and a shaken Jack Murtha called Hugya to break the news that it all was a hoax and there would be no fund to help the region.

"He called me and said, 'You know those Arabs I told you about who were going to pump all that money into the region? They weren't real. It was an investigation and they tried to get me to take a bribe.'

I knew he would never have taken the money. He was upset that he was a target of this thing.

"He was real upset, but he was just as mad the Arab money wasn't real. He had already started setting up the account with business leaders in the area. He was excited about what that Arab money was going to mean to the people who needed jobs," Hugya said. "People get upset he didn't storm out of the room or yell at these guys, but he didn't want to scare them off. He wanted them to help out here at home. These people (who criticize Murtha on Abscam) have no idea what it was like with twenty-four percent unemployment.... Hell, no, he didn't yell at the Arabs. People here were out of work. He didn't take their (personal) money, though, did he?"

Nonetheless, the scandal cost Murtha a leadership post at the time and undercut his chances for a leadership post two-and-a-half decades later when the Abscam tapes, having disappeared for many years, showed up in the hands of a conservative magazine that was out to discredit him for his opposition to the Iraq war.

While Murtha had great respect in Washington, he also had developed some antagonistic relationships. One that lasted virtually until his death was with Steny Hoyer, the Maryland Democrat who Murtha challenged for House majority leader in 2006.

Murtha's distrust of Hoyer dated back to 1982. When Ronald Reagan was elected president in 1980, Republicans took a big bite into the Democrats' majority in the House. In their television commercials, an actor portraying Tip O'Neill laughed off warnings that his vehicle was low on fuel until the car sputtered, gasped, and stopped, and the voice proclaimed, "The Democrats have run out of gas."

Although the Democrats continued to hold the House majority through the 1982 election, a mutiny was brewing. In his memoirs, *Man of the House*, O'Neill summed up the episode:

"A few of the younger members actually called on me to resign as speaker, although nobody ever said so to my face. But I had no intention of giving up – not for a minute. Anybody who wanted Tip O'Neill out of office would have to vote me out.

"Still, there were rumblings of dissent, and Dave McCurdy of Oklahoma led a small band that wanted to run somebody against me for speaker in 1982. The candidate they preferred was Richard Gephardt of Missouri, but Dick came in to tell me he had nothing to do with this plan," O'Neill wrote.

In his interview with Professor Remini, Murtha recalled, "Tip was able to get through rough spots because everybody liked him; he was friendly. He was on the floor. Tip presided when he became speaker. He presided every single day. He had a news conference every single day. If you wanted to see him, all you had to do was walk up to the podium and there he was.

"When things changed, he was the most unpopular guy in the country, at one time. They ran ads against him. They ran him as a big, fat politician. And he understood that. He hired a guy named Chris Matthews. Chris Matthews came in and Chris Matthews turned it around. I give him full credit. He told him (Tip) how to say it, be more concise, and when to say it, and Tip did it. And when he left, he was the most popular politician in the country," Murtha said, calling Tip a liberal who took on tough issues.

O'Neill called Murtha on Thanksgiving night of 1982 and said, "'Are you part of this Goddamned cabal?' I said, 'What are you talking about?' I didn't know a thing about it."

Murtha snooped around, identified those involved, and called and raised hell, he said, adding, "They all denied they had anything to do with it. They were just 'having a meeting.' They weren't trying to overthrow the speaker and so forth."

Hoyer was part of that group and Murtha, always loyal to friends, never got over his distrust of Hoyer.

Murtha survived a major challenge in 1982, when reapportionment forced him to run against another incumbent Democrat. Murtha beat then-Congressman Donald A. Bailey by a wide margin, even though Murtha's integrity was questioned because of Abscam.

In 1983, Murtha was elected chairman of the House Steel Caucus and used that position as a forum from which to push "buy American" legislation and appropriations to require that domestic steel be used in roads, bridges, office buildings, and military equipment.

Subsidized steel imports were devastating the economy in Johnstown and other steel-making cities across America. Johnstown's unemployment rate hit twenty-four percent because of cutbacks at the sprawling Bethlehem Steel Plant and two smaller mills. Foreign plants benefited from the subsidies that allowed them to sell steel for less than the cost of production, and they had cheaper wages, newer and more efficient equipment, and less expensive pension plans and other benefits.

As the nation shedded steel jobs, President Reagan agreed to meet with Congress members from steel-producing states. Although Reagan was a staunch free-trader, opposing any tariffs or other protective measures, Murtha argued with passion that America needed a steel industry for its national defense. Japan and Germany both were subsidizing the cost of steel imported into the United States, so it was fair for the United States to use quotas or tariffs to counter-balance the subsidies. The only time in his eight years as president that Reagan approved measures to protect an industry was when Murtha convinced him that domestic steel was a national defense issue.

Murtha's closeness with O'Neill was only part of his power.

Congressional Quarterly, in a 1987 profile titled "Hidden Influence," said Murtha derived his power from the Appropriations Committee; his leadership of a bloc of votes from Pennsylvania, Ohio, and West Virginia; his "renowned talent" for whipping; and "the gratitude of senior members for his repeated efforts at winning pay raises, higher limits on outside earnings and pension benefits for members."

He curried favor not only with the House leadership, but also with many rank-and-file members of Congress by being the sponsor of some of the most politically dangerous bills, such as pay raises. Currently, Congress and the executive branch get annual raises based on the federal Cost of Living Index, but then, Congress needed to vote to increase the pay of all civil servants, including cabinet members, federal judges and, yes, Congress members. Members facing tough elections could not be associated with pay raises and often voted against them.

Matthews said Murtha "would always be the member who would look out for the other members." After years without getting even a modest pay raise, many members "were living in two houses (in Washington and back home) and living in basements, going back and forth. Some of these guys had a lot of kids in school; had to pay for clothes and shoes; and Murtha tried to look after those guys."

Murtha also engineered deals to get allies on powerful committees, in part through the Democratic Steering and Policy Committee, which recommended committee assignments.

In an almost legendary battle in 1984, Murtha got fellow Pennsylvania Congressman Bill Gray elected as chairman of the House Budget Committee, Pennsylvania Congressman Bill Coyne elected to Ways and Means, and Illinois Congressman Dick Durbin elected to Appropriations, with all of them beating other Congressman who were backed by Majority Leader Jim Wright of Texas.

In an interview with the *Wall Street Journal*, Congressman George Miller talked about losing a fight to get a fellow Californian elected to a chairmanship, saying, "Murtha should have played middle linebacker. He's the monster of the midway." An unnamed Texas Congressman told the *Journal*, "The majority leader ought to have more influence than Murtha. I'm worried about him."

A key to Murtha's success was relationships he developed with

Southern Democrats based on defense and foreign policy issues, and he even occasionally whipped for Republicans to win funding for the MX missile and aid to Nicaraguan rebels.

Murtha also had connections with Democrats from other ethnic and working-class districts in New York, New Jersey, and Illinois, including Dan Rostenkowski of Illinois, chairman of the House Ways and Means Committee.

A 1987 *Congressional Quarterly* profile said, "Enhancing his effectiveness is his almost unique aversion to the media.... Murtha declines interviews routinely. Ambushed by a reporter as he left the speaker's office in mid-September, he rejected a request for information for this article, protesting on the run, 'I have so many people I talk to, it would be self-serving to discuss it.... I know what the deals are; if I talk about it, there might not be any more deals.'"

Murtha became chairman of the Defense Appropriations Subcommittee in 1989, giving him huge influence on which weapons systems and defense projects got funded – or not. He knew how to use the power of the purse and was never hesitant to use it, although at the end of the day, if he believed that a system or a project was needed by the troops, he made sure it got funded.

That year, Murtha got Gray elected as whip, making Gray the highest-ranking black leader in the history of the House.

When Murtha became chairman of Defense Appropriations, *Congressional Quarterly* wrote, "Many members and staff across the political spectrum attribute to Murtha an extraordinary prowess at making the wheels turn by shooting straight, dealing smart, and leaving the credit to others.... 'Jack Murtha, in his mind and heart, looks at defense from the foxhole up,' Les AuCoin, Democrat of Oregon, one of the defense panel's leading doves, said of its most influential hawk. 'You never see his attention more focused than when the welfare of the guy in the field is at risk.'"

Throughout the 1980s, Murtha was a force in Washington – little known because of his aversion to publicity, but well-known in the insider worlds of politics and defense.

He faced one of his toughest elections in the 1990 Democratic primary election, when attorney Kenneth B. Burkley of Greensburg, Pennsylvania, painted him as spending too much time in Washington, losing touch with the district, and using his influence more to benefit big defense contractors than the economy back home. Murtha survived with fifty-one percent of the vote to Burkley's forty-three percent.

Murtha felt that if he did things in the district, he did not need to talk about them because the people who had benefited would know. His classic example of the lesson he learned in 1990 involved Elliot Turbomachinery, which employed more than a thousand workers in Irwin. The struggling company had a buy-out offer that would have kept just a shell of the business in his district. Murtha intervened, convinced the company owners to find other investors, and kept the company whole.

Despite saving more than a thousand jobs there, Murtha was beaten by Burkley in Irwin and in surrounding Westmoreland County, where Murtha had gone to high school.

Murtha hired a press secretary, made a point of visiting each corner of the district regularly, and attracting local media coverage when he did. He never had another tough race until reapportionment redrew the district lines and he faced incumbent Democratic Congressman Frank Mascara in the 2002 primary.

Against Mascara, Murtha emphasized his ability to attract jobs and proclaimed he had created a whole new economy in computer science, robotics, biotech, health care, and defense manufacturing and research. Although the national media and watchdog groups constantly badgered him about pork-barrel, he funded some big projects in Pittsburgh and other areas beyond his district where the spin-off would build the broader regional economy.

For instance, he helped attract a supercomputer to the University of Pittsburgh and Carnegie Mellon University, and the Software Engineering Institute to Carnegie Mellon, which one study showed had created an estimated 10,000 spin-off jobs. He also supported Carnegie Mellon's world-renowned robotics program, which worked directly with a company in Fayette County, which then was part of his district, creating two hundred jobs there.

His 2002 campaign emphasized his efforts to help Timken Latrobe Steel, Johnstown Welding & Fabrication, and Gautier Steel expand their workforce through defense contracting.

Mascara was infuriated when Murtha came to a construction project on the locks and dams of the Monongahela River, which had been the very heart of Mascara's old district, to tell Pittsburgh television news stations that it was Jack Murtha who had added millions of dollars to rebuild the inland navigation system that supported 45,000 direct jobs, many in mining and other basic industries.

Murtha also emphasized his efforts to improve health care, such as initiatives to combat the epidemic of Type II diabetes and cure Type I diabetes and various cancers, especially breast cancer, which was the focus of work he was funding at the Windber Research Institute. The Institute, by the way, employed a hundred people near Johnstown, something Murtha was never shy to remind constituents when he talked about health care.

Even though the new district had as many voters from Mascara's old district as from Murtha's old district, Murtha won with sixty percent of the vote.

Murtha was now feeling confident that he had a strong message that played well back home in a conservative, but heavily Democratic district. That confidence and his record as a military hawk would give him more courage to speak out nationally when he took issue with the Iraq war just a few years later.

Chapter 5

Hawk

May 26, 1980, was a splendid day in Somerset, Pennsylvania. Sunshine and mild temperatures brought out a big crowd for the traditional Memorial Day parade and service to honor those who had sacrificed to defend the nation.

In rural Somerset, a typical small Pennsylvania community, many people had served in the military. World War II veterans were just retiring, while others had served in Korea or Vietnam, so Memorial Day here was a big deal.

This Memorial Day event featured twenty-nine units in the parade, including the high school and junior high bands, the Kiltie Kadets, the New Centerville Spinnettes, Somerset Saddle Club, and Cub Scout Pack 131.

The service included the traditional drum roll, moment of silence, tolling of the bells, and placement of wreaths on the courthouse monument. Many of the veterans stayed for a picnic lunch before moving on to family gatherings.

Before the parade, Jack Murtha ascended the ten-foot-high stage adorned with red, white, and blue bunting, his six-foot, four-inch frame towering over the audience.

Murtha said it was not good enough for the United States to be equal to the Soviet Union in power: we needed to hold a significant advantage over them.

This was the height of the Cold War, but the bitterness of Vietnam weighed heavily on the politics of the time as the former California Governor, Republican Ronald Reagan, was running for president on a platform that then-President Jimmy Carter had cut the military too much. Reagan won, and if Democrat Jack Murtha cast his vote that year based on military issues, he would have sided with Reagan.

At the time, fifty-three Americans were being held hostage in Iran. While Murtha expressed concern for them, his speech did not focus on the crisis of the moment. Ever mindful of the big picture, Murtha saw Iran as a symptom, but the Soviet Union as the disease, and did not offer a verbal picnic on America's place in the world.

"For the past few years I have been saying the Soviet Union and United States are roughly equivalent in strength. Now I am changing my position. I no longer believe the United States is even equal, and I think it will take four to five years of concentrated effort and spending to return our superiority," he said.

"And that superiority is essential. Our entire economy is now dependent on a thin line of oil tankers making their way from the Middle East. If we cannot defend that route and insure our tankers' safety, then we can be thrown into a massive depression at any time by the Soviets interrupting that oil flow. And meanwhile, the Soviet Union has invaded Afghanistan in a blatant power move. They are now poised on the edge of the Middle East countries. For our own safety and for the safety of the free world, we must make it clear to the Soviet Union that we will not tolerate their aggression, and that we will take whatever military steps are necessary to defend our interests and the cause of freedom. That is why we need military registration and may need the draft," Murtha said.

This was not a speech to military leaders at the Pentagon, but rather a speech to the regular folks back home. This was quintessential Murtha – the type of speech that leaves little wonder how the man developed his reputation as a hawk.

Murtha also spoke of the "trouble mobilizing quickly in case of war," noting, "It would take us over one hundred days just to find out who we could draft, much less begin to train them. That's a key reason why I recently voted for a return to registration," he continued, adding that if the manpower trends continued, "we may have to return to an actual draft."

He spoke of Soviet superiority in tanks, missiles, planes and submarines, and called for a five-year, trillion dollar spending plan, saying, "There's no first, second, and third in defense. There are no medals for coming in second."

Murtha wanted to double military personnel. He wanted more tanks, more war ships, more strategic missiles, and more nuclear submarines.

"Hawk" is an inadequate description of the Congressman some would want to label as a defeatist decades later.

Murtha's position on the military was more aggressive than his fellow Democrats and most of his Republican peers at the time. Virtually no one in Congress likes to talk about the draft, and that was especially true in 1980 with Vietnam so fresh in the nation's psyche. But Jack Murtha was different.

The political right commonly criticized what had become of American military might under President Carter and touted Reagan's presidency for bringing down the Berlin Wall.

Jack Murtha had a lot to do with that, too.

The Soviet invasion of Afghanistan was central to their downfall because the fighting dragged on from 1979 to 1988 and helped to bankrupt the communist nation. Murtha was more hawkish than Reagan and had to force Reagan to take stronger action to support the Afghan rebels.

Before he died in 2010, Murtha occasionally had a staffer write down his reflections. One reflection was on the Afghanistan

Mujahideen rebels and provides insights into the popular movie, *Charlie Wilson's War.*

"Representative Charlie Wilson prodded me on the Defense Appropriations Subcommittee to furnish Stinger missiles for the Afghan Mujahideen fighters," Murtha said. "The United States was already secretly supplying the Afghan fighters with Soviet weapons purchased from other countries, but these weapons proved incapable of bringing down the large, low-flying Soviet gunship helicopters. The Afghan fighters had no real defense against these helicopters and they gave the Soviets a distinct advantage over the poorly equipped resistance. The Stinger missile, which Charlie so vehemently pushed, is a U.S.-manufactured, shoulder-fired, surface-to-air missile with a range of over 15,000 feet.

"At first, President Reagan wasn't convinced," Murtha continued. "He was hesitant to supply any weapons system to the Afghans that could be directly traced back to the United States. After several attempts to make the administration supply the missiles, we forced the issue by threatening to take money from the CIA's priority programs to let the administration know how serious we were about the Stingers."

The Stingers had an "immediate and obvious" effect, Murtha said, explaining, "The Soviets lost many helicopters and were forced to fly at much higher altitudes, which resulted in much poorer accuracy for their weapons. The tide was beginning to turn in the Afghan-Soviet War, and Charlie was right in believing it would give the Afghanis the defense they desperately needed."

Two years later, with the Soviets desperately trying to move their beaten troops out of Afghanistan, Murtha was asked by then-Secretary of State George Shultz to accompany him to the funeral of Pakistan President Zia ul-Haq, who had died in a plane crash in August 1988. Murtha was to meet afterward with some Mujahideen rebels to encourage them to let the Soviets retreat unattacked.

"The day after the funeral, Charlie and I met with thirteen of the

Mujahideen leaders," Murtha recalled. "The first thing I noticed was their attire. They came to the funeral dressed in turbans and carried guns, knives, and magazines of ammunition. I couldn't tell their age because their faces had been blistered by the weather."

Murtha recounted his experience in Vietnam, praised the rebels for defeating the Soviets, and assured them of continued U.S. support.

"They cheered and pumped their rifles up and down in enthusiasm," Murtha said. "Then I made the second point, that since the Soviets were withdrawing from Afghanistan, the guerilla fighters should hold fire and let them leave. When I finished, one of them stood up and thanked our delegation for its assistance. But, he said, 'No Soviet soldiers will ever be safe in Afghanistan. We will not allow them to march out of Afghanistan with their heads held high, their bands playing, and their flags waving. We will continue to attack and kill them until every single Soviet has left Afghanistan.'"

Murtha was impressed by how brutal and tenacious the Afghanis were against the Russians and throughout their history. When the British retreated from Afghanistan in 1842, only one of over 4,000 troops retreating down Khyber Pass survived to reach British-held Jalalabad. Looking clear back to Alexander the Great, no one from the outside had been able to hold Afghanistan, Murtha recalled.

Murtha often said the Soviet Union had overextended itself during its ten-year occupation in Afghanistan, which caused major economic problems and helped to bring down the Berlin Wall in 1989.

He would make this point later in questioning President Barack Obama's decision to ramp up the U.S. commitment to Afghanistan.

But his role in the Afghan-Soviet war, even decades later, is known to very few people. The action was classified at the time. Murtha occasionally told the story of the leathered faces of gun-toting rebels at Zia's funeral without the details about the Stingers, and the most exposure he received on Afghanistan may have been the brief mentions in Charlie Wilson's War.

Other examples of Murtha's firm support for military power are far too many to recount. But one striking example was in 1987, when the House was considering a cut in funds for chemical weapons or CW.

Both the United States and Soviet Union talked about destroying their CW. Some Americans were so anxious to take the terrible weapons off the planet that they argued for the United States to get rid of its chemical weapons before the Soviets got rid of theirs. That provided no bargaining leverage, and Murtha turned to the Reagan White House to make his point.

Murtha had asked then-Secretary of State George P. Shultz about the impact on those negotiations if Congress would eliminate funding to modernize the U.S. arsenal. He read Shultz's reply on the House floor.

Shultz wrote, "Once the Soviets saw that the U.S. was serious about acquiring an adequate deterrent capability, the Soviet position began to take on an air of realism."

They began building a facility for destroying chemical weapons, and agreed to an exchange of visits to CW destruction facilities. But they did not agree to allow inspections.

"Our judgment is that the elimination of funding for the U.S. chemical modernization program could cause a significant setback in the negotiating process. It was only after we made clear that we would no longer tolerate a situation wherein our CW stockpile continued to deteriorate as the negotiations dragged on, that the Soviet position began to change. We believe that our binary (CW) modernization decision has provided a useful incentive to the Soviets to negotiate somewhat more productively," Schultz wrote, adding that if verifications would be achieved, all CW would be destroyed.

After reading the long letter, Murtha was succinct in adding, "We torpedo the current negotiations and lose our chance of getting rid of chemical weapons" if we adopt an amendment to cut CW funding.

To some, it may have seemed counter-intuitive to clamor for funds for chemical weapons as a means of eliminating them, but that made perfect sense in Murtha's mind.

He and Reagan, the quintessential hawk, were on the same page. The Soviets would talk seriously about eliminating such weapons only if they knew we were serious about making our arsenal more potent than theirs.

Barely three years later, with President George H.W. Bush in the White House, Iraq invaded Kuwait. While many in Congress argued that economic sanctions should be given more time to work, Murtha disagreed.

Urging Congress to authorize military action to force Iraq out of Kuwait in 1991, Murtha began his remarks on the House floor by praising President Bush:

"He sent in the 82nd Airborne, he sent in the Marine Expeditionary Force, he deployed carriers, he sent in F-15 fighters, and he consulted with Congress. I personally, in my job as chairman of the Defense Appropriations Subcommittee, met with him eleven times on this crisis. I have talked with him on the phone, and we gave him advice. He did not talk to us; we talked to him. We said to him, get the allies involved; seek burden sharing; don't repeat Vietnam. We said, everything must be done under the auspices of the United Nations. President Bush, with his background in diplomacy, as former ambassador to the United Nations, did a brilliant job."

Troops had been deployed under Operation Desert Shield to make sure Saddam Hussein would not try to march into another country and provide a base from which to launch a counter-invasion. Allowing time for sanctions to work meant that the troops would be left in a nasty place:

"I visited the 82nd Airborne one month after the deployment. Let me tell you something: there is no harsher environment. I have been in the jungles of Vietnam. I have been in the jungles of Central America.

There is no harsher environment than the deserts of the Middle East. If you sit here in an air-conditioned office and you say, 'Let our soldiers sit out there in the sand,' you do not know what it is like. You put your hand on metal and you get a third-degree burn. It is so hot they have to train at nighttime and sleep in the daytime. Many of them are getting just one hot meal a day and infrequent showers.

"It is easy for the Congress to sit back here and say, 'We are going to allow these troops to sit out there in the sand for an unlimited period of time.' We cannot do that, and they cannot sustain that physically," Murtha said, calling on the nation "to be united against Saddam Hussein and united in support of the international community arrayed against Saddam Hussein."

Murtha delivered eighty-seven Democratic votes to pass that war resolution, and President Bush personally called him at home that evening to thank him.

A decade later, Murtha often recalled his eleven meetings with "Bush I," a president who listened and considered recommendations, to draw a stark contrast with "Bush II," president in the second Gulf War. But that gets ahead of the story.

Perhaps the only thing that Murtha was more passionate about than a strong military was taking care of the people who serve in the military.

In 1994, he bucked President William Clinton, a fellow Democrat, when Clinton wanted to freeze the pay on federal employees. Using his great skill at shepherding key legislation through Congress, Murtha engineered a military pay raise of more than two percent.

"I've always concentrated on pay (and) quality of life," Murtha told *Congressional Quarterly* at the time. He said his efforts to upgrade medical care for military personnel was "probably the premier thing I've done."

This was just two years after the major deployment to remove Saddam Hussein from Kuwait, where troops remained. Yet Clinton was cutting the budget while troops were also deployed to Somalia and debate was focused on whether to deploy more troops to Bosnia.

Murtha understood better than anyone how much pressure was being placed on the defense budget. But there was also pressure on the troops, and he understood that morale would be affected if they did not get a raise – and that morale affects performance.

In 1998, Murtha beat back a proposal to reduce military pensions to forty percent from fifty percent for personnel who joined the military after 1986. Murtha argued that the pension cut was resulting in many sergeants and other experienced, upper-level military personnel refusing to re-enlist. The budget savings in reduced pensions would be offset by the need for more training as career soldiers, sailors, airmen, and Marines left the services, by higher recruitment costs, and reduced performance resulting in lower morale and lower-quality people joining the services.

In 1999, working shoulder-to-shoulder with Republican C.W. "Bill" Young of Florida, who had just moved up from Defense Appropriations Subcommittee chairman to chairman of the full Appropriations Committee, Murtha again battled for a military pay raise as part of the supplemental appropriation that was needed to support the deployment to Kosovo, where the Serbians were battling with Albanian guerillas.

Murtha was always concerned about veterans, too. And that concern extended far beyond the programs that provide veterans with health care and other benefits. The debate over whether burning the American flag is free speech protected by the Constitution is often a heated one.

In 2001, Murtha sponsored a Constitutional Amendment to prohibit the desecration of the American Flag.

"The American Flag is recognized around the world as a symbol of freedom, equal opportunity, and religious tolerance. Many thousands of Americans fought and suffered and died in ways too numerous to list in order to establish and preserve the rights we sometimes take for granted, rights which are symbolized by our Flag. It is a solemn and sacred symbol of the many sacrifices made by our Founding Fathers and our veterans throughout several wars as they fought to establish and protect the founding principles of our great nation," he said.

"Most Americans, veterans in particular, feel deeply insulted when they see our Flag being desecrated. It is in their behalf, in their honor, and in their memory that we have championed this effort to protect and honor this symbol.

"We are a free nation. No one would disagree that free speech is indeed a cherished right and integral part of our Constitution that has kept this nation strong and its citizens free from tyranny. Burning and destruction of the flag is not speech. It is an act. An act that inflicts insult, insult that strikes at the very core of who we are as Americans, and why so many of us fought and many died for this country. There are, in fact, words and acts that we as a free nation have deemed to be outside the scope of the First Amendment. They include words and acts that incite violence, slander, libel, and copyright infringement. Surely among these, which we have rightly determined diminish rather than reinforce our freedom, we can add the burning of our Flag, an act that strikes at the very core of our national being."

Murtha always said what he believed, not the party line. He wanted more soldiers, tanks, and aircraft than the Soviets had. He secretly forced Reagan to provide Stinger missiles to the Afghan rebels. He fought for chemical weapons. He delivered the votes to pass the resolution for the first Gulf War by a sizable margin. He sponsored a law to ban the burning of the American Flag – largely because that was such an emotional issue to veterans. On top of it all, he was a decorated combat veteran.

Over the years, Murtha was asked three times to become defense secretary. He twice was approved for promotion from colonel to general in the Marine Corps, but under federal law, a Congressman cannot also be a flag officer. On all of these occasions, he chose to remain in Congress because he felt he could have more impact there over the long haul.

So when Murtha called for redeployment of American troops from Iraq in 2005, the flurry of epithets painting him as a cut-and-run coward did not stick and even made many Republicans cringe. Perhaps one could make the case that Murtha was wrong or misguided, but weak? A liberal Bush basher? That was so far off the mark, more serious members of the House and Senate, even Republicans, defended Murtha or at least distanced themselves from such attacks.

For many, November 17, 2005, was the first time they heard of Jack Murtha. Many of those people were quick to call him something less than patriotic. To those who knew him for decades inside the beltway or at Memorial Day services and other events in rural Southwestern Pennsylvania, the "cut-and-run" shoe never fit because this was a man who had taken every opportunity for three decades to stress the need for American military power.

That is why Murtha's call for redeployment carried so much weight. That is why, when this man said there was something wrong with this war, both constituents and other members of Congress were inclined to believe that, indeed, there was something wrong with this war.

Chapter 6

The Warrior, Not the War

By November 1982, America was trying to heal itself from the divisive Vietnam War that had brought out massive anti-war protests and bitterness, not only against the war but clearly against the warrior, many of whom served not by choice, but because they had been drafted.

That November 13, during a weeklong national salute to Americans who had served in the war, 150,000 Vietnam veterans, family, and friends of veterans and of those who had died in 'Nam marched in the nation's capital. They came not to protest, but to say thanks and witness the dedication of the first phase of the Vietnam Veterans Memorial in Washington, D.C.

The black-granite wall was inscribed with the names of the 57,939 Americans who died in the conflict and arranged in order of death. Although it was controversial, "The Wall" soon became the nation's most-visited memorial.

Jan Craig Scruggs, wounded as an infantryman in Vietnam, was the inspiration for The Wall. He was joined at the dedication by one of the very few in Congress who had been of much help, Jack Murtha. The controversy that day was that President Reagan was not there, which angered the veterans and made them once again feel slighted.

Scruggs and Murtha had met in 1979, according to Scruggs, who described Murtha as a morning person and generally a very pleasant man. Murtha had worked with him in getting funding to remove land mines in Vietnam and was frustrated that Congress was not more supportive in funding the design and building of The Wall, leaving most of the fundraising to Scruggs and other veterans.

"To me, this was a guy who always seemed to try and do the right thing for veterans and the military. I would think those who look at such things would have to give the guy a pretty high grade in that regard," Scruggs said later.

In 1977, Murtha entered into the *Congressional Record* the words that Scruggs had penned for the *Washington Post*. The words had struck a chord with Murtha, who had often spoken of the challenges those who served in Vietnam faced at war and then back home, how many of them would never be at peace.

In inserting the column, Murtha said that it "eloquently adds to many of the comments I have been making over the past few years about the treatment of Vietnam veterans."

Scruggs' article was titled, "Forgotten Veterans of that Peculiar War."

"Just as the Vietnam war was unique in the way that it was waged – and lost – so, too, that conflict had subjected our youngest-ever crop of war veterans to pressures unparalleled in American military history. The victory parades and hero status awarded to previous generations of military returnees were simply not present. The national turmoil surrounding the war made one's status as a Vietnam veteran a dubious distinction at best," Scruggs wrote.

"Probably no aspect of the war has been more exploited, misunderstood, and officially neglected than the readjustment problems of Vietnam returnees. In the past two years, the psychological and academic communities have finally started taking an interest in the effects of having participated in that conflict. We are seeing research indicating that serious and prolonged adjustment problems exist for many Vietnam veterans."

He wrote that as a naive teenager, a profound sense of duty had compelled him to enlist.

"After my tour, the wounds and medals I received as an infantryman in Vietnam became slowly transformed into reminders of my part in a cruel and meaningless conflict. My naive acceptance of America as a great and noble land gave way to more critical thinking as my conventional beliefs, attitudes, and values were shaken by the war," he continued. "I sometimes felt a deep bitterness toward this country, as I reflected back to a quiet Sunday in 1970, when two very special friends of mine, a young black and a Jewish draftee, suddenly lay dismembered and motionless in the dirt of Vietnam."

Scruggs wrote about the poor treatment of military personnel returning from Vietnam, the burden on the youth who saw combat, and the long-term impact on those who served. He also saw that the war itself had a negative impact on the minds and hearts of a nation. He suggested a national monument as a means of helping to heal those wounds, and became the driving force who made the Vietnam Veterans Memorial a reality.

Also in 1977, President Jimmy Carter proposed a plan in which anyone who had received a less-than-honorable discharge during Vietnam, including those who fled to Canada or elsewhere to avoid returning to military duty, could have their discharge upgraded and become eligible for veterans benefits. Carter was reaching out in a spirit of compassion with the goal of helping the nation heal from the bitterness of the divisive war.

In a heated debate that June, Congressman Robin L. Beard Jr., Republican of Tennessee, argued that these veterans should not be eligible for veterans benefits, no matter what their circumstances were. "It is one thing to provide for removal of the stigma associated with undesirable discharges, but it is an altogether different matter to provide a reward of benefits for these individuals," he said, arguing that these veterans might receive $200 million or more in benefits.

Murtha, in an emotional speech, claimed that the program was needed because the domestic political turmoil surrounding the Vietnam War had placed those veterans under enormous strain.

"These fellows have had as much as they can stand," Murtha said. "Everybody thought the criticism was directed at them.... I do not know that there is one other person in this House that has served with the ground forces in Vietnam and saw the tragedy and suffering these young fellows went through, while everybody back here in this Congress were in their air-conditioned offices telling these soldiers what to do."

Murtha had such respect for the war fighters, he recognized the extraordinary extra stress that these young men faced when they were ridiculed and spit on by people on the street, just because they had been drafted and chose not to flee to Canada. Many of those who served in Vietnam, he believed, had earned benefits, even if they failed to complete their time in uniform. It was the highest respect for the sacrifice of service in war.

The biggest lesson that America learned from Vietnam, many believe, is that we can respect the warrior, even if we oppose the war.

Thirty years later, many argued that to oppose the war in Iraq was to insult the American war fighter. Those people either failed to learn the lesson from Vietnam or ignored the knowledge for the sake of political expediency. Murtha believed that war fighters deserve respect because they are answering a call to duty, and it is wrong to argue that respecting the war fighter required one to support the war. Murtha embodied that belief. He lived and breathed it.

As the Iraq war evolved, Murtha struggled to rationalize the American dead and wounded, the Iraqi civilian dead and wounded, the political realities that were being ignored, the financial implications, and effectiveness of this war effort. But there was more. Murtha saw the long-term impact on the war fighters who survived and on the families of those who came back dead, alive, or half-dead from the physical or emotional scars. He saw their service as patriotic, but came to see the mission their country had sent them on as flawed.

Murtha was attacked for turning his back on the war fighter in calling for redeployment. One could argue Murtha's military strategy was wrong, but to argue Murtha was dishonoring members of the military was childish name-calling. Few have served their country in battle and in thought the way that Murtha and Jan Craig Scruggs had over the years, and no one can argue that either man is anything less than pro-veteran. In a phone interview, Scruggs spoke about Murtha and his service and impact for veterans.

"Well, it is safe to say it is a passion of his, veterans and the military in general. Making certain their needs are looked out for, that those in the field have the equipment and protection they need. Some people have opera or national parks. Murtha has veterans and the military," Scruggs said with a chuckle.

Scruggs recalled a conversation not long before Murtha's 2005 call for redeployment.

"He seemed very concerned. I mean, I am sure everyone was concerned about the people doing the fighting, but it seemed to really be eating at him. He talked about meeting the wounded and the families of those hurt or killed and how it was weighing on him about the whole thing. He was definitely wrestling with the benefits being worth the cost in terms of that (Iraq). Of course that is the issue that one always wrestles with in terms of war. Is it worth it? Look at Gettysburg. It was one of the deadliest, bloodiest days of war ever. Was it worth it? Certainly even as bad as it was, it was worth it because it was a pivotal moment in saving the Union."

Scruggs recalled being confused when Murtha called for redeployment. What should we do, "get out, look for peace with honor, do we owe the Iraqi people this level of commitment in perpetuity, or was it time for the Iraqis to take more control, or when would that time be? These are the things running through my mind and I think most people were confused at the time – except for the truly partisan, of course."

Scruggs never doubted Murtha had the best interest of the country, and especially the military, at heart when he called for redeployment.

"First off, it is wrong to condemn any man for speaking his opinion, even though there certainly were those who did just that to Murtha," Scruggs said. "I know he was expressing his opinion in good faith, and the criticism of some that he was just seeking fame or notoriety just does not fit the man. There is no doubt Murtha's action and expression led to a more open, honest, and frank debate on the war and what was best to do next. Agree with the man or not, he carried such a level of credibility because he was a veteran and had always fought for veterans that his stance forced a conversation. That is a good thing, and certainly others with credibility as the same sort of military veteran, most notably I think would be (Senator) Lindsey Graham (Republican of South Carolina), argued the other side of the issue. But you are right in that I think Murtha's courage to take such a stance brought about those needed debates.

"There are a lot of people in Washington who manage to make a living by never taking a stand or putting themselves in a position to take such criticism as he (Murtha) did. It takes a great deal of courage sometimes in Washington to not just sit back, but to force an issue. You need leaders who are willing to speak out," he added.

Murtha's willingness to speak out, especially for veterans, was a hallmark of his thirty-six year career in Congress. The vast majority of veterans, and especially veterans from Murtha's area, believed that he was, had been, and would always be there for them. His comments on the Haditha incident did anger some veterans later. But for the most part, the attempt to paint him as a traitor or somehow anti-military never stood up, especially back home, where people knew better from the firsthand accounts of his words and actions.

One such firsthand account was offered by Elaine Boxler of

Johnstown. Her husband John served in Vietnam, and she said he was spit upon the day he returned. Still, that first day back would be a good one for John Boxler because he was home safe and that was the day he and Elaine first met. In 1991, John Boxler would again serve his country, but this time Elaine would meet his remains at the airport as a widow.

John Boxler's Army Reserve support outfit sustained the largest number of U.S. hostile deaths during the first Gulf war. Some two hundred miles behind the front lines, in Dhahran, Saudi Arabia, an Iraqi Scud missile landed on a converted water bottling plant and dropped through the roof. It was 8:23 p.m. on Feb. 25, 1991.

That plant was housing members of at least five Reserve units. Among them was the sixty-nine-member 14th Quartermaster Detachment based in Greensburg, Pennsylvania. The water purification unit had just arrived a week earlier.

"It was an awful time, really. I mean we knew there were a lot dead in the attack, but they couldn't tell me if John was one of them. Three days we waited, and all we were told was 'missing in action, missing in action.' At least I had hope that maybe he wasn't there when it hit," said Elaine.

John Boxler, at the age of forty-four, was the oldest serviceman to die in the blast. The final count was twenty-eight dead and another ninety-nine wounded. Because of this one scud strike, twenty-five percent of all Americans killed or wounded due to enemy action in the Persian Gulf War were Army Reservists.

The missile caused hideous wounds. Men sent to the desert to purify water would be blinded by their own blood; their faces peppered with shrapnel; their legs ripped off; blood flowing from their eyes and ears. It is described as a scene of chaos and pain. Some died instantly. Others suffered for a while with massive wounds. John Boxler was so mangled by the explosion that he was listed as missing in action for three days because it took that long to identify his body.

"Those were three awful days, not knowing. I hoped that by some miracle he was some place else and because of the confusion, they just didn't know where. His wounds were so bad, they didn't know who he was. The military came once they knew.

"John Murtha was one of the first people to call when they left," Elaine continued. "His office had been great and was really pushing to find out what was John's story during those three days. I think he (Murtha) found out first and when the military came and told us, he called right after. He said a lot of things and, to be honest, I don't know if I remember much of the actual words, but I do recall how good it felt that he called. I felt like he was with us and that he really appreciated John. You get the kindness of a lot of people when you lose someone, and it doesn't make the hurt go away, but it does make you a little stronger. Murtha calling as soon as he did helped me get through those first few days."

John Boxler's death had brought the Persian Gulf War home to the region. For folks from Southwestern Pennsylvania, when talk on television would center on how few American deaths had occurred in that military action, there was a sort of stillness. America had done a fabulous job in forcing Iraq out of Kuwait, but even such overwhelming victory comes with a cost.

For Elaine Boxler, the price was her husband.

"He died in service to his country, and it was hard, but we are all proud of him. Everyone was. We had to move his funeral to a church and I think over 2,000 people came. It was like that phone call from Mr. Murtha: it helped to know people cared," she recalled.

In the days and weeks that followed, Elaine Boxler dealt with her depression and loss, and while she had help from many, she gladly offered up praise for Jack Murtha and his work for veterans and their families.

"He and his people were there the whole time. I can recall meeting him, and his arm around me, and how he said if we needed anything we should call. He talked about how John died bravely and how honored he was to meet us. You know, to this day when he sees me, he asks how I am, calls me by name, asks about my family," she had told a reporter shortly before Murtha died.

"You would think with all the people he meets and places he goes and how busy he is, that my face would just kind of get forgotten, but he has never forgotten me. He spoke at my son's high school graduation a while after John died, and he spoke about sacrifice and country, and he talked about John. It meant everything to us that he spoke that day and that he used John in his speech. He promised me he would always be there for my family and me, and he has never forgotten us."

When America again returned to war in Iraq, Elaine Boxler worried for future widows. When Murtha eventually called for redeployment, she trusted immediately his instinct and his motives.

"Oh, when we went back in, I did think of John and what other wives might go through. I think back then, to be honest, I thought maybe we had left the job a little undone, so part of me liked that we may have been finishing the job now. Then we found out things weren't what we thought going in, and more and more of our guys were dying, and it seemed like nothing was getting better. When Mr. Murtha said we needed (to get) out of there, I thought he was right. He always knows what is going on, and I was sort of thinking we needed out of there, anyway," she said.

"People started saying all kinds of bad things about him but that's just politics. Nothing anyone has said about the guy has changed my opinion of him. He is a good man."

Political critics attempted to paint Murtha as old and out-of-touch after his call for redeployment, but Boxler summed up how most people in the 12th Congressional District reacted to his words and that criticism.

"I will say he (Murtha) sometimes says things that get him hot water. He puts his foot in his mouth. You could say he does it because he is older now, but really he has always spoken his mind when he believes something, and he doesn't care who he ticks off if it needs to be said. I worry about him getting, you know, attacked for speaking his mind, but I am a bit more shy about such things. I like that he speaks his mind and I can't tell you when I thought he was wrong about something. Like I said, I think he is honest, hard-working, and really cares about us, you know, the region, like he is supposed to do," said Elaine.

As for the complications of war, redeployment, and seeing the world in black and white, Elaine Boxler adds a perspective and clarity that only a war widow could. Scholars, politicians, and the media wrestle with how to support the troops, if not the war. They try to name it or define it. Elaine Boxler, in her simple way and through her life's experience, did it better than most. Mission and service are two different things and all widows and widowers can be proud of their spouses' service, no matter what the mission.

"Everyone talks about supporting the troops, but there is more to it than when they leave; there is when they come home or, like John, not come home. Murtha supports the troops. People need to keep in mind – other widows is who I mean here: even if you think this war was wrong or a waste, the husbands who died over there died for a good cause. I don't know if this war was a good cause or not; I am not that into politics. It's just that their country called and they went, and that makes what they did a good cause, that they went when they were called. I just think of any young wife today and hope that she never thinks of her husband's death as less or a waste, no matter what they think of the war. He served his country and if he died today, they can be just as proud of him as we are of John or anyone who died in other wars protecting our country. They had a duty and they lived up to it, so be proud of that."

A seven-foot bronze statue was dedicated at the Greensburg Reserve Center in 1992. The surrounding community raised $165,000 for the memorial, and 2,000 area residents attended its dedication. John P. Murtha was among them.

Chapter 7

Looks Like Rain

In January 2001, President-elect George W. Bush invited congressional leaders to Austin, Texas, to talk about their national security concerns. Each of them offered some observations. When Murtha's turn came, he told the president-elect not to focus on a missile-defense system, as Bush's advisors were urging, but instead to focus on nuclear proliferation and terrorism.

"I recognize the highest priority defense issue in your party's platform is the rapid development and deployment of a limited national defense to counter the potential of a missile attack from a nation such as North Korea or Iraq. Personally, I think a much more probable danger is a terrorist attack," Murtha told the president-elect, according to his 2004 book, *From Vietnam to 9/11*.

In his typical, low-profile fashion, when Murtha returned to Washington, he did not talk to national media, but set up a conference call with local reporters from Southwestern Pennsylvania.

Those reporters were more interested in the hanging chads, Florida recount, and Supreme Court debacle that had made Bush the president instead of Democrat Al Gore. Could the two sides mend fences? Could Congress work with this president?

Eventually, a reporter asked about the purpose of the meeting: national defense.

Murtha had chaired the House Defense Appropriations Subcommittee and at the time, with a Republican House majority, was the subcommittee's ranking Democrat. He had been an intense student of the military and international affairs his entire life, so his grasp of these issues was arguably unmatched. He was a staunch military man who had supported Ronald Reagan's approach to rebuilding the military after the Carter administration, and he had been an ally to the first President Bush in foreign affairs and the first Gulf war.

But Murtha also spoke from the gut. When he spoke, he said what he believed to be the truth and, far more often than not, he would turn out to be right. So if Jack Murtha said it looked like rain, the smart man would get his umbrella.

When asked a simple, broad question about what he had told the president-elect, his answer was overlooked by most media, but would prove in a few months to have been a chilling forecast.

Murtha jumped into his answer leading with one of his favorite words, "Absolutely!" While many politicians often say, "I am glad you asked that question," and then proceed to say whatever they wanted to say, Murtha gave straight, often long answers, but he always, at one point in his ramblings, gave some sort of answer to the question. When he started with "absolutely," he was jumping straight to the heart of the question first.

He said he had informed the president-elect and advisors that they were too worried about missiles and missile defense. He told them the real danger was terrorists using domestic airplanes as weapons against us. What scared him was the potential of a nuclear bomb the size of a suitcase being brought onto a commercial plane and set off in America. He said this threat was real and was something we needed to focus on.

This was nine months before the terrorist attacks of 9/11. At the time, terrorism, Iraq, and Osama Bin Laden were occasional topics for news junkies or analysts, but were not much on the public mind.

There was no political advantage in talking about terrorism to local reporters.

So when Murtha told local reporters that he had told Bush that the real danger from abroad was our domestic airplanes being used as weapons against us, his comment made such a small impression that the next media question went back to hanging chads and the voting process. Eventually a follow up on planes as weapons was asked, and Murtha explained the reaction of the incoming president.

"He seemed surprised by it, really," Murtha said. "He had no idea. They were very much in a Cold War kind of mind set. I pointed out to Cheney on the way down that this is something he personally ought to look at. So I think he got the message, and I believe that he probably was a little startled by what I told him."

Some reviews of Murtha's book referred to the work as boastful, but given the information he shared with local media after that Austin meeting, quite the opposite seems to be true.

While Murtha did not talk about planes being hijacked and crashed, he did warn of the dangers in our skies. For most politicians of this era, that would have been close enough to say, "I told you so." The fact that Murtha never did boast of his pre-9/11 concerns in his book cannot be downplayed. He did warn of terrorism. He did warn of planes as weapons, and he did tell Dick Cheney to handle the matter himself, as vice president, since it was so urgent.

Murtha and Cheney had a good relationship and a strong mutual respect. One can easily imagine them sitting on a plane having this discussion, and Murtha pointing out to his old friend that an attack on the United States by terrorists through the use of our own domestic airlines was far more likely than a missile encounter with a nation that would know our response would be overwhelming.

While Murtha was a fan of George H.W. Bush, whom he called "Bush I", the younger Bush or "Bush II" was virtually a stranger to him. Murtha was aware that Bush II had come from a different background than his father, the former CIA director. Murtha's nature was to work behind the scenes in the manner he felt would be most productive and best received by those in charge. In the case of the new Bush White House, that would mean through Cheney.

John Hugya, Murtha's long-time Chief of Staff, described Murtha's opinion of Cheney, even after the full-blown political battle that unfolded after Murtha's call for redeployment from Iraq.

"Jack liked Dick Cheney; he did. He had a great deal of respect for him, and he said to always remember that Cheney was a man, a real man who always had the best interest of the country at heart. He respected Dick Cheney."

Cheney returned that respect and defended the character of Murtha when Murtha was called a "coward" on the floor of Congress.

Hugya reflected back to a time where he and Murtha were fly fishing. Murtha was an avid fly fisherman and, like many from Pennsylvania, found an escape and clarity that comes from standing waist-deep in the chilled and rolling waters in search of the perfect cast and the resulting catch of a beautiful brook or rainbow trout.

"We were at Rolling Rock and the phone rang. It was one of those big cradle phones you used to lug around, and when I answered, I said, 'This is John Hugya for Congressman Murtha.' The voice on the other end of the phone asked where the chairman was, and I told him we were fishing and that he was a few clicks up the river. And I asked, 'Who is this?' The voice on the other end of the phone said, 'This is Dick Cheney and I need to speak with him now.' I got his number in case I lost him on the way up river, but I kept the line open as I made my way to the Boss (Murtha). That's when Cheney told him Saddam Hussein had gone into Kuwait. That's where we were when we got word, and it was Cheney who called. He (Murtha) didn't talk long, hung up the phone, and said, 'We got to go.'"

Murtha had learned of the invasion of Kuwait by Iraq the way a father hears of a bloody nose at school for his son: a phone call out of the blue with bad news while he was doing the things one does with life outside the beltway. War and nations at peril had reached into an otherwise quiet Pennsylvania stream and demanded the old fellow in the rubber boots and funny hat transform once again from ordinary to extraordinary, and make his way quickly to Washington, D.C., to help map out what America should do next. The call did not come from a staffer or an assistant. It came from Cheney himself, who at the time was Secretary of Defense under Bush I.

Murtha and Cheney had met after Cheney was elected to Congress in 1978 and served on the House Intelligence Committee, whose programs often were funded by the Defense Appropriations Subcommittee, on which Murtha was a senior member. When Cheney became defense secretary under Bush I, coming from the House, he did not know the Senators who headed the Defense Appropriations

Subcommittee or the Armed Services Committee well, and he did not click with Congressman Les Aspin, who then was chairman of House Armed Services, according to Murtha's close advisors.

"Cheney recognized that the power rested with the money. Murtha was such a hawk and he was the guy you could deal with, so by default, they developed a good relationship," the advisor said.

Cheney at times testified before the committee and briefed Murtha at meetings on Capitol Hill, but Murtha and Cheney also had breakfast once or twice a week and frequently talked on the phone. They even went to see the movie *Hunt for Red October*.

They became good friends.

Murtha and Cheney developed such a close trust that Murtha sometimes got things done simply by asking Cheney – not by "earmarking" or inserting funding in the defense appropriation, according to Murtha's advisors.

So in Austin in 2001, it would be precisely Murtha's nature to not belabor the issue of terrorism with the president, whom he did not know, but rather discuss his concerns in detail with the man in the loop he did know. This conversation in Austin and even the personal dialogue between Cheney and Murtha in flight is not mentioned to say that 9/11 could have been avoided if only the Bush-Cheney White House had listened to Murtha. Murtha was not the only one sounding such alarms.

According to the 9/11 Commission's report, Bush and his principal advisers had all been briefed on terrorism, including Osama bin Laden. In September 2000, Acting Deputy Director of Central Intelligence John McLaughlin led a team to Bush's ranch in Crawford, Texas, to give a four-hour review of sensitive information. Ben Bonk, deputy chief of the CIA Counterterrorist Center, used one of the four hours to deal with terrorism.

To highlight the danger of terrorists obtaining chemical, biological, radiological, or nuclear weapons, Bonk brought along a mock-up suitcase to demonstrate how the Aum Shinrikyo doomsday cult had spread deadly sarin nerve agent on the Tokyo subway in 1995. Bonk told Bush that Americans would die from terrorism during the next four years.

In December, Bush met with President Clinton for a two-hour, one-on-one discussion of national security and foreign policy challenges. In the 9/11 report, Clinton recalled saying to Bush, "I think you will find that, by far, your biggest threat is bin Laden and the al Qaeda." Clinton also said, "One of the great regrets of my presidency is that I didn't get him (bin Laden) for you, because I tried to."

Bush told the commission that he felt sure President Clinton had mentioned terrorism, but did not remember much being said about al Qaeda.

The fact that Murtha was left with the impression that the incoming White House team was surprised by his talk of terrorism or airlines is its own commentary on how closely Bush and his advisors were listening during these briefings.

Donald Rumsfeld, Paul Wolfowitz, and Richard Perle had been associated with the Project for the New American Century, a conservative think-tank spawned by the American Enterprise Institute. Now all three were high-ranking officials in the Bush administration.

"Their big concern was nuclear proliferation and ballistic missile defense. That's what they were telling Bush when Murtha sat in that meeting in Texas and told them the threat was terrorism," said Dan Cunningham, a Murtha team advisor.

Nearly two years after 9/11, Murtha told a reporter off camera why he had never said anything about his warning, why he did not bang the drum and say "I told you so" over and over as so many would have.

"What good would it have done? I mean we talked, I told him, he did not listen. But to be fair, it's not like I gave him a date and said stop this attack. We all are responsible for this because of what we saw and did not realize was there, and for what we did not see. We have a hell of a mess to clean up, and that sort of public bashing only slows the process. That is not the way to get things done until it is absolutely necessary, until you have tried every way to get it right and the other guy refuses to listen," Murtha said.

Nearly five years later, when Jack Murtha said it was time to stand back in Iraq and let the Iraqis sort out their own mess, he believed it. When he called out the president on Iraq, he did so as a man who felt he had exhausted every other way to change course. When the political hate machine fired up and attacked him as a coward and media hound, they were wrong. That just is not who he was or how he operated. In the biggest "I told you so" ever, Murtha took a pass at turning up the political heat on the president because he did not think it was fair or that it served any purpose.

Murtha's book, published in 2004, noted that he had told President-elect Bush about the likelihood of a terrorist attack, but did not mention that he had warned Bush about planes being used as weapons or that he had urged Cheney to look into the matter personally. Even in his own book, Murtha did not make public his warnings that using domestic airlines as weapons was the most likely method of terrorist attack against the nation.

The fact that the warning did happen demonstrates Murtha's insight on national security and his preference for working behind the scenes. Those who would call him a media hound seeking glory, or attack him based on their politics or the image created by the right-wing hate machine may begin to recognize that he was not politically motivated on 9/11, the darkest day America has known since Pearl Harbor.

Murtha was making his assessment based on briefings and discussion he had with the top national security advisors inside and outside of the Pentagon. The commonly used phrase "pre-9/11 mentality" typically meant that no one had thought about the dangers in our skies. But Jack Murtha had a near dead-on opinion about what to fear as early as 2000, and others in charge of our defense had educated him.

If the events of 9/11 and his pre-9/11 warning to the Bush White House had a hand in his eventual call for redeployment, that role perhaps can be boiled down to a single word: regret. Murtha did warn of the dangers in the skies, he did ask Cheney to look into the matter personally. But he did not blame the president for 9/11, and why would he? He did, in part, blame himself because his decades of experience, the intelligence, and even his gut told him this was a priority.

Murtha, in a sense, had been there before. U.S. troops were sent to Beirut, Lebanon, after Israel had invaded Lebanon to drive out Palestinian guerillas. Murtha went to inspect the situation and returned with serious concerns that the U.S. troops were vulnerable because the rules of engagement required solders on post or patrol to keep their weapons with no bullet in the chamber, bolt closed, and weapon on safe. He urged military leaders to change the rules of engagement, but his recommendation fell on deaf ears. On October 23, 1983, 241 U.S. troops died when a truck loaded with explosives crashed through security and blew up the building where they were housed.

If only Murtha's warning had been heeded.

Likewise, Murtha warned of the risk from domestic airlines. Again, no one listened, and his worst fear became a reality.

Murtha's sensitivity and understanding of the threat of terrorism was impressive, by any measure, in January 2001, but it was hardly new for the man who had made defense and the military his life's work.

In 1995, after the poison gas attack in Tokyo and the bombing at the World Trade Center, Murtha added fifty million dollars to the defense appropriations bill to enable the National Guard and Reserves to counter bioterrorism. While the rest of America convulsed over the guilt or innocence of O.J. Simpson in the murder trial of the former football star's wife, Jack Murtha was carving out fifty million dollars to fight bioterrorism in the United States. He was standing guard. He was paying attention. Not only had he warned of planes as weapons months before 9/11, he was preparing to counter terrorism at home six years before most Americans had come to accept that such events could happen on U.S. soil.

Murtha's warning on terrorism, and even his urging of Cheney to look into the matter of planes as weapons, is not intended to say that Bush blew it and Murtha warned him. It is, however, important to know this was a priority for Murtha when Bush first took office, and that he did speak about it publicly, even if most of the country was more consumed with chads on ballots.

Murtha did not seek political advantage in saying such things. The fact that he had warned of these dangers a full eight months before planes crashed into buildings can be labeled only as an honest assessment by an informed Congressman to an incoming president.

Murtha had told Bush and Cheney it was going to rain. Bush and Cheney forgot the umbrella.

Chapter 8

9/11

When American Airlines Flight 11 crashed into the north tower of the World Trade Center in the heart of New York City on September 11, 2001, the immediate broadcast reports spoke about the size of the hole and the fire in the building. The reports did not call it an act of terrorism or even speculate on the size of the plane, let alone what may have caused the crash.

When the second tower was struck by another plane, and then a third plane hit the Pentagon, the world knew the United States was under attack. But no one seemed to know quite what to make of it when a fourth plane crashed in rural Pennsylvania.

With that fourth crash, 9/11 came home to the region that Jack Murtha called home. By air, Johnstown is about sixty miles east of Pittsburgh and fifteen miles north of a small town called Shanksville in Somerset County. When United Flight 93 went down shortly after 10 a.m. that day, emergency crews scrambled to Shanksville, with Johnstown news crews in hot pursuit. Another news-crew caravan was rushing to the John P. Murtha Johnstown-Cambria County Airport, where the air traffic control tower had been warned to evacuate because an extremely suspicious plane apparently on a terrorist mission was heading for the airport.

The whole country was rattled that day, but anyone listening to the chatter on the police and fire emergency system in Johnstown was even more alarmed. Two planes had crashed into the two World Trade Center towers in New York. Another plane had crashed into the Pentagon in Washington, D.C. Yet another plane had crashed into an old strip mine near Shanksville, Pennsylvania, of all places on the planet. And a fifth plane reportedly was headed toward the Johnstown airport.

As alarmed as the nation was at that moment, based on national media coverage, all of the police, emergency responders, media, and anyone else monitoring what was happening around Johnstown was in a state of shock. If Johnstown and Shanksville were under attack, the whole damn sky must be full of crazies crashing airplanes all across the country.

Those listening endured about ten minutes of surreal tension, monitoring minute-by-minute updates and feeling that all of this simply could not be happening; that it must be a nightmare.

Kids at Shanksville Elementary School were ordered to duck under their desks when a loud explosion shook the windows, and dozens of other people in the vicinity were panicked or puzzled by the loud explosion, with many of them calling 9-1-1.

The Boeing 757 had crashed into a reclaimed strip mine, where several layers of rock and dirt had been removed to get down to a layer of coal. After the coal was removed, the loose rock and dirt were put back to create a smoother surface, but that new surface was not like solid rock. When the plane crashed at a sharp angle while moving 563 miles per hour, it partially buried itself in the field as it sent a large mushroom cloud into the sky.

At virtually that same minute, the crew in the Johnstown air traffic control tower was scanning the horizon through binoculars looking for the plane that was reportedly headed its way. As they realized the Johnstown-bound aircraft was not visible by sight and was no longer visible on radar, they soon concluded that the two were the same airplane. The good news, if there could have been such a thing on such a day, was that there was no fifth plane.

In the next few hours, as no other crashes were reported and the entire nation's air-traffic system was shut down, fear and panic was replaced by sadness, bewilderment, and questions – lots of questions.

The crash site in rural Somerset County was starkly different than those in Washington and New York. Chaos and debris are the imprinted images of the two larger cities, but a smoldering quiet and the odor of burning fuel were all that the would-be rescuers found in Shanksville.

The first two people from the media on scene were Brad Lawrence, a radio reporter for a Somerset station, and Erik Grant, a camera man for the Johnstown Fox television affiliate. Grant was there to capture images of a fallen passenger plane, and did not find what he expected.

"There was, well…, like nothing. There was heat and some smoke, but it was like the whole thing just dissolved into the ground. There just wasn't much in the way of pieces. Brad (Lawrence) was doing a live report and some emergency crews were there, but there was no one to rescue," Grant said.

Murtha was in the United States Capitol that day in a room below the House chamber, where his subcommittee was working on the annual defense appropriations bill. He was evacuated with the other members of Congress at about the time American Airlines Flight 77 struck the Pentagon. Flight 93 was on a course that would take it past Johnstown and toward Washington, where authorities feared that the Capitol or the White House was the most likely target.

Murtha's widow, Joyce, happened to have a meeting that day in the Capitol for the National First Ladies' Library board, on which she served as vice president.

"On 9/11, I passed by the Pentagon about fifteen minutes before the plane hit," she said, noting that she did not know about the Twin Towers until she got to the Capitol because she did not have a TV on at home.

"Jack had gone in early as usual, and I went directly to the Rayburn Building, where the National First Ladies' Library board meeting was to be held. A few minutes after I walked in, someone came rushing in to say the Pentagon had been hit. We were immediately told to evacuate the building, no cars, and saw Congressman Regula, who told us to go with him to the Capitol Hill Club," she continued.

Mary Regula is founder and president of the library. As they headed toward the club, a Capitol Hill policeman told them they were too close to the Capitol and directed them to follow him to a safe house a few blocks away.

"As we are walking away from the Capitol, I saw Jack being interviewed on the corner, so I dropped off from the group and joined Jack. He and I walked several blocks away and found a restaurant with outdoor seating. The owner was there. He said none of his employees had shown up, but he could give us coffee and maybe sandwiches. We sat at the sidewalk tables for several hours, but it was eerie. It was dead quiet with few people walking by, no vehicles whatsoever, no planes flying over, no ambulances, nothing. Our cell phones were dead, no TV, so we had no way to know what was happening, except occasionally someone would walk by with a little information. We heard a plane had gone down in Western Pennsylvania, but didn't know where. Every time we asked, we were told we still could not get into the Capitol.

"Finally, we decided to walk back to the Capitol to see if there was any chance we could get our cars out of the Rayburn garage. We got special permission to get our cars, and by then, the 14th Street Bridge had been reopened. We drove past the Pentagon, where the building was still smoking and emergency vehicles were everyplace. This was about 3:30 p.m. When we arrived at our condo near the Pentagon, the answering machine was filled with messages from the family and friends, asking if we were okay," she said, adding,

"Needless to say, none of the library board members from across the country ever wanted to have another board meeting in the Capitol."

The next day, Murtha toured the crash site and, while some paper and pieces of cloth had been scattered up to eight miles away, the vast bulk of the aircraft was in or near the impact crater, and the image that stuck in his mind amounted to little more than a smoldering hole in the ground. He then went to the airport that bears his name and, under the tightest security, spoke with the media about what had transpired.

Murtha choked up and was moved to tears as he spoke. The events of that day had marked him as they had marked all Americans, but in his heart, Murtha was feeling a level of personal responsibility.

"There had to be a struggle, and someone heroically kept that plane from heading to Washington," said Murtha, describing how the plane had veered sharply and turned upside down before crashing. He spoke about the devastation in New York and Washington, and he may have been the first official to publicly proclaim that the passengers were heroes for fighting back, breaking into the cockpit and bringing down Flight 93 before it reached Washington.

"There is no question in my mind the Capitol of the United States is a symbol of freedom worldwide. There is no question in my mind, this airplane was headed towards the Capitol, and it would have been disastrous with the loss of life and the symbolism that it would have presented to the perpetrators of this tragedy," Murtha said.

When he opened the floor to questions, only two of the local media there had also been at the news conference when he talked about warning President-elect Bush about planes being used as weapons. Neither reporter mentioned the warning that day, thinking perhaps Murtha himself might bring up the conversation with Bush or his urging to his old friend, Dick Cheney, to look into the matter himself. Murtha did not say one word.

Murtha never saw the original television piece that included his comments about planes and terrorists, but he did know later that the story existed. He never asked for a copy, never pressed for a bigger deal to be made of the matter after 9/11, and played down the issue when pushed.

In the aftermath of 9/11, as the nation mourned collectively and a sense of national unity swept through the country, Bush led the pack of political leaders in Washington who insisted that we needed to respond and hold someone accountable.

By October 7, less than a month after the attack on America, Operation Enduring Freedom was launched by U.S. and British troops in Afghanistan. The military moved swiftly to attack the safe havens and take away the base of operations from which al Qaeda could stage terrorist activity. Despite the remoteness and difficult mountainous conditions, they were by many accounts surprisingly successful in putting the Taliban regime on the run in the first stage of the war.

That success pumped up the president, the cabinet, the Pentagon, and pretty much the whole country. But it especially pumped up Donald Rumsfeld, Paul Wolfowitz, and Richard Perle. Associated with the right-wing Project for the New American Century, they had been advocating for a missile-defense system and fomenting the idea that if the United States controlled Iraq, the rest of the Middle East would be far more accepting and willing to deal with the United States. Now, all three of these graduates of the project had prominent roles in the Bush administration.

While there were serious rumors that people inside the Pentagon had been "gaming" invasions of Iraq before 9/11 and were planning to invade at that time, team member Gregory R. Dahlberg, who was acting secretary of the Army early in the Bush administration and staff director for the Defense Appropriations Subcommittee previously, said, "I heard that, too. The Army does war games all the time. It's not all that unusual to do war games.... But it's different than saying they were going to go do it (invade Iraq). If you look at the writings of Wolfowitz and the neo-cons, they were hung up about it. That group felt we should have gone into Baghdad the first time, and we didn't. They felt it would change the balance of power if there was a friendly Iraq that would be a buffer between Israel and Iran."

In their minds, 9/11 was just the perfect handy excuse to do what they wanted to do anyway: invade Iraq. The real juice for these guys was that Afghanistan held nothing of value to the United States, but Iraq was rich in oil – the fuel of the American economy.

A drumbeat of reports hit the media talking about how Hussein had weapons of mass destruction and was harboring terrorists, how the Iraqi people were thirsting for freedom and would welcome U.S. soldiers with flowers in the street. When asked the obvious questions about how long it would take to liberate Iraq and how much would it cost, the administration painted a rosy scenario of a quick military victory and a deployment that would be paid for almost entirely by Iraqi oil.

To most people, Saddam Hussein was almost as villainous as bin Laden for having invaded Kuwait just ten years earlier, his renowned cruelty and ruthless murders of political opponents, and his arrogance in refusing to allow United Nations inspectors to determine whether he was making chemical or biological weapons that could destabilize the entire Middle East.

Invading Iraq was an easy sell to some Americans.

Jack Murtha was less than impressed.

Murtha was not inclined to support a war resolution in Congress, his team of advisors said. He had said many times that the country should go to war only when our national security was threatened. He insisted that in any military operation, we needed clear and attainable goals, we should go in with overwhelming force, and we needed an exit strategy. He readily agreed that Hussein was a nasty character, but he was not convinced that Iraq posed an immediate and direct threat to our nation's security.

On September 24, 2002, as pressure was building to invade Iraq, Murtha joined Republican Senators Arlen Specter and Rick Santorum at the White House for a ceremony at which President Bush signed Murtha's legislation, House Resolution 3917, which created a National Memorial at the Flight 93 crash site.

"I'm pleased that we've been able to move this legislation so quickly and that it'll be signed into law so soon after the one-year anniversary," Murtha said in a news release. "The heroes of Flight 93 certainly deserve a National Memorial recognizing the supreme sacrifice they made in fighting back so courageously against terrorism on a date that none of us will ever forget, 9/11."

Murtha's staff was miffed that in the official White House photograph of the president signing Murtha's bill, Murtha was hidden from view behind Santorum, who had done little if anything to support the memorial.

But later that day, September 24, 2002, something else happened that had huge significance as the nation moved forward. That afternoon, at about two o'clock, Jack Murtha met privately with his old friend, Dick Cheney, the vice president of the United States.

A few days later, a member of Murtha's team heard him speak at an event at La Colline, a Capitol Hill restaurant.

"He suddenly went from saying, 'They haven't convinced me; I don't see where it's a threat to our national security,' to (saying) 'We need to push for inspections or else use military force,'" the team member said, adding that when he asked Murtha what had happened, Murtha said, "I can't go into details, but I met with Cheney, and based on what they told me, we've got a problem."

Cheney, it turns out, had told Murtha that Hussein had weapons of mass destruction, and had the means to deliver them to distant targets. The administration had been talking publicly about these supposed weapons for a long time, but the assurance from his old friend, Dick Cheney, was enough to convince Murtha.

Cheney had told Murtha that they had clear evidence that Iraq had chemical and biological weapons, as well as a "means of delivery." That "means" was not missiles, but unmanned aerial vehicles or UAVs, from which they could drop tubes that worked like an aerosol spray or crop duster, the Murtha advisor said.

"Later, when we asked experts, they said (chemicals or biological agents) would dissipate quickly and wouldn't be effective," he said, adding with biting irony, "In fairness to Cheney, maybe he believed that shit."

But based on what Cheney had told him, Murtha began to accept that what he was being fed was true, or at least that he needed to give the benefit of the doubt to Cheney.

On October 10, 2002, the Authorization for Use of Military Force Against Iraq Resolution of 2002, which was unofficially called the Iraq War Resolution, passed the U.S. House of Representatives on a vote of 296 to 133. Jack Murtha voted for the resolution, as did 81 other Democrats, many of whom supported the war resolution in large part because Murtha was voting for it. If Murtha had voted "no," many of them likely would have been emboldened to vote "no," too, more confident that they could withstand the political name-calling they knew would come.

Looking back at what prompted Murtha to call for redeployment three years later, Gabrielle Carruth, who was Murtha's Defense Appropriations aide, said, "He trusted Cheney as a friend and former colleague, but it kept coming out that most of the stuff was exaggerated."

Carruth noted that a different type of intelligence-gathering group had been created in the Pentagon that would skip the normal review processes and send the information directly to Cheney. "I think that had a lot to do with it: he was realizing that they were kind of creating their own intelligence. He was remembering his own experiences in Vietnam," she said, recalling that his commanding officers had threatened to have him court marshaled unless he would exaggerate the body-count numbers.

The inaccuracies and exaggerations started to get to him, and he became obsessed with comparing their "intelligence" with other reports.

"It became clear in his own mind that he simply wasn't being told the truth and the American people weren't being told the truth, and eventually he couldn't be silenced," Carruth said.

Much of that phony intelligence was being provided by Ahmed Chalabi, who had been part of the Iraqi National Congress, which began advocating for the overthrow of Hussein in 1992. Chalabi was the son of one of Iraq's wealthy power elite, part of a prominent Shia family that left Iraq in 1956. He had spent most of his life in the United States and United Kingdom, not in Iraq. So while the CIA distrusted Chalabi, Cheney and Bush were spoon-fed by Rumsfeld, Wolfowitz, and Perle, defending whatever Chalabi said about weapons of mass destruction and ties to al Qaeda, information that later was recognized as false.

As noted, if Murtha felt betrayed by taking Cheney's word in voting for the Iraq War, he never said so, not publicly and not even privately to his closest associates.

"They respected each other," said Joyce Murtha. "He always got along well with Republicans. They worked well together when Jack was Chairman and Cheney was Secretary of Defense. After Cheney became vice president, Jack would say, 'I don't know what happened to him.'"

Immediately after calling for redeployment from Iraq, Cheney made a crack about Murtha, who fired back that he liked "guys that got six deferments," a reference to Cheney's ability to avoid service during Vietnam. But aside from that one time, apparently the worst thing Murtha said about Cheney was that he had become "more ideological." Normally, he would say simply, "We used to be good friends" or "he's changed."

But without Cheney's influence, Murtha would have voted against the war resolution, those close to him agreed. The House vote would have been much more along party lines, not bipartisan, and the friction and tensions surrounding the war at home would have been far more heated and intense from the start.

The Pentagon began positioning troops for an invasion, but Murtha and many others still held out hope that Hussein would back down, rather than let the invasion proceed.

One night, Murtha came home and was really down, which was unusual for him, Joyce said. "He said to me 'This president is going into Iraq, no matter what cooler and more experienced heads are telling him.' He was getting calls from high-level people in the Bush I administration asking Jack if he couldn't do something to stop the president. When he asked them why they didn't stop it, he was told, 'This president won't listen to us.'"

On March 20, 2003, U.S. troops invaded Iraq and won a quick military victory. But that was the easy part.

A member of Murtha's team, who believed that some people in the Pentagon were planning to invade before 9/11, said, "The reason there was no after-war planning is that would have meant (acknowledging) they were planning to go to war – they were trying to do this charade to make it look like they hadn't made up their minds ahead of time."

While others on the Murtha team disagreed that there was "no" planning for how to get out of Iraq, they all agreed there was far too little realism in planning that exit strategy. Bush refused to set any timelines and refused to hold anyone accountable, so the war dragged on and on amidst a constant attrition of hearts and minds.

The administration had phonied up arguments to claim that Saddam Hussein presented a threat to the Middle East and, therefore, to the security of the nation and world. But while they did adhere to at least one of Murtha's tenants about going to war – they went in with overwhelming force – they went in ill prepared to "win the peace."

Winning the peace was the optimal exit strategy. But winning the peace required a large enough force to keep violence under control all over this enormous country until a viable government was established that could take over that control. Winning the peace would prove to be far more difficult than Bush or anyone in his administration seemed to recognize. Winning the peace was far more difficult than winning the war.

Chapter 9

"Energize, Iraqatize and Internationalize"

On Sunday, August 17, 2003, nearly four months after President George W. Bush had triumphantly landed on the U.S.S. Abraham Lincoln to give a rousing speech under the huge "We Have Prevailed" banner, Jack Murtha and a small delegation of congressional staff road out to Andrews Air Force Base near Washington, D.C. They boarded a military aircraft and departed. After a night stop to refuel at Shannon Airport in Ireland, they continued on to Kuwait Airport, where they took a long drive into Kuwait City. They arrived at the hotel late.

The next day was unbelievably hot. The delegation was driven back to the airport and boarded an empty C130 cargo plane for the flight to Baghdad International Airport.

At this time, things were relatively under control in Iraq. The delegation was able to ride in a convoy of vehicles down to the Green Zone. On four subsequent trips Murtha took to Iraq, they always had to take "the cowboys" – helicopters with an escort of Apache attack helicopters to protect them.

The drive went smoothly, although the scenery was surreal: damaged buildings along the way, debris along the route.

The delegation went to the one place in Baghdad that had air conditioning, a section of an otherwise bombed-out palace in an area with other bombed-out palaces.

"It was hot as the blue blazes," recalled David Morrison, who then was the top staffer on the Democrats on the Defense Appropriations Subcommittee. "In fact, I remember coming out of the meeting with (Brigadier General Martin) Dempsey (Commander of the 1st Armored Division). They were all in combat gear; we were all huddled in this little office because it was the only place that was air conditioned. I remember just about all of us in the delegation almost passing out because it was so hot."

They met with the Iraqi Provisional Authority and heard that many Iraqis did not feel safe and secure. They heard about the lack of progress in restoring the roads, electricity, and water infrastructure. They heard about unemployment rates at sixty percent – much higher than before the war.

Murtha came out of the meeting with concerns that he would soon convey to the president – concerns that there was only a narrow window of opportunity to improve security, the economy, and the infrastructure. The longer those concerns went unaddressed, the more hearts and minds of Iraqis would be lost.

Murtha also heard about shortages of critical equipment, which were endangering the lives and limbs of the troops – concerns that he would soon convey to Defense Secretary Rumsfeld.

But getting home was a bit of a challenge.

After the meeting, they went back to the airport. Morrison went to the C130, concerned because it was so hot, he recalled, drawing out the word "hot."

"I said, 'What limits do you guys have temperature-wise before they won't allow you to take off?' 'We can't take off if it's over 139 on the tarmac,' and I said, 'What temperature is it?' They said, 'It's above 139 degrees' and I said to him, 'No it isn't, it's 139 degrees,' and they said, 'We got ya.' I was not going to have our guys stay out there," he continued.

"Our guys" included his boss, Jack Murtha, who certainly appreciated how miserable such heat was making life for the troops. But Murtha the retired Marine Corps colonel also would have been up one side and down the other of everyone in sight if they could not come up with a way to get this delegation back to a more hospitable environment.

By Thursday, August 21, Murtha was in his Washington office, talking with his team of advisors about what he had seen and heard. They helped to frame issues that Murtha wanted to articulate in two letters he wanted to send promptly.

On August 27, 2003, Defense Secretary Donald Rumsfeld got one of those letters.

"As you are aware, I recently returned from the Iraq Theater of operations during which I met with Ambassador (L. Paul) Bremer and our senior military leaders in the region," Murtha's letter began. "In a matter of days, the president will receive a letter from me outlining my broad findings, conclusions, and recommendations. In the meantime, however, I want to raise with you several specific items that I believe require your immediate attention. In my discussions with our senior military leaders, I received information about parts and equipment shortages that are adversely affecting our troops' ability to conduct their mission and provide adequate protection for them and others."

With just that brief introduction, Murtha described six problems that were jeopardizing troops' lives, including shortages of spare parts and gear for personal protection.

"Some 40,000 troops in theater lack protective Kevlar plates for body armor vests," Murtha wrote, adding, "Many of the troops I've visited in military hospitals that were wounded in Iraq claim that these Kevlar plates saved their lives."

Kevlar vests could protect much of the body, but putting Kevlar in pants to protect the lower extremities did not allow flexibility to run, jump, and do the other things that war fighters routinely need to do. Troops traveling in HMMVSs or "humvees" could cover their legs with Kevlar blankets, but these, too, were in critical shortage, Murtha reported.

Remotely-controlled radio devices were detonating many of the improvised explosive devices or IEDs, killing or seriously injuring many troops. Portable radio-frequency jammers had been developed as an effective counter-measure against this threat. "Yet, the Army division patrolling the so called 'Sunni Triangle' has a total of only nine portable jammers, and the 2nd Brigade of this division only had one. The division leaders with whom I met reported that these jammers are urgently required for convoy and patrol protection," Murtha wrote.

He then noted that, within the 1st Armored Division, forty-six of the 140 Bradley fighting vehicles had been "dead-lined" with no vehicle tracks, and eighty humvees were out of service in need of spare parts. In addition, the division was still waiting for 125 "up-armored" humvees, personnel carriers on which armor had been added to better protect against roadside bombs and IEDs.

Murtha's letter continued: "Mr. Secretary, if there is anything the subcommittee can do to assist, please have someone contact us."

Murtha ended this correspondence with an offer of help. He was anxious to get things done right in Iraq. He felt that way before his visit to Iraq and, after seeing the battle on the ground, came back deeply troubled that we had gone in unprepared and appeared to have no game plan.

Murtha identified the problem with equipment shortages and was actively seeking a behind-the-scene solution long before it became a hot topic in the media. He was accused of being a media hound when he talked publicly about these problems, but he had been protesting privately about these issues for some time.

Later, when Murtha's comments on Haditha created a big stir, his critics contended that there was a personal war with Rumsfeld and that Murtha had used Haditha as a tool against the defense secretary.

In the end, certainly, there was bad blood between the two men. Murtha was unhappy with Rumsfeld because Rumsfeld did not take advice, and Rumsfeld was unhappy with Murtha because Murtha offered it. But this letter was simple and straightforward: our troops are inadequately protected and these shortages "require your immediate attention." The letter displays Murtha's eagerness to help solve the problems that were costing lives and limbs. How could a defense secretary ignore such a plea?

Within a week of writing to Rumsfeld, Murtha also wrote to the president addressing the larger issues of the war and emphasizing the need to "finish the job as quickly as possible" or risk losing the hearts and minds of the people – both the people in Iraq and those here at home.

In his letter to President George W. Bush, dated September 4, 2003, Murtha wrote:

> I recently returned from an inspection in Iraq and believe we have severely miscalculated the magnitude of the effort we are facing. Clearly we have no choice but to go forward and finish the job as quickly as possible. To accomplish this goal, however, we must "Energize, Iraqatize and Internationalize" our efforts.
>
> I cannot overly emphasize the importance of a robust public works program for rebuilding the Iraqi infrastructure and restoring its economy. In order to energize our efforts, the economic rebuilding program must be front loaded and fully funded. The estimates for costs of rebuilding are staggering, yet this great challenge cannot be approached in a piecemeal manner.
>
> I am in agreement with Dr. John Hamre's assessment concerning the narrow window of opportunity available to deliver progress in terms of economic infrastructure,

security and basic service improvements. Rather than seeing an improvement in areas of vital concern, the Iraqi people are experiencing a worsening in pivotal areas. The unemployment rate is currently sixty percent versus forty percent before the war, and those living in and around Baghdad receive less than eight hours of electricity daily, as compared to eighteen hours prior to the war. While these numbers may be rationalized, the situation is not improving at the rate needed to win the "hearts and minds" of the Iraqi people.

The support of the Iraqi people is critical to a positive outcome. We must engage the Iraqi population and provide them with a sense of ownership in the rebuilding process. Establishing a well-trained Iraqi security force, providing employment opportunities in construction and rehabilitation efforts and ensuring the success of the Iraqi Governing Council are crucial to gaining the support of the Iraqi people and in securing a positive outcome.

Murtha then emphasized the need for "significant" international troops to join the effort because of the "monumental task" we faced, adding, "It is vital that substantive forces from countries with proven armies and leadership join the stabilization efforts."

His letter concluded:

"Mr. President, while some talk boldly about a generation-long commitment to bring democracy to Iraq and the Middle East, the near term reality is that on its present course, we are in danger of losing support of both a significant portion of the Iraqi people and the American public. The administration and Congress must act together to address the needs in Iraq. To make significant progress we must 'Energize, Iraqatize and Internationalize' our efforts."

This was September of 2003 and in his very first sentence to the president, Murtha stressed that "we have severely miscalculated the magnitude of the effort we are facing." This conclusion was not followed by a call for withdrawal. Murtha emphasized the need to "move forward and finish the job" by adding "substantial" international troops, in essence a surge in troop strength.

More than two years later, Murtha's critics screamed that his call to redeploy was a mistake and that the right thing to do – echoing Murtha – was to finish the job. Those critics claimed Murtha wanted to get out of Iraq because he lacked vision and global understanding of what was at stake. They failed to recognize that he had advocated the same approach very early in the conflict. The difference was that Murtha understood that the United States had only a limited amount of time to win the hearts and minds of the Iraqi people. Not until early 2007 did Bush finally support a surge in troop numbers, but by then, those hearts and minds had already been lost.

If Bush would have come forward in 2003 and said what Murtha had told him – that we had severely miscalculated the magnitude of the effort we were facing and needed more troops – Murtha, no doubt, would have stood behind him at the podium.

The end of Murtha's letter notes concerns about losing the support of the Iraqi and American people. He does not say without these changes "you" will lose that support. When addressing the president, he says that "we" are in danger of losing that support.

Murtha saw himself in league with the president in his commitment to "finish the job" in Iraq, but he felt major changes were needed quickly in order to properly finish that job.

Murtha's call for a surge did not happen in a vacuum. In February of 2003, General Eric Shinseki, testifying before the Senate Armed Services Committee, was asked by Senator Carl Levin how much manpower he believed was needed to keep the peace in a post-war Iraq. Shinseki, the U.S. Army Chief of Staff, replied that several hundred thousand troops would be needed.

Rumsfeld went ballistic and, along with others in his circle, called the estimate wild and way off base. Rumsfeld had been telling Congress and the American people that the war would require relatively few ground forces and that our costs would be paid by Iraq. Shinseki's position clearly suggested otherwise.

Shinseki was a graduate of the U.S. Military Academy at West Point and a thirty-eight-year military veteran who retired with four stars and half a foot, courtesy of his time in Vietnam. He had been promoted from lieutenant general to four-star general in 1997, when he became commander of the allied land forces in Europe, including the NATO force in Bosnia. He was charged with keeping the peace after warring factions had halted the war based on the Dayton Accord. Keeping the peace, Shinseki knew from first-hand experience, was not as easy as it might sound when three separate factions harbored long-standing bitterness against each other. While Bosnia was in Eastern Europe and Iraq was in the Middle East, both countries had three ethnic groups that had fought and struggled against each other throughout their histories.

So, when asked how many troops it would take to keep the peace in Iraq, Shinseki noted the history of ethnic tensions and the logistical challenges of keeping the food, water, medicine, ammo, spare parts, and other essentials flowing to both the people and the troops, as well as the "significant" geography of Iraq. Iraq has nearly 170,000 square miles, making it more than eight times bigger than Bosnia.

Yet without regard for Shinseki's education, military training, and experience, his observation was promptly dismissed as wildly off the mark when it did not conform with the political parameters in which Rumsfeld needed to operate.

Within six months, Shinseki had been replaced as Army Chief of Staff. Other military officers soon would face similar fates, or would choose to retire rather than to work in silence in support of plans that they saw as seriously or fatally flawed. They effectively had no voice, just as many members of Congress had no voice while they were intimidated into silence by the fear of being labeled as cowards or weak on terrorism.

While Jack Murtha eventually managed to change the dialogue and thus change the direction of Iraq, he was building his case, in part, on the experience and courage of others like Shinseki, who decided to not just walk quietly along the party line. Even at the cost of his own career, General Shinseki tried to avoid much of what had gone wrong in Iraq.

Rumsfeld was able to essentially force the general's retirement, counting on the military's ethic of remaining silent when they disagreed with those who out-ranked them – either in the military or politics. Most media totally missed this story, and even the *New York Times* and other large newspapers gave the issue little ink.

Nonetheless, Murtha was a military insider. Murtha certainly knew what was going on. He and Shinseki had talked many times.

Murtha's team of retired military officers recognized two key factors behind his keen grasp of global military issues.

First, Murtha always talked to the troops on the ground at military bases and in the theater of combat – the rank-and-file sergeants and even the privates – to see the conflict through the eyes of those who were seeing it up-close and personal.

Second, Murtha had lots of "back channels" into the Pentagon. He never stopped at getting the sanitized official version from the defense secretary or others at the very top – he talked privately to a broader range of military leaders and strategists, prying into their personal thoughts and concerns.

He was able to do that because, through the years, he had demonstrated repeatedly that anything conveyed to him in confidence would remain in confidence. "Always keep your word" was one of those pearls of wisdom that had been bestowed upon Murtha in his very first days in Congress, before he even had a committee assignment. And Murtha's friends in the military trusted that when he promised to not reveal his sources, his word was gold.

Murtha also visited the wounded at Walter Reed Army Hospital and Bethesda Naval Hospital almost every week. He would walk into a room and bark, "What the hell happened to you?" Before he left that room, Murtha knew the details of the incident, what equipment might have made a difference, and how the training – or lack thereof – might have resulted in a different outcome.

When Murtha wrote to President Bush, his view had been built on his years of experience shaped by the position of General Shinseki and other military leaders, and by observations from soldiers in the field, the wounded in military hospitals, and everyday folks back home, where many people were beginning to question the ultimate cost in money and lives.

Murtha received no immediate reply. He was essentially dismissed much as Shinseki had been dismissed. The difference is that Murtha was not going away and ultimately was not bound by a soldier's silence the way the four-star general was.

Chapter 10

Rebuked and Ignored

"Democratic Hawk Urges Firing of Bush Aides." That headline appeared in the *New York Times* on September 17, 2003, as the patience of John P. Murtha was wearing thin.

Murtha almost always chose to work behind the scenes, but on this occasion, the old warrior Murtha chose a major frontal attack through the media, rather than the quiet stealth maneuver that he had used so effectively throughout his career.

With the war dragging on, the steadily rising cost in cash and warriors, and the understanding that sooner or later the hearts and minds in Iraq and America would stop supporting the war, Murtha called on Bush to hold someone in his administration responsible for giving such bad advice and misleading information.

A week after this story appeared, Murtha issued a detailed assessment that started with a typical story about how much the war was costing:

"I recently visited a young Marine at Walter Reed Army Hospital. He had lost his eye, left hand, and two fingers from his right hand in an explosion in Iraq, as he was disarming unexploded bomblets. His left leg ultimately required amputation at the kneecap. I've visited our troops in several military hospitals and I've talked to the families of those who have died in Iraq. Every day, we see our casualties mount and our financial costs grow," Murtha said.

"The price we are paying is indeed a heavy price and yet, the architects of this deployment have paid no price. Forty-eight percent of our Army is currently deployed. One third of our Guard and Reserves are currently activated and have been ordered to extend their deployment in Iraq from six months to one year," he continued before outlining the equipment shortages, miscalculations in post-war planning and costs, the difficulties in rebuilding infrastructure of the huge nation of Iraq, and the degree of resistance to the U.S. occupation.

"Yet the architects should have known," Murtha insisted, adding, "Former Secretary of the Army Thomas White was right on the mark when he said, 'Clearly the view that the war to liberate Iraq would instantly produce a pro-United States citizenry, ready for economic and political rebirth, ignored the harsh realities on the ground.'"

Secretary White, like General Shinseki, paid the price for providing an honest assessment. White had been fired by Rumsfeld for agreeing with Shinseki that several hundred thousand troops were needed.

The silence in the Pentagon and among the generals was virtually deafening – about as deafening in Murtha's mind as the response he still had not received from the president to his letter of September 4.

Then on October 30, 2003, Jack Murtha found himself on the floor of Congress urging his colleagues to support a defense appropriation of sixty-five billion dollars for the war and another twenty billion dollars toward the reconstruction of Iraq.

"We took care of the money for the troops, but if you do not get the electricity back, if you do not get the water running right, if you do not get the people who are unemployed," an angry Murtha said on the House floor.

"There is sixty percent unemployment. I just got a briefing yesterday and they told me there is still sixty percent unemployment. If we have sixty percent unemployment in this country, we are not going to be able to solve the problem," he said, insisting that the United States needed to fund the reconstruction of the water and electric infrastructure, and get the international community engaged to maintain support in Iraq, which then would allow for a diplomatic solution.

"If we do not do that, we are going to lose this war," Murtha said. "I believe the key to winning this war is to win the hearts and minds of the people.... I think it is on the edge now. I am not as optimistic as a lot of people are. I know an awful lot of people who were optimistic initially are much more realistic than they used to be. But I tell my colleagues one thing: if we were to let this legislation not pass, we sure would not win this war.

"So I would urge the members of this House to vote for this sixty-five billion dollars for the troops and the twenty billion dollars for the reconstruction effort in order to get our troops back home as quickly as we can."

"Cut and run?" Hardly. Murtha was calling for war funding, but with a warning that we needed to be realistic about what it would take to win the hearts and minds of a distrustful Iraqi people.

With Murtha's leadership, the spending bill passed overwhelmingly, and another month then passed with still no reply to his letter to the president. But by then, a sense of urgency was building in Murtha's mind. Our troops were over-extended, military personnel and their families were struggling with the stress of long deployments that separated families and tightened their finances, and they were witnessing or suffering brutal injuries that, in general, were more horrific than those in wars past. IEDs were creating an alarming increase in traumatic brain injuries, blindness, and multiple amputations that, in prior wars with less rapid and advanced field care, would have left the warriors dead.

On November 21, 2003, another letter was sent to President Bush, but this one was signed not only by Jack Murtha – it was signed by one hundred and fifty Members of Congress.

The letter was put together in a bipartisan way by Duncan Hunter, the California Republican who was chairman of the House Armed Services Committee, and Ike Skelton, the Missouri Democrat who was the committee's ranking member.

"Dear Mr. President," the letter began. "We are concerned that our Armed Forces are over-extended and that we are relying too heavily upon members of the Guard and Reserve in continuing the war on terrorism."

The letter urged the president to "significantly increase the number of people on active duty in the military and revise the missions given to the National Guard and Reserve during the up-coming budget year."

"Making these changes would be met with broad bipartisan support in Congress," the letter said.

The letter warned that the "operational tempo" of the forces was unprecedented because we were fighting one war in Iraq and another in Afghanistan while maintaining other troops in the Balkans, Korea, and other places where we had committed to maintain a peacekeeping force. The troops just had to keep going and going.

So this second letter to Bush, which Murtha joined in signing, talked about the current tempo with the added caveat: "This will be a lengthy war that will define entire careers. We must size and structure our forces to prevail over the long haul."

The citizen-soldiers of the National Guard and Reserves were simply being used too much, the letter said. "Many of the units currently serving in Iraq will have served for nearly fifteen months, in some cases longer, by the time their tours are finished. When they come home, the nature of this war is such that they know they are quite likely to be called up again sometime in the near future."

As a result, the Army National Guard was not going to meet its recruitment goal for the year.

"Unless these burdens are reduced, we may find ourselves in the midst of a recruiting and retention crisis in the reserve components. We need to send a clear message in the coming budget to members of the Guard and Reserve that help is on the way," the letter said, calling for two more combat divisions to reduce the pressure on the Reserves and Guard.

The letter concluded, "Mr. President, our military needs help now. We ask that you show strong leadership and take the necessary steps to increase the end strength of our Armed Forces and adjust the mix of active and reserve component forces in the upcoming budget year. We stand with you ready to confront any and all challenges to our great nation."

Nearly one hundred and fifty members of the House, including Jack Murtha, signed on to "We stand with you." Could it have been more emphatic? Do this differently. Make the changes you must make to win this thing and secure our long-term future. The letter did not blame Bush for the way the military was structured or for the failings of his appointees. It acknowledged that no one had seen such a war on the horizon. The people who signed this letter talked about bipartisan support if the president would budget such changes. Several Republicans on the House Armed Services Committee were among those who signed, including Joe Wilson of South Carolina, Walter B. Jones of North Carolina, Edward "Buck" McKeon of California, and Ron Kline of Minnesota. These people could not be called cowards who prefer to "cut and run."

Despite the urgent nature of the letter, despite the bipartisan tone, their plea for a new direction fell on deaf ears.

Another four months passed with no direct reply from the White House to Murtha's letter, and this was a time when Murtha did what he usually did: kept a low profile, working behind the scenes. He made no speeches of any significance on the House floor. His name rarely if ever showed up in the national media. Until March 17, 2004.

"Mr. Speaker, I am indignant, I am insulted, and I am embarrassed that no one came to me and asked me about this resolution. Nobody said, 'Do you have any input?'"

Jack Murtha's remarks on the House floor that day were more like a tirade than a speech. He was infuriated again, but this time by the tactic of the Republicans in Congress.

House Resolution 557 said, in essence, that the Congress "affirms that the United States and the world have been made safer by the removal of Saddam Hussein and his regime from power in Iraq."

The resolution was a variation on the old loaded question, "So when did you stop beating your wife." They were daring Democrats to vote against a resolution that said Saddam was horrendous. The resolution had no fewer than nine "whereas" clauses: whereas Saddam Hussein committed crimes against humanity, whereas Hussein's regime had killed 5,000 Kurds, whereas 270 mass grave sites had been found....

During a long debate on the House floor, Murtha spoke several times, and several times said, in essence, just because we say it, that doesn't make it so.

He called on his Republican colleagues to withdraw their resolution and reword a few things so that a meaningful and bipartisan resolution could be passed.

He mentioned a recent bombing in Baghdad, an attack in Spain that killed a few hundred people and injured 2,000, and surveys showing that residents of France, Italy, Germany, Spain, Canada, and other countries all believed there were increased threats in the world.

"I am concerned that we are making a statement that just exacerbates the very problem we have," Murtha said of the Republican resolution. "The world is not safer today than it was before they captured Saddam Hussein.... Just because it says on paper that it is safer, does not mean it is safer throughout the world."

Murtha more than once that day stated that he had voted for the war because he had believed there were weapons of mass destruction in Iraq, that Hussein was a threat to the world, and that there was an al Qaeda connection – none of which had turned out to be true, he emphasized.

"We do not go to war unless there is a core national security interest, and now we are trying to justify why we went to war by some of the things that are in this resolution," he said, later reflecting on the first Bush president, George H.W. Bush, whom he usually referred to as Bush I.

"George Bush I, the first George Bush, knew there were mass graves. And he did not go into Iraq, and he said, 'I do not want to rebuild Iraq; I do not want to occupy Iraq....' So we are trying to revisit history. I mean, we cannot change it: we went to war because we thought we were threatened. These things were terrible things, we are glad to get rid of Saddam Hussein. That is not the point. We cannot revisit and change history."

A bit later in the debate, Murtha returned to this point:

"Well, let me tell my colleagues: the preamble to this paper is what makes me so upset. We are trying to justify what we did. Look, no question about Saddam Hussein being a bad guy, but that is not why we went to war. If we took the preamble and we put that as a resolution, there would not have been a resolution. When they ask me if you would have voted for this (war) resolution if you (had known) what you know, I said there would not have been a resolution because the resolution would not have come up because there was no threat to our national security.

"This is going to be a long war, and I am going to be right there," Murtha continued. "I am going to be voting for something that means something. I am going to be voting for the money, for the troops, for all the things they need."

He noted that he had worked closely with then-chairman of the Defense Appropriations Subcommittee, Republican Congressman

Jerry Lewis of California, in passing that defense-spending bill with only sixteen Congress members voting against it.

"So we are for the defense of this country, but we should not mislead the people. I have said over and over again, do not be overly optimistic. This is going to be a long haul. And if we are overly optimistic, and we tell the American public and the international community and they lose faith in us, we cannot win this war on terrorism. We have to have the support of the American public, which has dropped dramatically. And if you tell them the cost, it drops below fifty percent. Internationally they do not support us because they do not believe many of the things that we say now, and we have to have them (international support) if we are going to win this war on terrorism."

Murtha was saying that the people behind this war had been wrong so many times:

Wrong about weapons of mass destruction.

Wrong about an al Qaeda connection.

Wrong about how long it would take to restore peace in Iraq.

Wrong that the Iraqis would pay for the war with revenues from their oil.

Wrong about how much it would cost America – both in dollars and in lives.

The war's architects had been wrong so many times that America had lost credibility around the world. America was now dangerously close to losing credibility with its own citizens. But America needed the support of both to bring about the type of diplomatic resolution that ultimately was required.

The resolution passed 327 to 93. Despite Murtha's vehement urging, he was out-voted by nearly three to one.

And then just five days later, on March 22, 2004, Murtha finally got a reply to the letter he had written to the president back on September 4, 2003. However, that reply came not from the president, not from the White House, not even from the defense secretary. It came from someone several pegs down the Pentagon chain of command, someone Murtha angrily described on many occasions as a Pentagon "staffer."

Murtha was livid, even more indignant and insulted than he had been on the House floor a few days earlier. Those close to him who heard his first reaction do not repeat it verbatim because he peppered his remarks with the salty language of a former Marine drill instructor.

Recall that in his letter, Murtha had told the president that we had "severely miscalculated the magnitude of the effort we were facing" and were in danger of losing the support of both the Iraqis and the folks at home.

The seven-month time lapse was inexcusable to Murtha, but that was only part of what was so infuriating to him. The reply from the principal deputy under secretary of defense essentially said that much of what he was worried about had already been fixed, and as for your help, thanks but no thanks.

"Thank you for your letter to President George W. Bush regarding your trip to Iraq last fall and the need to step up our efforts there," the letter began.

"Since that time, we have made substantial progress in the very ways that you suggest. There are now more than 200,000 Iraqis under arms in the various security services and armed forces. The Transitional Administration Law, an interim Iraqi constitution, in effect has been unanimously approved by the Iraqi Governing Council. And some 2,200 projects are in the process of being funded in the reconstruction program, thanks to your and Congress's support of the supplemental funds for Iraq.

"As a result of these and other things, the Iraqi people have begun 'to believe that their situation is improving.' As the February ABC/Oxford research national poll of Iraq revealed, a majority of Iraqis feel things are better now than before the war, and seventy percent or more feel life is going well or very well, and will be much or somewhat better a year from now. I think this indicates that the Iraqi people have the growing 'sense of ownership' that you so rightly suggest is necessary for the success of our efforts."

The letter ended, "Thank you for your sound advice and support," and was signed by Ryan Henry, principal deputy under secretary of defense.

When Henry wrote this letter, the question of how things were going in Iraq was at best debatable. If things were going as well as Henry indicated on March 22, 2004, then why would the president call for a surge in forces a few years later?

Although the numbers from the ABC/Oxford poll and Iraqis under arms were encouraging, the overall evaluation was way off. More troops were needed, much of the reconstruction that was funded never happened, and there was no realism in assessing what was required to succeed. As Murtha's original assessment said, we had miscalculated.

Perhaps by the pre-war standards set by Secretary Rumsfeld and President Bush – standards many military men felt were way off – this level of achievement in Iraq by March of 2004 was acceptable. The course of events in Iraq over the next few years clearly showed that Murtha was closer to the truth than Bush, Rumsfeld, or Ryan Henry.

The responsiveness of the White House under George W. Bush is worth comparing with that of President Ronald Reagan. As noted, Murtha's letter to Secretary of State George Shultz in 1987 was inquiring about chemical weapons funding. Schultz received that letter April 22, and Murtha was reading his response on May 7 that same year. A little over two weeks and written by the secretary of state himself. Murtha's letters to Bush and Rumsfeld were either not answered or were not answered for seven months – and then by someone who in Murtha's world was just a staffer.

Murtha anguished as he realized that this administration was either clueless about the reality in Iraq or was so ideologically driven that it was blind to the reality.

He anguished over the soldiers and Marines returning with shattered nerves, missing limbs, blind eyes, or heads so badly shaken that their brains had swelled and shut down much of their ability to function.

He anguished as he saw careers of generals come to a screeching halt just because they gave honest advice that was unwanted.

This was the landscape that would lead Murtha to a point where he was convinced that he had no choice but to publicly call out the Bush White House. While those who supported Bush would clamor about Murtha and his cut-and-run strategy, the fact is that Murtha had been quite the hawk. Where the war-fighting effort was concerned, he wanted more and better. Where the war-fighter was concerned, he insisted on nothing but the best. Murtha was not calling to get out: he was calling to "go forward and finish the job." He wanted sweeping changes in how the war was being handled and he was willing to put his name on those changes to bring about a bipartisan triumph.

What he got was rebuked and ignored.

Chapter 11

Political Payback

As Murtha expressed more and more concerns about losing the hearts and minds of the Iraqis because they lacked such necessities as clean water, electricity, and jobs, his frustration with the administration was building. So, too, was their frustration with his continued criticisms.

Although Murtha's concerns drew relatively scant attention in national media, in early 2004, President Bush's proposed budget called for closing the National Drug Intelligence Center in Johnstown, Pennsylvania, and moving its missions and its three hundred and forty some jobs elsewhere.

The move was pure political payback.

The beauty of the deal was how it played to the NDIC's two sets of critics.

Most of these critics simply equated the NDIC with "pork barrel" and refused to believe that any such facility located in a small rural city like Johnstown – hundreds of miles from the battlefronts in the war on drugs – could be doing anything truly connected to drug trafficking.

They acted like they never heard of computers, the internet, or telephones. These critics refused to acknowledge that if the NDIC had been located in Washington, D.C., its original proposed location, its analysts would not have been located in the poppy fields of

Afghanistan, or killing fields of Colombia or Mexico, or the nasty street corners of U.S. cities where gangs controlled their turf. These analysts would have been behind a desk compiling and sorting information to draw conclusions based on the facts provided to them from numerous sources across the globe.

The other set of NDIC critics questioned the center's worth. Some of them were academics who could get their fifteen minutes of fame by rapping the NDIC. Others often had connections to the El Paso Intelligence Center or EPIC, where people were jealous that their "tactical" mission to handle the U.S.-Mexican border did not seem to be as sexy as the NDIC's "strategic" mission in assessing drug movements globally.

Prior to the 2004 budget, criticism had not come from the White House, the Attorneys General, the nation's Drug Czars, or others who looked at the big picture and had no political ax to grind. Although they typically were not out front objecting when the issue came up, when they did talk publicly, they consistently credited the NDIC for playing a vital role in tracking the movement of illegal drug money, in providing overview reports on where drugs were being produced and moved to market, and in something called "DOCEX" or later "DOMEX".

With Document Exploitation or DOCEX and later Document and Media Exploitation or DOMEX, any documents such as address books, lists of phone numbers, cell phones, computers, or other media that had been found through drug raids or search warrants were quickly scanned and/or dumped into a database and matched against names and numbers or people who were known to be involved or suspected of involvement in the illicit trade.

DOMEX was so effective and impressive in the War on Drugs that, when the nation declared War on Terrorists after 9/11, they promptly expanded the NDIC's role to utilize the same methods in tracking how terrorists and terrorist organizations moved money, arms, and other instruments of destruction.

"Pork" and "waste" are labels the media use mindlessly to criticize anything outside of Washington or anything that any member of Congress manages to get in his or her district or state. So it is not surprising that national media reports on the NDIC created the impression that the NDIC was not performing a single task of meaning.

On the local stage, the NDIC represented some 340 friends and neighbors. They are smart people who go to work, take out their trash, mow their grass, and wave hello to neighbors who walk by their yard.

In other words, to those in Pennsylvania's 12th District, such attacks were not just targeting Jack Murtha, but were also targeting fellow members of parent-teacher groups or people who coached their kids in Little League. Yet on the national stage, people seemed to be surprised when the voters of the 12th did not rise up in revolt against a man who was fighting for those Little League coaches.

Certainly, good people might work at the NDIC and not do good work. Jack Murtha, however, is not the only government official who had praised the NDIC. In fact, a mere two years before the Bush White House proposed to kill the NDIC, that same Bush White House was singing its praises.

In August of 2002, Attorney General George Ashcroft visited Johnstown and the NDIC.

The *Johnstown Tribune-Democrat* on August 21, 2002, began its coverage saying, "Intelligence gathering and document analysis developed in Johnstown by the National Drug Intelligence Center are vital not only in the battle against traffickers, U.S. Attorney General John Ashcroft said yesterday. Protocols developed in Johnstown are key to the war on terrorism, the nation's top prosecutor said during a stop in the city. 'The program developed here has become an important part of targeting terrorists,' Ashcroft said."

Ashcroft called the center "very important" to the war on drugs and the war on terror. "You actually have direct linkages" between those wars, Ashcroft said during a press briefing at NDIC. "The work that is being done here is commendable work."

Ashcroft personally thanked the analysts, computer specialists, and other NDIC employees, shaking the hand of every staffer and posing for photos.

Ashcroft's speech to employees was even more gushing than the news print account indicated. He paused frequently to thank the men and women of the NDIC and almost seemed like a college football coach at a pep rally the night before the big game, urging them to keep fighting the fight and stressing that they could make a difference in the outcome.

Ashcroft, the man President George W. Bush handpicked as Attorney General, clearly was speaking from the heart and from a position of understanding of the value of the NDIC. Did the agency really fall from being a vital tool in the war on terror to an unneeded agency in the seventeen months between August 2002 and early 2004?

The NDIC's history goes back to 1989, when the first Bush, George H.W. Bush, proposed it. Bush I's proposal foundered for two years. The Justice Department supported the idea, but creating this new entity meant taking money from something else.

They continued to insist that a new strategic intelligence entity was needed to assess activity in the drug war. One day, Jack Murtha dropped a solution in their lap:

In 1991, Murtha inserted twenty-eight million dollars into the defense appropriation bill to create the NDIC within the Department of Justice, but funded by the Defense Department. Murtha justified the funding because the defense appropriation bill that he shepherded through Congress each year funded military intelligence as one of the nation's premier sources of raw intelligence information and a huge "black budget" for the CIA and other global covert operations.

The FBI, CIA, DEA, and other Justice Department entities were well-known at the time for not sharing their own intelligence with each other, but the central purpose of the Bush-proposed NDIC was to share key intelligence across agencies to improve the effectiveness of all of them.

By cross-referencing all the raw intelligence data, they could create a better understanding of which regions of the globe were producing drugs, how they were delivering those drugs to markets, and what those who made the drug money were doing with it: were they relatively harmless nouveau riche fat cats, or were they funneling large amounts of cash into paramilitary or outright militant organizations that were taking de-facto control of nations such as Afghanistan, Colombia, or Mexico?

Big questions. Issues that the U.S. government had a legitimate interest in tracking. Issues that justified a need for a National Drug Intelligence Center. And given that the CIA had lots of intelligence on drug production, drug movement, and the flow of the resulting cash, these were issues that made it valid to fund this organization through the mechanism that funds much of the CIA budget: the defense appropriation bill.

Although much of the criticism was based on a provision in the appropriation requiring that the NDIC be set up in Johnstown, not Washington, D.C., Murtha understood that the raw intelligence that would be fed to the NDIC could be sorted and analyzed at lower cost in annual salaries and overhead in a relatively small city like Johnstown, Pennsylvania.

Given its history and Ashcroft's glowing praise as late as 2002, as comments from Murtha were becoming increasingly critical of the war in Iraq, the 2004 budget was clearly a warning shot from a political machine known for heavy handedness: if Murtha did not back off on Iraq, his district would pay the price in the form of jobs, even if it was a program heralded by the Attorney General as critical

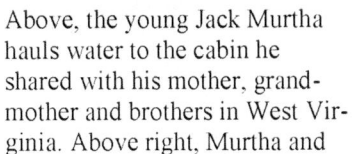

Above, the young Jack Murtha hauls water to the cabin he shared with his mother, grandmother and brothers in West Virginia. Above right, Murtha and his family await a train in the 1940s. Below, Murtha receives the American Spirit Honor Award upon conclusion of basic training in 1952. Murtha often said that award was the one he was most proud of because only one in 100,000 Marines received it.

At right, Murtha on patrol behind a fellow Marine in Vietnam in 1967. Below, Murtha receives the Bronze Star with Combat V, for his service in Vietnam. Murtha also received two purple hearts and the Vietnamese Cross of Gallantry.

Above, leading a 1975 Congressional delegation to Vietnam, Murtha brings back the remains of military personnel who had been listed as missing in action (MIA). Below, Murtha joins President Ronald Reagan and Senator Strom Thurmond in presiding at a 1984 ceremony honoring the Unknown Soldier from Vietnam. The ceremony took place in the Capitol.

Above, Murtha is sworn in by his mentor, Thomas P. "Tip" O'Neill, in 1974. Below, Dick Cheney and his wife, Lynne, join Jack and Joyce Murtha at a dinner in the U.S. Capitol. As chairman of Defense Appropriations, Murtha held the dinner to honor Cheney after Cheney became defense secretary in 1989. Murtha and Cheney were very close then, especially during Operation Desert Storm in 1991. During the Iraq war, rather than criticize his old friend, Murtha would say such things as, "He's changed."

Above, Gen. Colin Powell joins Murtha in singing at a program on Capitol Hill. As chairman or ranking member of the Defense Appropriations Subcommittee, Murtha was on a first-name basis with virtually all top generals, and often talked to them in confidence about their concerns. He also had a good sense of humor, evident in the photo below as he shares a light moment with Gen. Norman Schwartzkopf.

Above, Murtha talks to troops in Kuwait during Operation Desert Storm in 1991. At right, on a 2005 tour of Iraq, Murtha and Congressmen John Larson, Democrat of Connecticut (partially visible behind Murtha), and Congressman Dave Hobson, Republican of Ohio, talk with an Air Force colonel. Behind Hobson in a red scarf is David Morrison of the Appropriations staff. Below, Murtha poses in 2003 with his nephew, Col. Brian C. Murtha, at Ali Al Salem Airfield in Kuwait at the tent city for Marine Medium Helicopter Squadron 365, which Brian Murtha served as commanding officer.

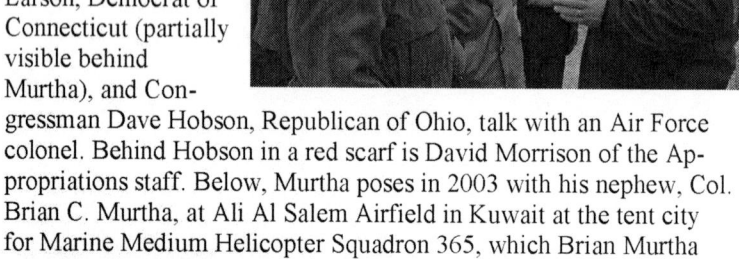

Above, Major General Richard Huck walks with Murtha during a 2005 inspection in Haditha, Iraq. Walking behind them are, left to right, David Morrison, top Democratic staffer for the Defense Subcommittee; General Jessica Wright, head of the Pennsylvania National Guard; and Congressman David Hobson, R-Ohio. Below, Murtha walks with General David D. McKiernan, now retired from the Air Force, who was commander of forces in Afghanistan from 2008 to 2009. The photo was taken on November 30, 2008, in Kabul, Afghanistan.

Above, former U.S. Senator Max Cleland revs up the crowd during a veterans rally in Murtha's 2006 campaign. Cleland was one of the first veterans who was "swift boated" by attacking his military record. He came to two Murtha rallies that year to help prevent Murtha from being swift-boated, too. Below, Murtha and then-Senator Hillary Clinton greet people after a rally in her 2008 presidential campaign.

Above, Murtha receives the Profile in Courage Award from Caroline Kennedy and the late Senator Edward M. Kennedy on May 22, 2006. This photo is from the John F. Kennedy Presidential Library and Museum, Boston, Massachusetts. Below, New Years Day 2008, a rare day when Murtha got away to fish. This photo was taken by Col. John A. Hugya, U.S.M.C.-ret., Murtha's long-time chief of staff.

to fighting both terrorism and the war on drug.

As this book was in final editing in early 2012, the NDIC was once again on the chopping block, although this time the issue was more about money in an extremely tight budget driven by an agreement that the budget deficit needed to be radically reduced.

President Obama's budget allocated only enough money to close the NDIC. Pennsylvania's senators and congressmen came together in a bipartisan way to support the center, but were unable to stop the appropriation that included the closure. They were, however, working to keep the DOMEX program alive as an office of the Justice Department in Johnstown.

But in 2004, the effort to ax the NDIC was not a budgetary or policy move: it was pure politics in the worst sense of the word. It was pure and simply a political payback.

Chapter 12

Darby Rules of Engagement

Cumberland is a quaint, small city in Western Maryland on the edge of the Cumberland Narrows, where Wills Creek carved through the Allegheny Mountains. Named for the son of King George II, also known as the Duke of Cumberland, the historic fort located here was key to supplying the French and Indian War. Cumberland has many connections to Western Pennsylvania, the heart of Jack Murtha's congressional district: history dating to George Washington's explorations and the French and Indian War, logging and coal as industrial legacies, tourism on the National Road and the Great Allegheny Passage, and photographs of naked prisoners being humiliated in an Iraqi prison called Abu Ghraib.

These communities are close enough that many members of the Cumberland-based 372nd Military Police Company resided in Murtha's part of Pennsylvania.

When Cumberland was vaulted onto the national political scene as the Abu Ghraib prison scandal broke in the spring of 2004, the two biggest players in that scandal came from Murtha's district. One moved from the district to Cumberland after high school, and the other still lived in the district when the scandal took place. While the entire country became fixated on the prison-abuse scandal, no place other than Cumberland, Maryland, was more torn by the disgrace than Murtha's 12th Congressional District.

Only a few of the two hundred members of the 372nd Military Police Company were photographed abusing Iraqi prisoners. The abuse painted a very ugly picture of Americans around the globe and infuriated many Iraqis, turning them against what was now increasingly viewed as an American occupation of Iraq. The scandal also played a significant role in shaping Murtha's outlook on the war in Iraq that spring.

Allegations of torture, humiliation, and even death were the proverbial final nail in the coffin of the Bush administration's belief that the United States would be treated as liberators in Iraq. Murtha immediately recognized it would be a watershed moment in losing the hearts and minds of the indigenous population – a concept that he knew first hand from his days as a field-intelligence officer in the villages and jungles of Vietnam.

Murtha also understood the broader implications of how such abuse lowers the United States to the same level as terrorists and gives the country no moral high ground from which to object if American prisoners are abused, a position that will be articulated in depth in the next chapter. This chapter looks at how the scandal rocked the area that called members of the 372nd its sons and daughters.

Sergeant Joe Darby was credited with coming forward with the photographs. He had been handed a disc with the electronic images, for the most part by accident. Darby looked on his fellow members of the 372nd as friends, so he agonized before providing those photographs to his superiors. After months of soul searching, he decided the right thing to do would be to report the abuse. He was a hero to many, but something far less to some people in Cumberland.

The man who handed him the disc was Army Specialist Charles A. Graner Jr. Graner was labeled the mastermind behind the abuse and, despite testimony that he had been following orders, he was tried, convicted, and sentenced to ten years behind military bars. Graner was painted as a monster by most, but as a victim by others. Many shared Murtha's view that he was largely a victim of poor leadership in a military spread so thin that it failed to provide adequate training. Others saw him as a victim of Joe Darby's treachery and attacked Darby for choosing the enemy over his fellow soldiers.

Many of those whom Darby considered to be "friends" felt betrayed and lashed out against him. He faced ridicule, scorn, and hate, and at one point, when Cumberland was holding a vigil for the members of the 372nd, he was specifically named as one of the troops for whom prayer was not being offered. The military feared for his safety and even his life. He and his wife were forced to leave Cumberland, the place they had come to call home until Abu Ghraib.

Rules of engagement define how soldiers in battle zones react when confronted: Do they have a live round of ammunition in the chamber of their weapon or need to chamber the round before they can fire? Do they immediately react with deadly force or do they assess the situation first?

The unwritten rules of engagement for Joe Darby, the man who did not torture other human beings, called for keeping hate and anger loaded and ready to spew without hesitation. In an interview with CBS, Colin Englebach, head of the Veterans of Foreign Wars in Cumberland, said of Darby, "He was a rat, a traitor. He let his unit down. He let his fellow soldiers down and the U.S. military. Basically he was no good."

Englebach was not officially speaking on behalf of the VFW post, but certainly he was not alone in his thoughts. "Do you put the enemy above your buddies? I wouldn't," Englebach said.

By military rules, Darby had done the right thing. There is widespread agreement that our treatment of those prisoners was wrong. Even in Congress, when the issue came up for a vote more than a year later, 107 Republicans supported a resolution that passed 308 to 122 to approve a bill endorsing tough anti-abuse language drafted by the former Vietnam prisoner-of-war, Senator John McCain. Murtha, not surprisingly, introduced that measure in the House.

Yet some people, including many closest to the situation, still feel that what Darby did was wrong and vilified him for his actions. These people called Joe Darby and Jack Murtha traitors because they acted out of conscience, instead of "patriotism," as defined by those who do the hating and those, such as Bush's deputy chief of staff, Karl Rove, who were masters at manipulating the political debate.

Graner is hardly a sympathetic soul. The media reported that he had been accused of abusing prisoners when he worked at state prisons near his home in Southwestern Pennsylvania. In speaking with the local media, Murtha said that Graner had told his superior officers that he had abused his wife and that, therefore, he should not be kept in his assignment at Abu Ghraib prison. That left Murtha and others with more questions about Graner's superiors than about Graner.

In an interview with the *Pittsburgh Tribune-Review* in May 2004, Murtha said he had been told by another soldier who worked in Abu Ghraib that military-intelligence officers were in control, not the military police. Graner's attorney argued that he was not guilty because military-intelligence personnel had encouraged him to abuse prisoners through psychological manipulation that was demeaning and degrading to the Iraqis.

Certainly, Graner had a dark side before Abu Ghraib, but he informed his chain of command and they took no action to remove him from a situation ripe with temptation to abuse again.

Murtha, with his personal connection to abuse in families, was obviously troubled by this failure, but what irked Murtha the most was that the troops who were serving as prison guards had not been given proper training in how to run a military prison.

Troops were serving as military police with no training in how to do that mission – one of numerous cases of inadequate training that troubled Murtha throughout the war.

Murtha demanded an investigation of who had been in charge, but ultimately, no greater heads would fall. Later, in May 2004, Murtha was joined by Pennsylvania Congressman Curt Weldon, a Republican, in introducing a provision calling for demolishing the Abu Ghraib prison and building a modern detention facility in its place. They argued that the abuse of Iraqis had so infuriated the Iraqis that only a dramatic statement – as dramatic as destroying the site of the crime – could stop the further erosion of the hearts and minds of the people.

Under such circumstances, there is cause to wonder why Graner did more jail time that anyone else. In fact, many did no jail time, and the officers in charge were barely reprimanded. Graner was guilty, so the term scapegoat is perhaps unfitting, but certainly others were not punished by the same standard.

Graner and Darby, one a villain and the other a hero, share a common bond in history. They share more than Abu Ghraib: they share Congressman John P. Murtha. Darby graduated from North Star High School in the tiny town of Jenner in Somerset County; Graner called Uniontown, Fayette County, his home. Both places were in Murtha's district.

While it would be easy for a politician to only praise the whistle blower and hang the villain out to dry, Murtha was a statesman who did not take the easy road. His message was that our troops were being asked to do too much, that such failures occur when the limits of men are tested beyond their training and ability, that there was no excuse for what had happened, but the core cause was not the failings of any one prison guard. The failings of these individual soldiers had resulted from the failings of a war plan that disregarded the human condition of the war fighter, providing inadequate training and equipment to personnel who endure two, three, and sometimes four or five long and difficult deployments to a barren, far-away land that, in hindsight, inarguably posed no direct threat to the security of the United States.

Being a prison guard took specialized training, and few of the people at Abu Ghraib had such training. Murtha knew that giving a gun and absolute authority to someone not trained to handle the position was a recipe for disaster. Graner was responsible for his own actions, but those planning and prosecuting the war were responsible for Graner.

A Marine drill instructor himself, Murtha was big on proper training for the job at hand. In his earliest days as an elected official, he made training one of his first priorities. As late as 1973, anyone could become a police officer in Pennsylvania if a local official simply pinned a badge on his chest.

The old West scene of deputizing someone in the field may provide great drama in movies, but police officers without proper training were a problem on several fronts. First, there were those who meant well, but could bungle an investigation. Then there were those who meant well, but did not handle dangerous situations well or perhaps made relatively harmless situations dangerous. Then there were those who did not mean well and would use the gun and badge to bully or abuse people.

As a state legislator before being elected to Congress, Murtha fought for Act 120, which would require specialized training in order to be a police officer of any kind in Pennsylvania. The State Police lobbied successfully against the measure in 1973, but Murtha went to the wall and was promising to withhold five million dollars in funding for the State Police if they fought Act 120 again. The law passed in 1974. Today the idea of having a police officer with no formal training seems absurd, but such was the case in Murtha's home state when he first took office.

Abu Ghraib had international implications, but it was the same simple problem. People put in a situation for which they are not trained are more likely to fail or abuse their power. Murtha recognized immediately that abuse of this nature would turn many Iraqis against the United States, and his frustration with yet another failure in this war effort was even more aggravating because those connected to Abu Ghraib were from his own district.

Murtha, a product of Vietnam, was certain that this incident would be a tidal wave in turning the hearts and minds of Iraqis against the U.S. forces. "I'm appalled by the mistreatment of Iraqi prisoners. It's hard for me to believe that American soldiers would commit such acts, even if they were ordered to," Murtha told the *Tribune-Review*.

Graner's life was now a mess, and although he had brought much of that on himself, Murtha felt strongly that people far up the chain of command had put the man in a position to fail by failing to provide adequate training, even if they were assigned to new jobs because of the lack of personnel.

Darby's life was a mess as well, despite having done the right thing, and he was unable to return to his hometown. In large part, that was due to the political notion that "supporting the troops" meant saying nothing and doing nothing to question either the war or the warriors. The consequence was to be branded as a wimpy liberal or worse, a traitor. Darby's action, while morally sound, made many feel that he did not support his brothers in arms – that it would be better to not know such human rights violations had taken place than to see men like Graner behind bars because of crimes committed against Iraqis.

In calling for redeployment in 2005, Murtha firmly believed that he was supporting the warriors without supporting the war. Many disagreed, arguing that Murtha was aiding the enemy with talk of redeployment, much as many would acuse Darby of aiding the enemy. But Murtha's action gave voice to many more who had quietly felt a sense of loyalty to those in uniform, but a sense of frustration with this war.

Both Darby and Graner came from lower or middle class families.

Neither would be considered wealthy by any standard. Murtha had long felt the demands on the war fighter were not shared equally among Americans because people from lower-income families were more likely to see the military as "a way out" through a military career or training that would open job opportunities later. Further, without enough troops, an unfair burden was being placed on those who did serve – and on the families of those who served.

The families of Darby and Graner both suffered in the aftermath of Abu Ghraib. Watching a son or a brother, a husband or a friend be reviled as a traitor is its own form of torture. The fact that Darby and his family suffered such a fate speaks volumes about what it meant to use one's voice to simply state what was right.

Darby's identity should have remained a secret, but in a national address, Rumsfeld mentioned him by name for having come forward and done the right thing. Darby and others would come to feel that it was the defense secretary's way of exposing him, a payback for the criticisms of the war effort that resulted when the atrocities were exposed. Darby even told the BBC that Rumsfeld had written him and apologized for the outing, claiming that he had not known that Darby's name was supposed to have been kept confidential.

Rumsfeld aside, a member of the military who exposes torture and abuse should not have to fear that his name will be revealed in a situation that forces him to move his family far away to avoid facing the daily scorn of neighbors. Doing the right thing should bring honor. But in this politically charged environment, the domestic rules of engagement were to keep a round in the chamber and shoot first, think later.

Chapter 13

Troops, Torture and Twisted Words

The fallout from Abu Ghraib produced one drama in the mountains of Maryland and Pennsylvania, and a very different drama in the nation's capital.

In the Super Tuesday primaries of March 2, 2004, decorated Vietnam veteran John Kerry won a major victory that soon cleared the field in the Democratic primaries and left him cruising toward the Democratic presidential nomination.

Kerry supported the war, so the majority of Democrats in Congress, even if they did not feel the war was going well, had another reason not to come out against the war.

That year, March 20 marked the one-year anniversary of the U.S. invasion of Iraq. In April, intense fighting was under way in the Iraqi city of Fallujah, and May 1 marked the anniversary of President Bush's dramatic landing and speech on the carrier Abe Lincoln under the "Mission Accomplished" banner, prompting the national media to note the irony and the prospects of a long, drawn-out conflict.

May 6, the *New York Times* summed up the situation this way: "For months, Democrats and Republicans on Capitol Hill tap-danced around the war in Iraq. With the election looming, and both sides uncertain about the way the war would go, a kind of uneasy truce reigned. Democrats shied away from criticizing the war too forcefully, while Republicans shied away from making it a centerpiece of their campaigns."

The second paragraph of the *Times* story read simply: "On Thursday, the Iraqi prisoner abuse scandal shattered that delicate peace."

Although photos of the parading and taunting of naked prisoners in Abu Ghraib had surfaced at the end of April, the political flashpoint ignited May 6, set up by a headline that morning in the Capitol Hill newspaper *Roll Call*:

"Murtha: Iraq 'unwinnable'."

A virtual firestorm of news conferences by both sides of the aisle unleashed that day, with Democrats taking hard shots at the administration and Republicans attacking Murtha for undermining both the war and the morale of the troops – even before Murtha had said a word on the record. Murtha had offered an assessment to Democratic colleagues at the closed weekly "leader's lunch" on May 5, but declined to talk to *Roll Call* for their May 6 article, which quoted other Democrats who had heard Murtha speak at the lunch.

In the May 6 parade, House Minority Leader Nancy Pelosi called for Secretary of State Rumsfeld to resign or be fired.

Representative Charles Rangel, the New York Democrat who months before had called for Rumsfeld's ouster, now called for Rumsfeld to be impeached.

Pelosi and other Democrats were righteously indignant that the torture and abuse by American soldiers had been allowed to happen and perhaps even outright encouraged by those in charge of the war. The abuse by Americans, they feared, threatened to lower America to the hideous standards of terrorists.

Murtha did not appear with others when he spoke to the Washington media that day. He was simply introduced by Pelosi as one of his party's most respected voices on military affairs.

In typical Murtha style, he spoke for more than ten minutes about General Shinseki's position that 200,000 troops were needed but only 30,000 were deployed; his letters to the defense secretary about equipment shortages and to the president about how to earn support from the Iraqis; a subsequent letter to Rumsfeld about the many troops in Iraq who were assigned to missions for which they had not been trained; various problems in the 372nd Military Police Company at the center of the Abu Ghraib scandal; and the fact that a protection-from-abuse order had been issued against one of the people most involved with the abuse at Abu Ghraib, Charles Graner Jr., who therefore should not be allowed to carry a weapon, let alone be in charge of a prison.

Murtha finally concluded:

"We cannot prevail in this war (with) the policy that's going on today. We either have to mobilize or get out."

Mobilize or get out. Murtha wanted to put more troops and equipment into the war effort. He did not join fellow Democrats in calling for Rumsfeld's resignation. He said the nation needed to mobilize or get out.

That was how he felt, how he had long felt. From his first letter to Bush until this moment, more troops were needed to do this right. Again "cut-and-run Murtha" was talking about sending more troops.

Murtha also briefly noted the slow progress toward establishing a firm Iraqi government and the increasingly dismal prospect of attracting more international support for the war before repeating his central conclusion: "The direction's got to be changed or it's unwinnable, in my estimation."

As too often happens in Washington politics, perception and reality are separated by vast canyons.

Saying that the United States cannot prevail with the current policies or that unless the direction is changed, the war is unwinnable, is quite different than saying simply, "The war is unwinnable."

But the "unwinnable" headline that appeared the morning before Murtha spoke provided great fodder for the slam-bam, "policy by bumper sticker" approach of Karl Rove and the Republicans, especially given that Americans hate to not win or be told they cannot win.

Representative Tom DeLay, the Texas Republican and majority leader known as "the Hammer" for beating people to follow the party line, held his own press conference May 6 to accuse the Democrats of undermining the war effort. Delay rolled them all up in the same flag: "Calling for Secretary Rumsfeld's resignation is as bad as saying the war is unwinnable."

Another Texas Republican, Representative Michael C. Burgess, said the Democrats had "embellished our enemy, and basically are giving aid and comfort to the enemy."

Neither man recognized that in his actual remarks that day, Murtha had neither called for Rumsfeld's resignation nor called the war flatly unwinnable.

There were no shades of gray to the political combatants, while Murtha saw many shades.

The subsequent media coverage was more about the Republicans' push-back than about Abu Ghraib.

"From GOP, Zero Tolerance for Democratic War Critics," blared the *Washington Post* headline.

That headline pretty much summed things up: to Republicans, the war on words was more important than the words on war.

This was the typical political play of the time, a time when voice was feared and trampled. Calling for more troops was unpatriotic? Comforting the enemy?

When Americans in 1776 decided fighting the British in standard columns head-to-head was an unwinnable way to approach that war, were they cowards? Abe Lincoln wanted a decidedly more aggressive approach to hunting down and destroying the Confederate Army than had been used when he finally put General Ulysses Grant in charge of Union forces. Did Lincoln's action constitute aiding the enemy?

Murtha recognized that with inadequate troop numbers, personnel were being stretched to the breaking point by the long and repeated deployment and service extensions. The situation was worsening as the military was forced to re-assign whatever troops were available to undertake whatever mission had the most critical need.

Infantrymen were being assigned as military police, truck drivers, and prison guards. Many personnel were being assigned to protect convoys. The personnel working outside of their military specialty or MOS numbered 6,300.

In the May 6 news conference, Murtha used the 372nd Company from Cumberland as a prime example of how badly the war was being executed. He read the following e-mail that had been forwarded to him from the father of a deployed soldier:

> This letter is to address serious concerns I have as a member of the 372nd Military Police Company. As a bit of background information, the 372nd MP Company was mobilized in February 2003, cut orders for 365 days for mobilization to Iraq. In January 2004, the unit was extended for 100-day extension orders and told they would be released as soon as possible. Now the 372nd has been held in theater awaiting a 120-day extension of orders they have not received yet. This call comes on the heels of an eight-month deployment in Bosnia in 2001-2002.
>
> While being extended again is obviously a hardship on the military family, this is not our primary concern. The new mission is to ride shotgun on Kellogg, Brown & Root tractor trailers and do personal protection for these drivers on long-distance convoys covering roads that have been under heavy insurgent attack in recent weeks.
>
> This is not an MP mission and cannot be found in any

MP handbook or resources. There is no standard operating procedure for such a mission. We have no battle drills that cover shooting from cabs or trucks, dismounting from cabs and trucks, or any other drills that would apply. We would be alone in these missions, with no communication with other members of our unit in the MPs providing escort security in armored humvees.

The reason for this mission is because the civilian drivers, who have no military experience, are refusing to do their jobs until they get what they want from the U.S. Army. These civilian drivers are aware of the dangers their jobs can entail, can quit and leave their jobs at any time, and make large sums of money driving for KBR in Iraq.

This brings me to the current state of our unit. We currently have no officers left in our company. Our commander (and) the first sergeant were relieved of duty and are still in Iraq. Our other officers served on twenty-two months of active duty and were entitled to go home. Our commander is an enlisted sergeant first class E-7. Our first sergeant is also an E-7 and does not have the Military Police MOS. Without any officers, our unit suffers from a lack of commissioned leadership and leaves our company with no one to address the issues, to look out for our best interests.

Our unit has packed our personal and military equipment for shipment home, leaving us rushed into a mission without the proper equipment and supplies to succeed. We have no communications equipment, such as radios and GPS. All of our night-vision medical supplies for combat life-savers and weapons cleaning have been packed away in connexes. Many soldiers do not have the basic TA-50, such as sleeping bags, ammo pouches and other standard-issue gear. The 372nd Military Company is being rushed back into Iraq without the proper equipment, training and command structure. The unit is not being given the tools it needed to succeed, and the mission is not properly thought out.

After reading the soldier's e-mail, Murtha offered his assessment: "Now, this doesn't go to this small group (of soldiers). This goes to planning. This goes back to what I said at first. Shinseki said you need 200,000 people. You remember the riots that got out of control when this thing first started, because we didn't have enough people. And because of that, this prison didn't have enough people. How many other installations are undermanned, they don't have enough people in them, and how many people are sent over there without the proper training to do the job that they're doing?"

He continued, "Now why am I not going to the Defense (Department), why am I coming to you (the media)? I'll tell you why. I wrote this letter to the president in September, and I got an answer just a month ago, and he said everything's all right. It wasn't even from the president; it was from an assistant secretary of defense. That's the way they treat Congress: with absolute arrogance, pay no attention to the suggestions that are made by Congress.

"Our failure to surge in terms of troop level and resources needed to prevail in this war has led to what appears to be unattainable goals in our current path. ... And our troops are suffering because of the lack of planning by those people over there at the Pentagon. Bad intelligence, inept planning, careless mistakes made by the architect of this war has resulted in gross errors and underestimated distribution of resources that are needed."

Despite that scathing assessment, Murtha did not call for Rumsfeld's resignation. Yet the big fallout from Abu Ghraib, in addition to turning the Iraqis against the U.S. troops, was the collapse of support for Defense Secretary Rumsfeld.

Republican Senator John McCain said Americans had lost

confidence in Rumsfeld. Fellow Republican Trent Lott, Senate majority leader, said he was not a fan. To their credit, they and a few other Republicans had been pushing Rumsfeld on the low troop numbers that they also felt were a problem in Iraq. Of course, that responsibility really sat with the president, but no Republican dared to knock the White House in an election year. Rumsfeld took many hits over Abu Ghraib.

Murtha and others used much stronger terms than McCain or Lott, and Rumsfeld did offer his resignation to Bush over the scandal at least twice. Bush declined to accept.

Bush also declined to change direction. The Republicans seized upon the "unwinnable" word to repeatedly attack Murtha. When asked about the claims that he was undermining the troops, Murtha was typically blunt:

"Do you think the troops don't know about these shortages? Do you think the troops don't have…," he could not continue, just chuckling and shaking his head at the notion that the troops somehow did not know what was really going on.

He added: "I went over there, this general was telling me how good the morale was. I said, 'You don't need to tell me, General, how the morale is. I've been around too long. I'll talk to the troops to find out how the morale is.'"

Murtha did talk to the troops, especially those wounded and recovering at the military hospitals, which he visited nearly every week. He insisted that more troops were needed to win the war and continued to oppose the idea of leaving Iraq, ignoring the anger that was aimed at him by those who steadfastly refused to hear what he was saying because it was not their party line. Murtha went on for more than a year calling for more strength and a better plan, but he was continually slammed for "enabling the enemy."

Seventeen months later, Murtha offered an impassioned articulation of why torture and Abu Ghraib were wrong. On December 14, 2005,

Murtha took to the House floor to rally his colleagues to support an amendment mandating that the Defense Department adhere to the Army Field Manual for military interrogations, which specifically banned the use of torture. Murtha offered the following observations:

> The words "torture," "cruelty" and "abuse" elicit images of draconian and brutal dictatorship. These words are reserved for the worst of human rights offenders. It should never include the United States of America.
>
> The United States of America and the values we reflect abhor human rights violators and uphold human rights. No circumstance whatsoever justifies torture. No emergencies, no state of war, no level of political instability....
>
> Using the argument terrorists do much worse, that al Qaeda does much worse is a horrifying rationale. As Captain (Ian) Fishback argues, "since when did al Qaeda become any type of standard by which we measure the morality of the United States?" And that is a quote from Captain Fishback.
>
> Captain Fishback wrote to Senator McCain, "If we abandon our ideals in the face of adversity and aggression, then those ideals were never really in our possession. I would rather die fighting than give up even the smallest part of that idea that is America." And Captain Fishback was in Afghanistan for eighteen months and in Iraq.
>
> We cannot protect freedom abroad or at home while degrading our society and its political and legal systems. We cannot do it while trampling all over the values which have made this country strong, which define us all as Americans. These values do not belong to any party. They are not Democrat or Republican. They are American values.

At another point in his speech, Murtha talked about Abu Ghraib and how such abuse impacts innocent people and produces false confessions and unreliable results.

> We have irrefutable evidence of widespread use of unlawful interrogation techniques by American interrogators at Abu Ghraib and other locations. This has been absolutely disastrous to our credibility and our reputation as a nation that was built on the sanctity of individual rights. We have a legal and moral and ethical obligation to uphold the values of the Geneva Convention and the United Nations Convention against Torture.
>
> Furthermore, torture, cruelty, and abuse are not effective methods of interrogation. Torture may not yield reliable, actionable information and can lead to false confessions....
>
> Torture is not only used against the guilty; it often leads to unintentional abuse of the innocent. We cannot torture and still retain the moral high ground. Torture endangers U.S. service members who might be captured by the enemy. Torture brings discredit upon the United States.
>
> There can be no waiver for the use of torture. No torture and no exceptions. Gray areas in rules; lack of direction, training, and supervision from superiors; lack of standards and clear guidelines from leaders are dangerous and led to the abuse at Abu Ghraib and other locations. During times of war, clear guidelines governing the treatment of prisoners is imperative, especially when, due to the lack of manpower, people are put in jobs with little or no experience or people are put in jobs that are not appropriate. The alleged ring leader at Abu Ghraib

had a history of domestic abuse and therefore, by law, could not carry a firearm in the United States. Yet, he was a prison guard at Abu Ghraib, and he was not suited for handling prisoners.

It is now evident that abuse of prisoners took place because of lack of supervision, that our troops were given ambiguous instructions which, in some cases, authorized treatment that went beyond what was allowed in the Army Field Manual.

The definition of abusive treatment cannot be a matter of subjectivity and ambiguity.

Murtha concluded his speech with more impassioned words about honor and humanity:

War is about killing. For those sent to fight an enemy, that killing will stay with them for the rest of their lives. It is in the faces of friends lost, in the shadows the soldiers feel on their souls for having killed. This is the nature of war. But when torture becomes a part of war, when torture is condoned, if we allow torture in any form, we abandon our honor and the last shred of humanity. Visions of abuse and torture chill our conscience and sear our souls. Torture scars not only its subject; it scars those who perpetrate it and those who are witnesses to it.

Most military leaders know that allowing torture subjects our service members to similar acts if captured. We in Congress must never forget this because we are charged with sending our sons and daughters into battle. This responsibility is doubly heavy today when America is living in a time of great uncertainty and two wars.

In the case of Iraq, we are unsure of the war's rationale

and where it will lead us. In the war against terror, we are still struggling to fathom our enemy and are troubled by his tactics. It is all the more important now that we remember that America stands for the honor of those we have sent to fight this war.

The reaction was typical: ignore the depth and substance of Murtha's remarks and stick to the bumper-sticker approach of accusing the un-American Murtha of aiding the enemy.

Meanwhile back in the real world, Americans with sons and daughters in harm's way were increasingly agitated by the war of words and the mounting toll of the war itself in Iraq.

Chapter **14**

Mothers and Mission Accomplished

On November 1, 2004, just one day before President George W. Bush was re-elected to lead the nation for a second term, the Fox News station in Johnstown ran a story about Dawn Golby and Sandra Rusin, two women who had lost sons in Iraq.

In the broadcast, Golby said, "This war was supposedly declared over by President Bush when he was on that carrier."

"Mission accomplished?" the reporter asked.

"Mission Accomplished, correct," she replied. "Then if the war was over and the mission was accomplished, then why are all of them still dying? Why are they still dying?"

Golby was referring to one of the most theatrical events of the Iraq war, when Bush had hopped a ride in a military jet that landed on the deck of the aircraft carrier USS Abraham Lincoln on May 1, 2003. The president emerged dramatically from the cockpit wearing a jump suit and helmet. Under the huge banner that screamed "Mission Accomplished," he saluted the smiling men and women in uniform who had been possitioned on the carrier deck to provide the appropriate visual backdrop for such a dramatic announcement.

"In the Battle of Iraq, the United States and our allies have prevailed," Bush proclaimed.

Although Bush spoke about the challenges to come, the theatrics quickly became a controversy in itself. The sign, the declaration, and even the cost and risk of flying the president out to make the dramatic landing on the aircraft carrier drew fire from war critics and others who felt the president had gone too far.

It was a sign of the twisted political times: The debate about America's own propaganda seemed to be more heated than the debate about whether to go to war in the first place.

The White House claimed that the banner had been requested by the crew of the ship to signify the end of their ten-month deployment. Critics claimed the president was showboating and feeding the American public a false sense of accomplishment. The fact that the president used the jet landing, even though the Abraham Lincoln was only thirty miles from the U.S. coast, suggested grandstanding to those critics who felt the president's helicopter should have been used. Jet aircraft use a lot of fuel, and anyone who lands on a carrier earns the title of "tailhooker" because the boat is not long enough for a traditional landing: the aircraft drop a big hook that must catch a metal cable to stop it on the deck in a procedure that has far more risk than landing a plane on land.

Such heated banter over a banner demonstrates how focused Washington had become on the politics of war rather than the consequences of war.

Murtha understood that presidents have always used glowing terms and backdrops, in part to inspire the people, and that inspiring the people is important because real change and prosperity always comes from an inspired people who are willing to meet a challenge.

The speech delivered by the president was accurate in describing the major military operations as being over, since a standing army had been defeated. The president did talk about the work to be done, and if one looked only at his words, the moment would have drawn far less criticism.

But the banner, the jet landing, the jump suit worn by the president all suggested a far greater victory than his words had indicated. In fact, Bush was agreeing with much of what Murtha would say by 2005: the remaining solution in Iraq was not one for the military, but one for diplomacy since everything the military could achieve had been accomplished.

The banner, however, also came to represent something to a pair of mothers back in Murtha's 12th Congressional District.

Dawn Golby and Sandy Rusin both lost sons in Iraq. Neither used the time of their child's death as a platform to speak against the war, but both would come to a conclusion by November of 2004 that had a lot to do with "Mission Accomplished".

Specialist Christopher Golby was twenty-six when his Black Hawk medical evacuation helicopter went down near Fallujah, Iraq, on January 8, 2004. Golby was assigned to the Army's 571st Medical Company air ambulance and, on the day of his death, had been removing the injured from the battle.

His parents had remained silent, for the most part, except to say that they had spoken to their son just a week before and he was laughing and in a good mood. He was set to come home in March.

The media was permitted to attend the funeral, and they all stayed an appropriate distance from the actual service.

Golby was laid to rest at Richland Cemetery. It was a bitter, cold, January day that offered a wind only a grieving family could ignore. The retired Army bugler who played taps stayed inside his car to keep warm until the moment he was called into service.

When he exited his vehicle, he had a noticeable limp. Walking the short distance to the grave site appeared to be a real challenge for the elderly man, who perhaps had been injured in a prior war or perhaps was just dealing with the toll that the passing years can have on the human frame.

The region does not have many such musicians. This one usually played at any Veterans Day or Flag Day celebration. On the occasion of Golby's funeral, however, his sound was off and labored. When he returned to his car after taps, his eyes were full from sadness for the Golbys and, to some degree, from the physical pain.

He apologized to the media near his car, saying he felt badly that he had not played well, but that his lips were freezing to his instrument and he could not generate the moisture in his mouth to handle the bitter cold and get the horn to sound good.

This was a soldier who did his fighting decades ago, sad that in the moment a brother in arms needed him, his body could no longer fight off the elements. His remorse was a small demonstration of the brotherhood common among veterans. With one of the highest percentages of veterans anywhere in the country, Southwestern Pennsylvania has an especially tight-knit group, and the loss of Golby was a personal tragedy to this bugler and to thousands of area veterans who never knew the man.

The bitter cold and frozen landscape served as a stark back drop to the black clothes and as reminders of the completeness of such loss.

The American flag looked brilliant in the field of white. That image would prove to be a deception when Golby's mother, Dawn, spoke to a television crew a few months later.

Private First Class Aaron Rusin was only nineteen years old when he was killed by gunfire while driving in a military transport in Iraq in October of 2004. Rusin had enlisted right out of high school, in part to serve his country, and in part to extend the tradition of his family. Rusin's father, three uncles, and grandfather all had served, and he was proud to continue that chain.

He had always been in service, if not to his country then to his community, joining the local volunteer fire department in his early teens. He was described as enthusiastic to serve and dedicated to his department. Just as Golby was honored by the large population of military folks in the region, so too was Rusin. But young Aaron had an extended family as well among volunteer fire fighters, emergency medical technicians, and ambulance crews.

The region has many volunteer firefighters. They are a dedicated bunch who take what they do seriously and offer a life-saving service that local and state government could never afford. They work almost as hard at raising funds to keep their fire companies afloat as they do in constant training to stay prepared. Above all, they look out for their fellow firefighter.

Aaron Rusin died in a different sort of firefight, but he died nonetheless, and the tiny fire halls that pepper the region and make up perhaps the community's single largest fraternity, mourned his passing.

There is no good time to die for someone only nineteen years old, so saying there is a bad time seems to lack any real logic. But Aaron Rusin had been in Iraq only a month when he died, and the brief nature of his time there seemed to add to the shock and dismay.

His mother, Sandy, talked at great length about her son and the way 9/11 had inspired him to serve. She had exchanged e-mails with him and still had a message on her answering machine from her son, whose call she would miss only to have him call no more.

Sandy leads a simple life. She styles hair and lives in a quaint home that was wall-papered with pictures of her family, even before her oldest son's death in Iraq. Knick knacks and warm, worn chairs, along with those pictures, set the tone for her home. It is a familiar setting in the Johnstown area. Clean but jammed with small things that bring reminders of simple times, their homes offer both clutter and comfort. Family is almost always there when anyone enters the residence of the working men and women of the 12th Congressional District.

Sandra Rusin was understandably proud of her son, but in their last communication, Aaron said that Iraq was not what he had thought it would be. He was apparently unhappy about being more police than army, and felt unsettled by being an easy target in those transports. Aaron Rusin wanted to come home.

Dawn Golby would reach out to Sandy Rusin, and the two would forge a friendship born out of loss. On the eve of the 2004 presidential election, Golby would urge her friend Sandy to join her in reaching out to the local media because they had decided there was something they wanted to say.

Another woman joined them, Cynthia Shantz. Her son was alive, but currently serving in Iraq. She was a friend of Sandy Rusin.

The mothers of these boys had formed a common opinion based on their experience. That opinion was conveyed to Murtha and was among the seeds that eventually would lead him to assert that the American public was way ahead of the government on Iraq. These were the voices being heard in the 12th District.

The following is the transcript of the story, inspired in part by an ill-conceived banner on a war ship. The story aired on the local Fox affiliate almost one year to the day before Murtha would call for redeployment.

> RUSIN (weeping): They are sending our boys; they are not the mothers that are losing it. I know it's hard for fathers, but we carried this child for nine months and we brought this child into the world, and it's just not fair.
>
> REPORTER SCRIPT: Sandy Rusin lost her son, Aaron, to sniper fire in Iraq. He had been there less than a month. Tonight, in her Cambria County home, she sat with other mothers who share or feel her pain. Her son wanted to serve his country, but in an e-mail just eight days before his death, Aaron Rusin wrote that things had changed.
>
> RUSIN (READING FROM HAND WRITTEN COPY OF E-MAIL): It starts out saying that I'm definitely ready to

come home and be with you all. Being here, I really see how stupid this all is. I mean, we had a good reason for the war, but with the stuff we do now, it's kind of pointless to be here, so hopefully I can get home and spend time with you all.

REPORTER SCRIPT: Cynthia Shantz has been friends with Sandy for years. She also has a son serving in Iraq, and Aaron's death has left her shaken.

SHANTZ: It was devastating. It hit really close to home. I said, "Oh my God, that could have been my son," and that made it even worse.

REPORTER SCRIPT: Cynthia supports her son but says we were misled into war and that we have put 100,000 sons and daughters into the line of fire for no real reason.

SHANTZ: You know those people over there have been killing each other for thousands and thousands of years, and I don't feel we're going to make a difference because when we leave there, it's probably going to go back to the way it was.

REPORTER ASKED: So what do you say to your son?

SHANTZ ANSWER: Be safe.

REPORTER SCRIPT: Sandy is often consoled these days by Dawn Golby. Her son, Christopher, also from Cambria County, was buried in January after dying in Iraq. She not only feels the president misled about weapons, but misled when he said the war was over.

GOLBY: This war was supposedly declared over by President Bush when he was on that carrier.

REPORTER ASKED: Mission accomplished?

GOLBY ANSWER: Mission Accomplished, correct. Then if the war was over and the mission was accomplished, then why are all of them still dying? Why are they still dying?

REPORTER ASKED: Now you voted for Mr. Bush last election?

GOLBY ANSWER: Yes, I did.

REPORTER ASKED: You're not voting for him this election?

GOLBY ANSWER: I find it hard to vote for the man who sent my son to his death.

REPORTER SCRIPT: Dawn last saw her son via the internet, where she used the web cam to show him his home for the holidays.

GOLBY: I showed him the Christmas tree and I told him I wasn't going to take the Christmas tree down (weeping) until he came home, and it's still up.

REPORTER ASKED: So when does it come down?

GOLBY ANSWER: Never. The tree will never come down.

REPORTER SCRIPT: These three moms have each other. They share a feeling of betrayal and a sense of loss. As for home for the holidays? The newest member to this sad sorority cannot imagine what she might feel.

RUSIN (crying): I can't even think about it. Chris was just talking about decorating for Thanksgiving, I told her to do it. I can't do it.....I want my baby home.

Murtha was not bending to the will of grieving mothers when he spoke out on November 17, 2005. In fact, just days before Aaron Rusin died, Murtha voted in favor of reinstating the draft, which would, of course, send more sons and daughters into battle.

Internet rumors about reinstating the military draft after the 2004 elections were being fueled by some of the unabashedly liberal Democrats and war opponents to undermine support for Bush. With

Murtha and others now arguing that more troops were needed to succeed in Iraq, the draft rumors carried some weight. Those rumors certainly grabbed the attention of anyone with a son or daughter, a grandson or granddaughter who was at or soon would be at draft age and therefore might soon be drafted into service in Iraq or Afghanistan.

Legislation to reinstate the draft was political theater from both sides. The Democrats drafted the bill with no intention of voting for it; they only wanted to politically threaten the president. The Republicans then rushed it to the House floor as a political counter-measure to create the illusion of support for the president and to scream publicly that it was Democrats calling for a draft, not the president or Republicans.

Republicans saw the vote as damage control. Many of the Democrats who howled were more upset about Republicans controlling the damage than the real question of whether America should bring back the draft.

The bill was defeated with 402 members voting against it and just two voting in favor. Jack Murtha was one of the two along with Congressman Pete Starks, Democrat of California. Murtha offered an explanation in a news release to the local media on September 6, 2004.

"My vote for this bill shouldn't surprise anyone. I've always favored universal service because I believe the burden of our defense should be shared by all Americans, not primarily by low- and middle-income young people who join the military because they can't find a decent job, or because they need money to attend college under the GI bill. The responsibility belongs to all of us," Murtha said.

"Earlier this week, Ambassador Paul Bremer said we never had enough troops on the ground in Iraq. For the first time since 1994, the National Guard missed its sign-up goal for the fiscal year ending September 30. The Army is considering cutting the length of its year-long combat tours in Iraq and Afghanistan because of concerns about a possible decline in recruitment and retention. Right now, our troops are understaffed and in many cases, inadequately trained for the missions they're being asked to carry out," he said.

Murtha had remained consistent. More troops were needed to do this right. His view was consistent with General Shinseki's original assessment of necessary troop levels before the war. Without enough men, then more men would die. Murtha was in no hurry to have more grieving mothers in his district and, in his words and actions, he demonstrated that he felt the best way to protect the war fighter was with more war fighters. Eventually, after exhausting himself trying to get the White House to change its strategy, Murtha would finally decide to call for a change in mission: a redeployment from Iraq.

As for the war of words that followed the "Mission Accomplished" banner, whether the banner was the president's idea or not, one can certainly see how the sign and the president's speech would leave a mother with a son in battle with the notion that this war was essentially over. Someone on the Bush team of advisors should have known this was a bad idea. Anyone who lost family in the war could look back on this moment with the conviction that they had been misled. And more than ninety-eight percent of U.S casualties came after President Bush stood aboard the USS Abraham Lincoln in front of the red, white, and blue "Mission Accomplished" banner.

Christopher Golby's mother related another note about red, white, and blue. While all the media had access to the red-white-and-blue images of "Mission Accomplished," television cameras were not permitted to see the flag-draped coffins of the fallen as they came home. Dawn Golby scoffed at the debate and, in a near indignant tone through more tears, talked about how, when she went to get her son, no flag covered her boy. In fact, choking back tears, she said she would barely describe what her son arrived in as a coffin.

Golby claimed that when she arrived to meet her now-dead son, he was in little more than a cardboard box that was marked "Human remains." It can be said with absolute certainty that Dawn Golby felt this had diminished her son's contribution. Golby said it was like "now that he is dead, he is of no use to us (the military)." She said she was proud of her son's service and the people who wear the uniform, but that their sacrifice had been misused.

The contrast of that arrival with the funeral of Golby the previous January is stunning: the bitter cold, the limping and aging bugler, the black silhouettes walking across the frozen ground, the somber mood, and most vividly, the brilliant red, white, and blue American flag cast against the white canvass that winter had painted over the cemetery. Golby's words delivered with a blend of anger and sorrow in this mother's voice expose that image as a counterfeit portrait, a deception that put a priority on staging patriotism rather than a real picture of events. No camera, no flag, just a box and a label of "human remains."

Dawn Golby would die about three years after this interview, the result of a heart problem while on vacation. Sandy Rusin remains in the same home surrounded by photos. She is slowly healing, and looks back on the days after Aaron's death and burial as a blur. She recalls Jack Murtha coming to the funeral home to pay his respects.

"I never thought about him (Murtha) coming or anything, but there he was," said Rusin. "He put his arms around us (her and her fiancé, James) and stood there between the two of us and said how sorry he was for this. It was like he was one of the firemen talking about Aaron. Nothing really helps when you lose a child, time maybe, but him (Murtha) coming like that gave me comfort that Aaron mattered to someone. I never would have given it a second thought had Mr. Murtha not been there. The fact that he came at all made a difference to us."

Cynthia Shantz prayed her son, John, would come home alive. Her prayers were answered, but one could hardly call this mother or her son the lucky ones. John came back a different man than the one who left for Iraq. He would talk about nightmares. Children ages ten or nine or maybe younger who had to be shot. The images she described were of bodies and body parts littered through her son's dreams.

Agitated, angry, and unable to sleep, he became depressed and distracted. He was diagnosed with post-traumatic stress disorder. Eventually the new John did something a lot of angry men end up doing, time.

Cynthia's son, at age twenty-eight, would be charged with the armed robbery of a bank. He used a knife and claimed no recollection of the crime, but spoke of fantasies in which he did something to force the police to kill him: suicide by cop.

While his mother could not talk about the legal aspects of what her son may have done, she has no problem today saying too much was asked of her boy for too long, and it broke him.

"He was not the same. He was angry and could not sleep. He did not talk too much about the war, but would mumble about this huge blast and civilians blown apart. He would talk about this ten-inch hole blasted through the chest of some guy who turned out to not have had a bomb or been a threat, and it tortured him. He would ask me, 'What do I do? What do I do?'" said Shantz.

Interviewed in the Cambria County Prison, John said he had tried to kill himself once, but the gun he had placed beneath his chin did not fire. He still did not want to live, but never again worked up the courage to pull the trigger on himself. Suicide by cop seemed like a good option to this broken war fighter.

Just as Murtha complained about men who were sent to war ill-equipped, Shantz would say men were sent home from war ill-equipped, too.

"He was not the same, and he was lost, and it seems like there was no or not enough help for him and other men like him. He survived, but I don't think he lived. Some part of him died over there. I hope it can come back, brought back to life, but it won't happen without help. Nothing is worth this, but when you think about why and how these guys ended up over there, it makes you cry."

At the time of the first interview, these mothers had grown to see the effort mustered by their sons as heroic, but the call to duty that demanded such heroism as misguided and misleading. In November of 2004, this was the mood of a growing number of people in Murtha's 12th District. By November of 2005, it was the feeling of most.

Between those Novembers, Jack Murtha would visit Walter Reed or Bethesda military hospitals almost weekly; he would meet Sam Ross and stage a big rally to present Ross with a Purple Heart to help this young Connellsville man get over the bitterness of being blinded; he would earmark funding for traumatic brain injuries, post-traumatic stress disorders, and the nerve block that stops incredible pain; he would work tirelessly behind the scenes to help the wounded and everyone who proudly wore the uniform of this great nation, and to convince the Bush administration to change course in Iraq.

As that next November approached, he would see the U.S. death toll go beyond 2,000. He would see polls stating that eighty percent of Iraqis opposed the U.S. presence there and forty-five percent of them believed it was acceptable to kill American soldiers. To Murtha, it would become clear that the United States was now seen as an occupier in Iraq, and that U.S. troops were caught in the cross-fire of a civil war that was simply impossible for us to win militarily. Ultimately, he would come to believe that the war in Iraq had become a waste of blood and treasure.

One day, he would get himself worked up into such a funk that we would tell his good friend, Congressman Doyle, "I'm gonna shake this whole place up."

Chapter 15

November 17, 2005

"**The war in** Iraq is not going as advertised. It is a flawed policy wrapped in illusion.... Our military has done everything that has been asked of them. The U.S. cannot accomplish anything further in Iraq militarily. It is time to bring them home."

With those words on November 17, 2005, Congressman Jack Murtha abandoned the role of behind-the-scenes shepherd of foreign policy and took on George W. Bush and the Karl Rove smear machine in a frontal assault.

Murtha had tried repeatedly to be heard by the president and his top policy-makers. Every U.S. president for more than thirty years, from Gerald Ford through Bill Clinton, had sought Murtha's counsel on military and foreign affairs. Every president, that is, until George W. Bush. Murtha had never sought to speak to the world because he could have immediate impact by talking directly to presidents. Murtha was a close advisor to Democratic presidents and probably even closer to Republicans Ronald Reagan and George H.W. Bush or "Bush I", who talked to Murtha eleven times leading into the first Gulf War and did everything that Murtha recommended at the time.

But by November 17, 2005, after having waited seven months for a response to a letter to the president only to finally get an "everything's fine" reply from a Pentagon "staffer;" after having been shut out, rebuked, and ignored by Bush, the White House, the defense secretary, and even his old friend, Dick Cheney; after having publicly expressed his concerns in trying to get someone in the inner circle to hear his call for more troops and more honesty about the war; after two-and-a-half years of agonizing over the mounting deaths and devastating injuries to U.S. troops who were paying a tremendous burden. After all that, Murtha finally stood up and proclaimed, in essence, that enough was enough.

At 9:45 that morning, Murtha addressed the Democratic Caucus in Room HC-5 of the United States Capitol. Mike Doyle, the Pittsburgh Congress Member who was among those closest to Murtha, described the situation:

"When he spoke, there was a hush. Usually in caucus, people were talking; it was sometimes hard to hear. But when he spoke, you could hear a pin drop. The doves loved what he had to say, equally for the hawks and Southern Democrats, the Gene Taylors who looked up to Jack," Doyle said, referring to then-Congressman Eugene Taylor, Democrat of Mississippi. "There was shock on both sides, so everybody wanted to hear what he said. That rarely happens. You could hear a pin drop."

When Murtha finished, several members of Congress were crying, and they all stood and delivered a standing ovation.

Murtha then walked down the hall to HC-9, where, at 10:30 that morning, he spoke to the national media, or at least to those members of the national media who had either the foresight or good fortune to be close enough to get to this "presser" even on short notice.

Murtha's remarks to the media were well-rehearsed until he went off script and talked about the troops, at which time the old warrior became highly emotional, but tried to ignore the tears in his eyes.

War was hell, and this old warrior knew it.

His remarks that day were detailed and said it all:

> The war in Iraq is not going as advertised. It is a flawed policy wrapped in illusion. The American public is way

ahead of us. The United States and coalition troops have done all they can in Iraq, but it is time for a change in direction.

Our military is suffering. The future of our country is at risk. We cannot continue on the present course. It is evident that continued military action in Iraq is not in the best interest of the United States of America, the Iraqi people, or the Persian Gulf region.

General Casey said in a September 2005 hearing, "The perception of occupation in Iraq is a major driving force behind the insurgency." General Abizaid said on the same date, "Reducing the size and visibility of the coalition forces in Iraq is a part of our counterinsurgency strategy."

For two-and-a-half years, I have been concerned about the U.S. policy and the plan in Iraq. I have addressed my concerns with the administration and the Pentagon, and have spoken out in public about my concerns. The main reason for going to war has been discredited. A few days before the start of the war, I was in Kuwait. The military drew a red line around Baghdad and said, when U.S. forces cross that line, they will be attacked by the Iraqis with weapons of mass destruction. But the U.S. forces said they were prepared. They had well-trained forces with the appropriate protective gear.

We spend more money on intelligence than all the countries in the world together, and more on intelligence than most countries' GDP (gross domestic product). But the intelligence concerning Iraq was wrong. It is not a world intelligence failure. It is a U.S. intelligence failure and the way that intelligence was misused.

I have been visiting our wounded troops at Bethesda and Walter Reed hospitals almost every week since the beginning of the War. And what demoralizes them is going to war with not enough troops and equipment to make the transition to peace; the devastation caused by IEDs; being deployed to Iraq when their homes have been ravaged by hurricanes; being on their second or third deployment and leaving their families behind without a network of support.

The threat posed by terrorism is real, but we have other threats that cannot be ignored. We must be prepared to face all threats. The future of our military is at risk. Our military and their families are stretched thin. Many say that the Army is broken. Some of our troops are on their third deployment. Recruitment is down, even as our military has lowered its standards. Defense budgets are being cut. Personnel costs are skyrocketing, particularly in health care. Choices will have to be made. We cannot allow promises we have made to our military families in terms of service benefits, in terms of their health care, to be negotiated away. Procurement programs that ensure our military dominance cannot be negotiated away. We must be prepared. The war in Iraq has caused huge shortfalls at our bases in the U.S.

Much of our ground equipment is worn out and in need of either serious overhaul or replacement. George Washington said, "To be prepared for war is one of the most effective means of preserving peace." We must rebuild our Army. Our deficit is growing out of control. The director of the Congressional Budget Office recently admitted to being "terrified" about the budget deficit in the coming decades. This is the first prolonged war we have fought with three years of tax cuts, without full mobilization of American industry, and without a draft. The burden of this war has not been shared equally; the military and their families are shouldering this burden.

Our military has been fighting a war in Iraq for over two and a half years. Our military has accomplished its mission and done its duty. Our military captured Saddam Hussein, and captured or killed his closest associates. But the war continues to intensify. Deaths and injuries are growing, with over 2,079 confirmed American deaths. Over 15,500 have been seriously injured, and it is estimated that over 50,000 will suffer from battle fatigue. There have been reports of at least 30,000 Iraqi civilian deaths.

I just recently visited Anbar Province, Iraq, in order to assess the conditions on the ground. Last May 2005, as part of the Emergency Supplemental Spending Bill, the House included the Moran Amendment, which was accepted in conference, and which required the secretary of defense to submit quarterly reports to Congress in order to more accurately measure stability and security in Iraq. We have now received two reports. I am disturbed by the findings in key indicator areas. Oil production and energy production are below pre-war levels. Our reconstruction efforts have been crippled by the security situation. Only $9 billion of the $18 billion appropriated for reconstruction has been spent. Unemployment remains at about sixty percent. Clean water is scarce. Only $500 million of the $2.2 billion appropriated for water projects has been spent. And most importantly, insurgent incidents have increased from about 150 per week to over seven hundred in the last year. Instead of attacks going down over time and with the addition of more troops, attacks have grown dramatically. Since the revelations at Abu Ghraib, American casualties have doubled. An annual State Department report in 2004 indicated a sharp increase in global terrorism.

I said over a year ago, and now the military and the administration agrees, Iraq cannot be won "militarily." I said two years ago, the key to progress in Iraq is to "Iraqatize, Internationalize and Energize." I believe the same today. But I have concluded that the presence of U.S. troops in Iraq is impeding this progress.

Our troops have become the primary target of the insurgency. They are united against U.S. forces and we have become a catalyst for violence. U.S. troops are the common enemy of the Sunnis, Saddamists, and foreign jihadists. I believe with U.S troop redeployment, the Iraqi security forces will be incentivized to take control. A poll recently conducted shows that over eighty percent of Iraqis are strongly opposed to the presence of coalition troops, and about forty-five percent of the Iraqi population believe attacks against American troops are justified. I believe we need to turn Iraq over to the Iraqis.

I believe before the Iraqi elections, scheduled for mid-December, the Iraqi people and the emerging government must be put on notice that the United States will immediately redeploy. All of Iraq must know that Iraq is free. Free from United States occupation. I believe this will send a signal to the Sunnis to join the political process for the good of a "free" Iraq.

My plan calls:
- To immediately redeploy U.S. troops consistent with the safety of U.S. forces.
- To create a quick reaction force in the region.
- To create an over-the-horizon presence of Marines.
- To diplomatically pursue security and stability in Iraq.

This war needs to be personalized. As I said before, I have visited with the severely wounded of this war. They are suffering.

Because we in Congress are charged with sending our sons and daughters into battle, it is our responsibility, our obligation to speak out for them. That's why I am speaking out.

Our military has done everything that has been asked of them. The U.S. can not accomplish anything further in Iraq militarily. It is time to bring them home.

This was Murtha's prepared text that day. He went off script then and talked about his visits with wounded soldiers. He recalled his meeting with two young widows and a Marine who had lost two legs and an arm. Murtha fought back the tears as he shared these experiences in front of the national media. And those who knew Murtha as the tough old warrior were profoundly moved by his emotion.

Friend and critic alike had always recognized that he was someone who worked behind the scenes, never seeking such bright lights. Although he had spoken out to the media a few times on Iraq, that was contrary to how he had always handled himself. And on this day, he went far beyond what he had done previously because, this time, he launched a frontal assault that was certain to draw fire from those who would support the president. This was not something he wanted to do, and in an interview for a local television station a short time later, he made that abundantly clear.

"You never want to be out front and doing things this way. It is more productive and better for everyone involved if differences can be talked out, but this White House doesn't listen to any one. They don't see that there are people who know about this (war) who can help. I have been trying for years to get them to do things a better way. They would not listen. I have written, and they don't reply for months, and when they do it is some staffer," he said.

When asked about the accusation that he had adopted a "cut-and-run" strategy, Murtha was not shy about pushing back.

"This is a civil war. We cannot solve the things that are wrong in Iraq militarily. We need to redeploy, make certain those who would love to see Iraq in chaos or come into power from outside Iraq don't get involved. We need to do a better job of securing Iraq, of helping the Iraqis help themselves. Right now, our people are just targets and there is no real end in sight based on how we have handled the situation. I warned them (The White House) we are not winning the people, and only bad things can come out of a situation like that. Our military is being broken and they just don't seem to get it. We need a new way."

Gabrielle Carruth, Murtha's associate staffer on Defense Appropriations, likely was the first one to know what Murtha had decided to do.

Murtha had agreed to speak to the Democratic Caucus at its November 17 meeting, and Carruth knew that it would be her job to put on paper the thoughts that he would decide to articulate.

"Every day leading up to the speech, we talked for hours about what was on his mind, to the point where those discussions became more like a daily grueling exercise," Carruth said. "Although the war rarely made front page in the newspapers, it consumed him and everyone who was close to him. There were times when he became quite emotional. His compassion was surprising at first, but obviously necessary for the path he would ultimately take.

"I never really understood the reasoning behind what to me was becoming a daily obsession in fact-finding," she said. "Every day hashing out what was being reported as facts on the ground and comparing against what was being reported by the administration. Then one morning, instead of beginning with the familiar exercise, Mr. Murtha began with the statement that he could no longer support the war and had to speak out. He said he would first address the Democratic caucus with a prepared speech. So we began working on the speech that would change his life and the lives of everyone around him, a speech that would change the course of history."

She recalled vividly the morning of the speech.

"On the morning of November 17, we began our journey from the Rayburn Office Building to the Capitol," she said. "The mood was serious and tense, and I was consumed in apprehension. As we approached the elevators, to break the tension, I half jokingly said, 'You know, it's not too late to turn around.' Mr. Murtha erupted in one of his hearty laughs and said, 'No, we are doing this.' The elevator doors closed, and there was no turning back."

Few people had any notion what Murtha was about to do until right before he did it. Many national media were upset that they had barely any advance notice of the enormity of what was about to happen, so some national reporters missed the whole news conference.

Even Minority Leader Nancy Pelosi, who was a friend and close political ally of Murtha, found out only that morning what he was about to say.

"I knew he had concerns, but I did not know what his position would be because I had not supported the war; he had. So I did not know what presentation he would make about his concerns about the direction," Pelosi said in an interview for this book.

"He came to me and told me, 'This is what I'm going to do: I'm going to talk to the caucus and then have a press announcement.' I told him I thought that was good, to talk to the caucus first," she said.

Asked if Murtha had sought any sort of advice, even suggestions about how to present his rationale to the media, the leader said, "He had his own comfort level; he didn't need advice from anybody about how to talk about war. You have to remember who he is when you say, did he ask for advice.... This was pretty startling. He said he was absolutely convinced that this is what I have to do. It was emotional; he was emotional when he announced his direction."

Pelosi said she was somewhat surprised: "When I say surprised, I was not overwhelmingly surprised. He had questions about the war;

he had questions before.... It was really one of those very special times when you hear from a member who is giving voice to what so many had thought. And he had very substantial and significant reasons for what he did.... He had given his support (for the war resolution), he had questioned the generals, he concluded what he concluded, and then said, 'This is what I intend to do.'"

Congressman Doyle had learned of Murtha's intentions only the day before the news conference when Murtha told Doyle, "I'm gonna shake up the place."

"The next day he came out against the war. He called a press conference, and this was not Lynn Woolsey; this was not Dennis Kucinich; this was John Murtha saying it; and it changed the whole deal," Doyle said, referring to Woolsey of California and Kucinich of Ohio, who are among the most liberal members and had long argued against the war.

People interviewed for this book, when asked why Murtha called for redeployment, all offered multiple or complex reasons based on all the things he had said over time. But in the moment, one summary of Murtha's own view came in an e-mail to Murtha press secretary Cindy Abram from *Los Angeles Times* reporter Maura Reynolds.

On that bizarre day of November 17, 2005, Reynolds, like so many reporters, was trying desperately to reach Murtha. Her e-mail, sent later that day, said:

"Thanks so much for your call. I'm sure it's a busy day for you. I wasn't at my desk when you called because I was outside the House floor where I managed to talk to your boss (Murtha) for a few minutes.

"When I asked him what the trigger was for his decision to support withdrawal, he answered that more than anything else, it was his meetings with the wounded at Walter Reed. I asked him when he started doing that, and he said it was after two widows came to him and asked him to visit recovering troops to tell them how lucky they were to be alive, despite their injuries."

Chapter 16

"Cowards Cut and Run"

Jean Schmidt, Republican of Ohio, was the newest member of Congress, having been elected just three months earlier, when she decided to defend her president and take on Jack Murtha.

On November 17, 2005, as the shockwave of Murtha's call for redeployment was reverberating across Washington and spreading rapidly across the nation, Schmidt stood on the House floor and made her mark on history:

"A few minutes ago, I received a call from Colonel Danny Bubp (an Ohio legislator and Marine Corps Reserve officer) and he asked me to send Congress a message: Stay the course. He also asked me to send Congressman Murtha a message: that cowards cut and run, Marines never do. Danny and the rest of America and the world want the assurance from this body that we will see this through."

Democrats erupted with boos and catcalls, and more than a few Republicans recoiled, not just from Schmidt's words but from the energy bursting from Democrats.

Ten minutes later, Schmidt would have her words removed from the House record. Bubp would say he never mentioned Murtha by name and that Schmidt's words did not reflect their conversation. Schmidt would add that she meant no personal offense to Murtha.

The media made much of the angry words and the strong division on Capitol Hill. If Schmidt had attacked Minority Leader Pelosi or the late Senator Ted Kennedy, Democrat of Massachusetts, some people would have been upset, but it is impossible to imagine the backlash that was erupting in this moment. While Democrats fought back with verve, even a number of Republicans came to Murtha's defense.

There was much more to this moment than displaying the anger: it was proof that in all of Congress, only Jack Murtha could have changed the political dynamic and put the Bush White House on defense. Nobody else in Congress or in all of Washington, for that matter, had the credibility on national defense to withstand the onslaught as the angry, vitriolic attacks came flying.

Speaker of the House J. Dennis Hastert, Republican of Illinois, said, "Murtha and Democratic leaders have adopted a policy of 'cut and run.' They would prefer that the United States surrender to the terrorists who would harm innocent Americans."

White House Spokesman Scott McClellan referred to the ultra-liberal and controversial film-maker when he said, "It is baffling that he (Murtha) is endorsing the policy positions of Michael Moore. Nowhere does he explain how retreating from Iraq makes America safer."

White House Counselor Dan Bartlett called Murtha's position "out of the mainstream of his own party," and said that withdrawal would be "a recipe for disaster."

Vice President Dick Cheney said those who accused the administration of having manipulated intelligence were making "one of the most dishonest and reprehensible charges ever aired in this city."

President Bush was in South Korea, where he agreed with Cheney that criticizing the administration's handling of pre-war intelligence was "irresponsible," adding, "They looked at the same intelligence I did, and they voted, many of them voted to support the decision I made."

Murtha wasted no time in firing back. Aiming both barrels at his old friend, Cheney, who had avoided military service during the Vietnam War, he snorted back: "I like guys who got five deferments and (have) never been there and send people to war, and then don't like to hear suggestions about what needs to be done."

Ironically, the outcry against the Republican attacks was so strong that, as Murtha was lambasting Cheney, Cheney himself was publicly conceding, "I disagree with Jack, but he's a good man, a Marine, a patriot."

That was certainly one of the very few times, if not the only time, Murtha said anything bad about Cheney. He repeated that line about five deferments a few times, but almost immediately calmed down and took a far more tactful approach of echoing Cheney in saying that they simply had different opinions.

The backlash against those who had attacked Murtha came from many circles, and much it was aimed at Schmidt, who was promptly dubbed "Mean Jean." NBC's *Saturday Night Live* lampooned her. The editorial page of her hometown paper, the *Cincinnati Enquirer*, which had endorsed her congressional bid, said she was "way out of line."

Did she expect Democrats to sit and take it as they had for so long? Did she expect a chorus of cheers from her fellow Republicans? Schmidt was described as dazed as she sat back down with the fury going on around her. Back in Murtha's 12th District, sleeves were being rolled up and heels were being dug in.

Call Murtha "King of Pork," no sweat. People around Johnstown do not agree, but politics is politics. Call Murtha corrupt, big deal. Everyone shouts such insults at politicians, unless it is the politician who is bringing money to "their" district. But call Jack Murtha a coward? Then expect a fight.

The message was clear: a full frontal verbal assault on Murtha would not be tolerated, and for the first time in a long time, Democrats had won a shouting match. Wiser and more in-tune Republicans certainly knew that this time, they had gone too far.

Since 9/11, the Democrats as a party had been like frightened puppies. Murtha's bark reminded them they had bite, and when Schmidt slapped Murtha, Democrats finally flashed their teeth.

Perhaps the greatest irony of the episode is that, back on September 6, 2005, when Schmidt was first sworn into office, her maiden speech offered this humble address:

"Mr. Speaker, I stand here today in the same shoes, though with a slightly higher heel, as thousands of members who have taken the same oath before me. I am mindful of what is expected of me, both by this hallowed institution and the hundreds of thousands of Americans I am blessed to represent. I am the lowest-ranking member of this body, the very bottom rung of the ladder, and I am privileged to hold that title. This House has much work to do. On that we can all agree. We will not always agree on the details of that work. Honorable people can certainly agree to disagree. However, here today, I accept a second oath. I pledge to walk in the shoes of my colleagues and refrain from name-calling or the questioning of character. It is easy to quickly sink to the lowest form of political debate. Harsh words often lead to headlines, but walking this path is not a victimless crime. This great House pays the price.

"So at this moment, I begin my tenure in this Chamber, uncertain of what history will say of my tenure here. I come here green with only a desire to make our great country even greater. We have much work to do. In that spirit, I pledge to each of you that any disagreements we may have are just that and no more. Walking in each other's shoes takes effort and pause; however, it is my sincere hope that I never lose the patience to view each of you as human beings first, God's creatures, and foremost, I deeply appreciate this opportunity to serve with each of you. I very much look forward to getting to know you better," she said.

Schmidt apparently forgot her "second oath," although in the current political era, the trash-and-burn attitudes of Republicans certainly encouraged nastiness and personal attacks over statesmanship, tact, and respect.

The irony of Schmidt's maiden speech was not lost on those who follow politics closely. Murtha was fighting a bigger fight than dealing with a single Congress person who, in her first speech, swore not to be reduced to name-calling and in her second speech, resorted to name-calling.

Even though Schmidt's "coward" attack was countered, Murtha's stance on November 17, 2005, made him a target for many people, both inside and outside of Washington, and he would face the repercussions of his stance for the rest of his life.

A Republican, who was a long-time Murtha supporter from his district, summed it up this way: "Jack Murtha did what a lot of us felt needed to be done, but it cost him a lifetime reputation. He had always been seen as a statesman in the region, not a politician. Those who say you should never contradict the president would now see him as a politician. Murtha knew that and he did it, anyway, because he knew it had to be done. That is courage, and it seems to me even if you do not agree with him on the war, you still have to respect taking a stand you believe in at such a personal cost and promise of attack. It is something to be admired."

In Schmidt's defense, she was a newcomer to this political stage and she was doing what everyone seemed to be doing, spewing outrageous rhetoric that had been confused with patriotism. Her misguided attack on Murtha was in fact a tonic for Democrats who needed to win a fight. They won this one, and in this way, Jean Schmidt, quite by accident, helped Murtha's party.

History should note that the national debate and discussion that began on November 17, 2005, were to the credit of Congressman Murtha, who used his voice when others either would not or could not use their voice and be heard.

But the Republicans had another tactic that they used to try to keep Murtha in a box.

Murtha had introduced a resolution in Congress the same day he publicly called for redeployment of troops to the periphery, so they could quickly return, if needed. House Republicans immediately introduced a substitute measure that called for the total and immediate withdrawal of American forces from Iraq. This measure truly did amount to a cut-and-run strategy, but it was a simple partisan stunt to try to quickly quash the rising tide of Murtha's dissatisfaction with the war.

Of course, the substitute measure was overwhelmingly defeated, but it did not succeed as intended by its designers. It did not quash Murtha and it did not put the genie back into the bottle in terms of open debate about what to do in Iraq.

The many representatives who spoke on the Republican substitution bill that day included Congressman Jim McGovern, Democrat of Massachusetts, who not only defended Murtha, but also spoke in larger terms about the need for debate on Iraq. McGovern, who had opposed the war from the beginning, now joined the chorus of voices calling for something apparently feared by the White House: conversation.

McGovern said the House was "about to embark on a process that should dismay every single member of this House. This is not about debate on Iraq. This is about politics, clear and simple. I will go further to say that I believe this is a deliberate effort to attack a member of this House and his views because the majority is afraid of this man and afraid of his views and afraid of his words, so they believe somehow he has to be attacked, that we need to take some quick action here on the House floor."

McGovern continued, "Mr. Speaker, we should have a debate on Iraq. We should have had a debate on Iraq a long time ago. But what we are about to have is not a debate on Iraq. This (legislation) will not be able to be amended; there will be limited amount of time for members to be able to express their views, and quite frankly, it is demeaning to our soldiers, and it is demeaning to those who have raised questions about the war in Iraq. They want us to take this issue seriously and not just play politics with it."

McGovern went on to charge that the Republican House leadership was complicit with the White House in hiding the facts about the faulty intelligence and, most recently, the Abu Ghraib prisoner-abuse scandal. He called the Republican substitute "political theatrics," adding:

"There are none of us in this Chamber who are going to fight in this war, none of us are going to put our lives on the line and, with very few exceptions, none of our kids are going to be fighting in that war. So it takes absolutely no courage for anybody in this chamber to wave the American flag and to say, 'stay the course.'

"This is not about debate on Iraq. This is about political cover for you. This is about finding a way to not answer the tough questions. This is about a way to cover the administration's backside at a time when we should be demanding questions."

If Murtha's actions on November 17 created a seminal moment in our nation's history, then this speech was proof that Murtha's pebble in the pond had created a splash that was generating a growing wave. McGovern was not calling for a withdrawal, although that was his hope; he was calling for real and serious debate. He was urging others to offer voice to how they felt Iraq should be handled. He was fighting back against those who had for so long fought to silence any voice that was not in harmony with their own. He was calling for America as a nation to come to the collective kitchen table and talk.

In calling the Republicans' cut-and-run bill "political theatrics," McGovern hit the bull's eye.

Why were the nation and its leaders not talking about how things were going in Iraq? Why had the war cost so much more than our leaders had said it would? Why had we not seen the promised results? Why should such questions be met with attack?

When Murtha was back in Johnstown for a ribbon cutting for a new business, the buzz was about his actions and whether he had any doubts about his stand.

Murtha was a man who never second-guessed himself. But many in the community had doubts, doubts that were erased that day when working man after working man wanted to shake his hand and tell him how happy they were that somebody had finally done something about the mess in Iraq.

Now Murtha was in his own district and, of course, Johnstown itself was far more pro-Murtha than many other parts of the 12th Congressional District, but a sense of enthusiasm overshadowed the planned event.

When the Congressman was back in the district at such events, he never walked away from a hand shake, but this time he had to. There were just too many. Each time he took a hand, it was followed with words of thanks, and while usually people were excited to meet Murtha, this time Murtha was the one feeding off the energy. He seemed surprised by the enthusiasm and volume of the greetings. The Emperor had no clothes and Jack Murtha was the one who had told him so.

The editorial reaction also was extremely positive in area newspapers, despite the fact that they tended to be very conservative.

The liberal *Pittsburgh Post-Gazette* editorial used several Murtha quotes, including his observation that the war was "not going as advertised" and was a "flawed policy wrapped in illusion," adding, "Indeed it is."

"Coming from anyone else, these comments could be dismissed. Coming from Representative Murtha, they linger in the air with authority, despite the frantic efforts of Republicans to dismiss him as a defeatist," the *Post-Gazette* said.

In the heart of Murtha's district, the *Johnstown Tribune-Democrat* is owned by a very conservative chain that gives local editors leeway on local issues. The paper said Murtha had "fired a shot heard 'round the nation" and quoted Congressman Bill Shuster, a Republican from a district that almost encircles Johnstown, reciting the party line by saying an immediate withdrawal would be "irresponsible, ineffective, and premature." Of course, Murtha never called for "immediate" withdrawal, but the party line never let the facts get in the way of good one-liners.

Just south of Johnstown lies Somerset County, which had given President Bush almost sixty-three percent of the vote against John Kerry in the 2004 presidential election. The *Somerset Daily American* tends to be as conservative as its readers, but concluded, "John Murtha has never steered us wrong. If he believes it is time for troops to come home, then we agree. We hope a time table will be set and that our people will make it home without more loss of life."

The most conservative force in Western Pennsylvania media is not a single newspaper, but a man named Richard Mellon Scaife, whose middle name is connected to his wealth. The *Washington Post* has dubbed him the "Funding Father of the Right" because he gives hundreds of millions of dollars to all the best and brightest right-wing groups, including the Heritage Foundation and the American Enterprise Institute, the group whose spin-off became the breeding ground for the ideas of Paul Wolfowitz, Richard Perle, and Donald Rumsfeld. Scaife is a rich, right-wing intellectual.

Scaife also owns a bunch of papers that almost create a monopoly on editorial opinion in the region. The *Tribune-Review* publishes both a Pittsburgh and Greensburg edition, plus dailies in Connellsville and the Monongahela Valley south of Pittsburgh, and Kittanning and the Allegheny Valley north of Pittsburgh. The 12th Congressional District intersects with the circulation areas of all of those papers.

Jack Murtha knew Richard Scaife very well and, while those who had come to hate Jack Murtha may cringe to hear this, Murtha and Scaife agreed on many issues. Murtha occasionally spoke to some of the conservative think-tanks that Scaife funded and, frankly, Murtha was just that conservative on military and foreign-affairs issues. When he disagreed with those intellectuals, he was able to articulate damn good reasons for his differing view, so when Jack Murtha spoke, Richard Mellon Scaife was among those who listened.

Although the day-after editorials in the Scaife papers echoed the White House position, Murtha met with the *Tribune-Review* editorial board in Pittsburgh in January, and Scaife personally was there to hear what his old friend had to say.

The subsequent *Tribune-Review* editorial was headlined, "The war in Iraq: Time to move on."

The piece praised the Iraqi elections that had been held and talked of the Iraqis stepping up to take control. It warned of a growing Iranian threat and the need for U.S. forces to be prepared for what may come in Iraq, and said that preparing for another threat in the region meant relocating forces from Iraq. It explained why redeployment was not cowardly:

"This is not retreat. This is not 'cut and run.' This is a recognition of the reality in Iraq – one that has evolved into an Iraqi problem that only the Iraqis now can solve – and that the paramount world security threat now is Iran."

The *Tribune-Review* had not gone left-wing; it remained very much right-wing. But Scaife recognized that America could not resolve Iraq's problems militarily, that American forces had been stretched way too thin, and that America's military superiority was being jeopardized by that overextension, which might embolden other nations such as Iran and North Korea to do something crazy.

These were all points that Jack Murtha had been articulating. And when Scaife gave voice to the Murtha position in conservative political circles, while some certainly still disagreed with Murtha, there was a far more open debate about America's future direction. Murtha had brought America's right-wing intellectuals to the table to sit down and talk.

In his letters, public statements, and occasional news conferences prior to his call for redeployment, Murtha had been urging the president to get in there and do this right, to "finish the job," but the president was not taking any advice. In the end, with his own redeployment strategy, Murtha said if they would not get in there and do it right, then it was time to just get out.

Although the right-wing intellectuals were now at least talking, the right-wing political machinery remained singular in focus and was determined to make Jack Murtha a target until the day he died.

Murtha knew he would be targeted, but he did not care. He did not do this for political favor. He had no aspiration for the Presidency. He could have sat back, never said a word, and been re-elected by landslides in his 12th District as long as he wanted, if he had continued with his low profile. Murtha did what he did because he felt it was the right thing to do.

There were also people from both sides of the aisle who agreed with Murtha or at least shared his concerns, yet refused to use their voice. Democrats were bogged down by fears of accusations that they were not patriots or not supporting the troops if they were to use such voice. Some Republicans wanted a different approach, but were publicly silenced by the fear of being called unpatriotic and, worse yet, needing to face their party bosses and without the stomach for a tough fight.

Murtha was confident the voters in his district would support him, although that would be tested when the Republicans made a point of recruiting candidates to run against him in his next two elections. But Murtha knew his thirty-year career as a hawk, as a decorated war veteran, and a staunch supporter of the military had given him much more political body armor than the secretary of defense had provided to the real troops in battle. Murtha had tried his way, the quiet way, and nothing had changed.

One reason so many had been so silent is that the political attacks launched on those who dared challenge the Bush party line were vicious and relentless. Few wanted to deal with the full frontal assault they would face. Murtha was willing and, perhaps more importantly, Murtha was able to face the heat, end the silence, and get America talking openly about our direction in Iraq.

Chapter 17

Mavericks, Renegades and Troublemakers

The morning of November 17, 2005, Murtha's press secretary, Cindy Abram, was told that he was going to do a news conference.

But she had no clue what he was about to say, no idea what sort of firestorm was about to erupt. C-Span was covering Murtha's news conference live, so back in Johnstown, Abram went into Murtha's personal office, which also served as a conference room with a big television, to see what he would say.

Before he was even half-way through his remarks, her phone was ringing off the hook from local, national, and even international media. Many of the news people were angry that they had not heard anything about what he was going to say until it was on the air, so it was too late to get there and hear or record his comments directly.

"We were told he was going on TV to make an announcement, and at first I didn't realize just how big it was," Abram said. "The staff told me I was getting phone calls, so I went out to check. I had twenty-four messages, and the press conference wasn't even over. I'd take one call and by the time I got off, two more had come in. It was that kind of barrage."

CNN and all the cable channels wanted their own interviews, as did many of the national reporters, especially those who were not at the event.

About an hour after calling for redeployment, Jack Murtha was looking at a memo from Abram that said, "We have received at least twenty-five requests for you for interviews and TV appearances." The list included CBS *Morning News,* CNN, both MSNBC and the MSNBC show *Hardball, USA Today,* and one of the Sunday morning news shows.

That Thursday afternoon, Murtha did interviews with Wolf Blitzer at CNN and Margaret Warner for *The Jim Lehrer News Hour* on PBS. The next day, he appeared on *The Anderson Cooper Show* and *Hardball with Chris Matthews* while also doing some interviews with print media. On Sunday, he was live with Tim Russert on *Meet the Press.*

Within a few weeks of his call for redeployment, Murtha had heard from pretty much everybody who was anybody in news coverage, includng every network and cable TV show, National Public Radio, foreign broadcasters from Japan to Norway. He was, in a sense, an instant celebrity and darling of the media, which was new turf for Murtha, given his history as a behind-the-scenes player.

NBC's *Today Show,* CBS's *Morning News* and ABC's *Nightline* did interviews. *This Week with George Stephanopoulas, Meet the Press,* and *Face the Nation* with Bob Schieffer had Murtha on their Sunday-morning talk shows in three successive weeks. Schieffer politely warned Murtha to be careful: they were coming after him.

Chris Matthews, Wolf Blitzer, and Anderson Cooper had him on their cable-network shows a few times each.

The British Broadcasting Company did an in-depth interview, and *Newsweek* magazine's Washington bureau chief, Dan Klaidman, personally came in to interview Murtha.

Among the few shows he did not do were those on Fox Network, which were notoriously one-sided, pro-Bush, pro-Republican, and downright nasty with anyone who disagreed. Murtha never really said "no" to their barrage of requests to do their shows; he just conveniently had schedule conflicts he could not work out.

"The thing with Fox is, we just weren't going to do Fox," Abram acknowledged after his death. "Sheppard Smith called, said to me, 'Cindy, I'm not like the others.' I said, 'I understand that, Sheppard.' I thought it was funny that he tried to divorce himself from Sean Hannity or other right-wing commentators."

Former Congressman John Kasich, Republican of Ohio, was relatively moderate as Republicans go, and Murtha did agree to do Kasich's *Heartland* program, in large part because he felt he could trust Kasich to not be a typical Fox in-your-face jerk, and in part, his staff felt, just to be able to tell the other Fox folks that he had done their network.

The other shows Murtha repeatedly turned down were the biting comedy shows of Jon Stewart and Bill Maher. Maher personally called several times, but Murtha, who called his own shots about what shows he was willing to do, repeatedly said "no". Although Murtha never explained his reasoning to Abram and other staffers, members of his team felt that he simply did not want to be associated with television programs that used profanity, although they found that ironic given that the old Marine drill instructor would blister any man with profanity when he was not in mixed company. But Murtha, influenced by his mother and Grandfather Ray, always tried to be careful not to curse in front of women. That old-school ethic would carry over to programs on which women might see him.

Given his reluctance to do off-beat television and his straight-up approach to conventional news, many who knew Murtha well were downright shocked when he agreed to a profile in *Rolling Stone* magazine.

Rolling Stone is known mostly for its extensive coverage of music and culture, including the drug culture, and its political coverage is left-wing, pretty far left on the spectrum of left-wing. Just five months after running the Murtha profile, the magazine's cover story carried a banner headline, "The Worst President in History?" Historian Sean Wilentz from Princeton University noted that James Buchanan, Andrew Johnson, Warren Harding, Herbert Hoover, and Richard Nixon were contenders, adding, "Now, though, George W. Bush is in serious contention for the title of worst ever." The magazine's cover featured a cartoon caricature of Bush looking rather apish, wearing a dunce cap, and seated on a stool. The stool was much like the one he sat on in the school on 9/11 when a staffer whispered in his ear that the World Trade Centers had been struck by planes, and Bush sat there, seemingly bewildered for a good while.

Some thought Murtha probably just did not know what kind of magazine *Rolling Stone* was when he agreed to the interview. But judging by the way he answered the questions, maybe he did.

"What do you say to those who call your plan nothing but 'cut and run?'" asked writer Tim Dickinson.

"These damn people don't even pay attention to what I really say in my plan," Murtha snorted. "It calls for redeployment, an over-the-horizon presence in an allied country. I think terrorism will drop once we're out. But if terrorism other than the insurgency should arise and affect our national security, then we could send our troops back in a hurry to attack terrorist bases."

"These damn people...." The gloves were off and this was clearly not "the old Murtha."

"The president just unveiled a 'victory strategy' that commits us to an open-ended occupation of Iraq," Dickinson said.

"By staying the course, you're only going to lose more people, and a year from now, it won't be any better. One year ago, they kept saying it was going to be better, and it's not only not better, it's worse by far. So you can go on like we did in Vietnam, or you can change direction now. You have to do it. It's up to the Iraqis to win a political victory."

Comparing this to Vietnam really was taking off the gloves. Murtha came straight out in this interview and was much more direct than usual.

He called Abu Ghraib "an absolute disaster." Noting the shortage of 112,000 people in critical military specialties, he said publicly for the first time that the Army was "broken." Until then, he would say things like, "Some say the Army is broken."

He said the administration flat-out ignored plans that the military and the State Department had in place and refused to let the primary three-star generals in the room before the invasion, making decisions with only civilians in the room. And in a real slap at the president, he recalled the letter he had sent to Bush 2003, adding, "So what do we do? We hire Halliburton," the logistics company that became embroiled in controversy because of the many no-bid contracts it received for work that was, at best, poorly done in Iraq. Dick Cheney was chairman and CEO of Halliburton from 1995 to 2000.

The *Rolling Stone* article, titled "Mavericks, Renegades, and Troublemakers," highlighted a dozen people who were making waves in 2005, but did not say which of these applied to Murtha. Arguably all three, because he continued his rampage over the next several months, appearing routinely on all of the popular news shows, except Fox.

Murtha's staff was nervous before every interview because they knew he had a tendency to shoot from the hip. Sometimes he did not think through exactly what he wanted to say and how he wanted to say it before going on the air, and he often had so much going on in his head that he would start sentences and not finish them.

Tim Russert asked him on *Meet the Press* once, "Congressman, have you heard privately from people at the Pentagon who are supportive and encouraging of you?"

To which Murtha's recorded, verbatim reply was, "Oh, absolutely. I mean, there's nobody that talks to the people in the Pentagon more than I do. And they publicly…, they have to say what the administra…, and that's the way it should be. Soldiers in the field…, I'll tell you how bad it's gotten in the field. I talk to sergeants who said to me, 'We're afraid to say anything because we'll stand to be recriminated by our superiors.'"

Abram was glad that one of the first big television shows he did was with Chris Matthews. "I talked to him (Matthews) on the phone, talked to him a while. He practically gushed about Jack Murtha. They had a personal relationship…. I remember the first time I talked to Mr. Murtha when Matthews wanted him on. He said, 'Oh, I know him.' That was the first I knew that he knew Matthews. So he was comfortable going on there."

Murtha knew Matthews from years earlier when Matthews had been hired to improve the image of then-Speaker Tip O'Neil, who was Murtha's mentor.

"As things progressed, he seemed to get more comfortable with the media," Abram said. "He was not comfortable at first; that's why I was glad he went on with Matthews first."

She said she was particularly concerned when Murtha agreed to be interviewed by Mike Wallace, a host of the popular network-television show *60 Minutes*, but Murtha and Wallace seemed to have good rapport.

Overall, his rapport with the media was good, although she recalled once when he had a pretty nasty exchange with Wolf Blitzer. "He obviously didn't like the question and made it clear he wasn't going to answer it," she said. "He was often asked tough questions and, most of the time, he handled them pretty well."

Others close to Murtha admit they got nervous any time he got near a microphone because sometimes the things he would try to say just did not come out right. Prime examples are his comments on Haditha and race, which are covered in later chapters.

Dan Cunningham, a member or Murtha's team, said he was surprised when Murtha called for redeployment because it was "not his normal modus operandi."

"He was a very, very private person, really a shy person in some respects. He did not like any public exposure," Cunningham said, noting that Murtha found great satisfaction in getting things done, and that public confrontation was not the way to get things done.

But Murtha was fired up, really fired up in the first several months after calling for redeployment. Two weeks after his call for redeployment, he was again making headlines, this time by making the case that the Army was "broken, worn out" and "living hand to mouth."

USA Today covered Murtha's first public appearances back in his district, where he told a business group in Latrobe, Pennsylvania, that most troops would be out of Iraq within a year, in part, because they were stretched so thin that they would not be able to send fully-equipped units to Iraq the next year.

"I admit I made a mistake when I voted for war," Murtha said. "I'm looking at the future of the United States military."

As usual, Murtha was ahead of most people on defense issues. His assessment was reinforced two months later when a study for the Pentagon concluded that the Army had become a "thin green line" that could snap unless relief came soon, according to a study for the Pentagon.

The study said the Army could not sustain the pace of troop deployments to Iraq long enough to break the back of the insurgency. It suggested that the Pentagon's decision, announced in December, to begin reducing the force in Iraq that year was driven in part by a realization that the Army was overextended and was missing its recruiting goal.

In December 2005, two weeks after his comments in Latrobe, Murtha was back in Washington, where he engineered what the *New York Times* called "an unusual bipartisan rebuke to the Bush administration." Some 107 Republicans joined all but one Democrat in overwhelmingly approving legislation written by Senator John McCain that barred cruel, inhumane or degrading treatment of prisoners in American custody anywhere in the world.

Murtha had introduced the legislation in the House and made a long speech, covered in the chapters about Abu Ghraib, that concluded with the bottom line, "If we allow torture in any form, we abandon our honor."

By February 2006, Murtha was aggressively making the case that Iraq had become a civil war.

On *Hardball*, he said, "We're caught in a civil war, and I keep saying this administration is mischaracterizing what's going on in Iraq. Iraq is a civil war between two factions inside the country. Our troops are the targets, and they're unifying Iraq against us. There's a very small al Qaeda contingent in there and in Iran. Everybody else wants us in Iraq because we're spending so many resources, human and monetary resources, in Iraq itself.

"So what we're into is nation-building. You cannot nation-build inside an insurgency," he continued. "So we're not only not winning, we're spreading hatred towards the United States. Eighty percent of the people in Iraq want us out of there. Forty-seven percent of the people in Iraq say it's justified to kill Americans."

Then Matthews quoted the president calling him a defeatist, to which Murtha replied, "He answers substantive recommendations with rhetoric. This is the thing that's so frustrating. This war has been going on longer than our war against Germany in World War II. World War I went on for less time than this war, and the Korean War was less time than this war. So we've been there a long time. It's time to change direction. Our troops are the targets of an insurgency, and there's no way that we can get out."

Six weeks later on *Meet the Press*, Murtha said Rumsfeld should resign.

Tim Russert quoted Secretary Rumsfeld saying that leaving Iraq "would be the modern equivalent of handing postwar Germany back to the Nazis."

Murtha shot back, "Let me tell you how they mischaracterize these kinds of things. For instance, we're caught in a civil war.... Twenty-five thousand insurgents are fighting with each other inside the country for supremacy. That's the definition of a civil war. There's less than a thousand al Qaida. And when he says turning it over to al Qaida — and that's what he means, he's inferring it'll be turned over to al Qaida. I don't believe that (could happen) for a minute. The Iraqis will get rid of al Qaida the minute that we get out of there. And sixty percent of the people in Iraq believe the sooner we get out, the more stable Iraq will be, and that's what all of us want."

Murtha again admitted that his vote for the war had been a mistake, saying, "When I found out we didn't have a threat to our national security, we violated one of the principles I've always adhered to: You've got to have a national threat to our security before you go to war; then you've got to have overwhelming force, which we didn't have; and then, third, you've got to have an exit strategy. We violated all those principles. So we have gotten to the point where we lost the hearts and minds of the people: eighty percent of the Iraqis want us out of there; forty-seven percent say it's okay to kill Americans. When it comes to that stage, it's time for us to give them the incentive to take over their own country."

Asked what advice he would give the president, Murtha said, "Here, here's what you should do, Mr. President. First of all, you should fire all the people who are responsible for that, which gives you international credibility."

"Including his secretary of defense?" Russert asked.

"Well, he, he should—well, let's say he should offer his resignation, because he certainly..."

"And it's sure to be accepted?"

"I would accept it, that's exactly right," Murtha said.

"What about the vice president?" Russert pressed.

"Well, you can't fire the vice president, so I think he'll, he'll have to handle this himself."

Asked if Vice President Cheney should resign, Murtha replied, "Well, certainly the vice president has been the primary force in running, running this war, and many of the mischaracterizations have come about. You and I talked before the show about some of the things he said on your show, right before the war started. None of them turned out to be true. This is why the American public is so upset."

By mid-April, a small army of retired generals came forward and publicly called for Rumsfeld's resignation. The *New York Times* has a photo of six of them: Major General Paul D. Eaton, General Anthony C. Zinni, Lieutenant General Gregory Newbold, Major General John Batiste, Major General John Riggs, and Major General Charles H. Swannack Jr.

"Among the retired generals who have called for Mr. Rumsfeld's ouster, some have emphasized that they still believe it was right for the United States to invade Iraq. But a common thread in their complaints has been an assertion that Mr. Rumsfeld and his aides too often inserted themselves into military decision-making, often disregarding advice from military commanders," the *Times* reported.

General Swannack, for instance, called for continuing the war, adding, "But I do not believe Secretary Rumsfeld is the right person to fight that war based on his absolute failings in managing the war against Saddam in Iraq."

UPI Senior News Analyst Martin Seiff called the outburst of

the generals "unprecedented in modern times." General Douglas MacArthur criticized President Harry S. Truman's handling of the Korean War after he had been fired by Truman in 1951. Air Force Chief of Staff Curtis LeMay criticized the handling of the Vietnam War in the mid-1960s. However, neither of them was publicly supported by any other top brass and both spoke out "as self-avowed hawks arguing that wars should be fought with less restraint," Seiff wrote.

He added, "But the criticisms the retired generals are now making against Rumsfeld and, by implication, against President George W. Bush, are of a very different nature. They are charging that the defense secretary lacks basic competence and that he has made one wrong decision after another."

Generals historically have followed the tradition of keeping politics out of military operations and not publicly criticizing the president or other top civilian leaders of the government. But in this case, the frustration and aggravation within the military was through the roof. Would they have spoken out and given voice to their anger if not for Jack Murtha starting this national debate? Unlikely.

Perhaps he was "Murtha the maverick" or "Murtha the renegade," but he certainly was seen as "Murtha the troublemaker" by the administration. He continued to stir things up with regular public appearances on TV and occasional news conferences and floor speeches through early 2006.

Despite his thirty-some years in public life, Murtha did not anticipate how nasty the backlash would be. Some of those closest to him said they sensed that he was hurt by how personal the attacks were at times.

In an op-ed published in the *New York Times* titled "Purple Heartbreakers," former Navy Secretary James Webb wrote, "It should come as no surprise that an arch-conservative website is questioning whether Representative John Murtha, the Pennsylvania Democrat who has been critical of the war in Iraq, deserved the combat awards he received in Vietnam. After all, in recent years extremist Republican operatives have inverted a longstanding principle: that our combat veterans be accorded a place of honor in political circles. This trend began with the ugly insinuations leveled at Senator John McCain during the 2000 Republican primaries and continued with the slurs against Senators Max Cleland and John Kerry, and now Mr. Murtha."

Webb added, "The political tactic of playing up the soldiers on the battlefield while tearing down the reputations of veterans who oppose them could eventually cost the Republicans dearly. It may be one reason that a preponderance of the Iraq war veterans who thus far have decided to run for office are doing so as Democrats."

Murtha began to get the sense that the war was changing the political landscape; that people were fed up with Bush, Rumsfeld, and company; and that the potential was there for the Democrats to win the majority in Congress.

While the ire of the right-wing partisans was clearly focused on Murtha, the changing mood of the nation also made them fearful that the fallout from Iraq could bring down their president.

Chapter 18

Bush Bashing without the Bush

Thirteen days after Murtha's call for redeployment, Senator John McCain, Republican of Arizona, spoke at the Blackstone dinner in London, England. McCain began with the usual greetings and talked about the special relationship between the United States and Britain, but turned quickly to Iraq.

"I would submit that the stakes are higher than in the Vietnam War," he told the Brits. "We simply cannot afford failure in Iraq, with all the implications that a failed state in the heart of the Middle East would have for our security, not to mention the bloodshed that a true power vacuum would unleash on the Iraqi population. Defeat in Iraq risks giving way to a failed state and a terrorist sanctuary, one in which extremists could train and plan attacks with impunity. We could have, in other words, another pre-9/11 Afghanistan.

"I believe that, at a minimum, several corrective steps are critical," he continued. "We need to adopt a counterinsurgency strategy in Iraq that focuses on protecting the population and holding territory, instead of on invading towns and killing insurgents. The coalition needs to keep our senior officers in place, rather than rotating them out as if they were regular troops. We need to build ethnically mixed units within the Iraqi National Army. And we need more troops on the ground."

McCain did not envision success without an increase in troop levels, repeating what he had said in a *New York Post* op-ed piece he had done just two weeks earlier. In his multi-step plan for victory, he emphatically claimed, "We need more troops."

American politicians who travel abroad generally live by an unwritten code to not criticize the president while on foreign soil. McCain had been telling Bush for months, if not years, that more troops were needed. But in this case, he was trying to walk a fine line by openly criticizing Jack Murtha, not the president. Moments after saying that more troops were needed, he named Murtha to make it clear that he was addressing the congressman from Pennsylvania.

"At the same time, we must tend to our home fronts or we will have lost this war as decisively as if the coalition had suffered battlefield defeat. Anti-war protests, coupled with calls for withdrawals from my friends John Kerry and John Murtha, show that we need a renewed effort to explain to the American and British people precisely what is at stake in this war; not to alarm them, but so that they see the nature of this struggle for what it is. Part of this effort includes relying less on rosy aspirations for near term improvements in Iraq's politics or security situation, and more in accurately portraying events on the ground, even if they are negative."

Not only was McCain saying our troop levels were too low, as Murtha had said just months into the war, he was saying we needed to be honest in talking about the real conditions of the war. Arguably he crossed that fine line because saying that events on the ground needed to be portrayed accurately is another way of saying that, until now, descriptions had not been too accurate.

McCain offered this conclusion at Blackstone: "Every American who visits Britain would like to quote Winston Churchill, and like them, I must cave to temptation. An optimist, Churchill said, is one who 'sees opportunity in every difficulty.' As an optimist, I see great opportunities for leadership in the difficulties we face today. I'm sure many in this room see it the same way, and in this room we have leaders who can seize them."

The Churchill quote was appropriate on another front. Murtha's comments, which had created difficulty for the Bush administration, also presented opportunity for McCain and others like him because now they could take a more frontal approach in stating how they felt the war should be handled. Since early in the conflict, McCain had often expressed concerns, but he was not usually this direct.

The key point is that, after November 17, 2005, any Republican who disagreed with the president could now say so by couching his comments as criticism of Murtha. They had been given voice by Murtha's actions. They could raise their voice and push their cause for more troops and a more aggressive approach in Iraq because now they could do it as a counter to a "cut-and-run Democrat," instead of their own Republican president.

The tragedy is that some leading Republicans, with a few soft-spoken exceptions, knew much earlier that the war had been handled poorly, even disastrously, but they remained silent. Many staunch conservatives knew that President Bush did not represent true conservatism. The size of the government was huge, spending was out of control, and the Iraqi war was the kind of nation-building that never would have been undertaken by either the great Ronald Reagan or Bush's own dad. The current leaders knew all this, yet they were either silent or ineffectively mushy in questioning their current president.

Bush I managed political and social turmoil in the region during one of the most tense times this constantly troubled region had seen in decades. He consulted with Congress and especially the chairman of the House Defense Appropriations Subcommittee, Jack Murtha. He set clear and achievable goals for victory, and sold them to Congress and the American people in an honest and open way. He assembled a true coalition with other countries and then cut loose the whirlwind that is American military might to get the job done.

Some have argued the United States did not finish the job in the first Gulf War, but the reality is, as Murtha and many others recognized, the coalition and the international balancing act performed by Bush I would have collapsed immediately if the mission had been expanded beyond liberating Kuwait to invading Iraq. Bush I understood that occupying Iraq long enough to establish a stable government was a mission impossible.

Jack Murtha fully supported the first Gulf War and George H.W. Bush, and he personally delivered eighty-seven Democratic votes in favor of that war resolution. Murtha said many times that what Bush I did in the first Gulf war was magnificent foreign policy and some of the best presidential decision-making in his lifetime. Those were hardly the words one would expect from a left-wing, cut-and-run liberal.

But with Bush II, there was absolutely no dialogue, no discussion, no debate, despite the fact that many experienced political leaders in Washington had come to feel that the war in Iraq was misguided and/or mishandled.

If the bungling by Bush and his administration was not bad enough, Murtha was especially agitated by their arrogance, said Morrison, former Democratic staff director on Defense Appropriations.

"They touted Iraq as part of 'the global war on terror,' a phrase Murtha hated" because, by then, it was clear that Iraq had not been harboring terrorists before 9/11 and had nothing to do with the terrorist attack on America on 9/11, he said.

The phrase "global war on terror" was a key element of the administration's propaganda and a clever way to link the Iraq war to the war in Afghanistan, which was the base of operations for al Qaeda and the real terrorists. Using that phrase boxed in anyone who wanted to criticize the Iraq war because they would be attacked as "weak on terrorism," even though Iraq had nothing to do with 9/11.

So virtually no one in Washington was lending real voice to the crisis.

Back in October of 2003, Senator McCain had compared aspects of the conflict in Iraq to those endured during the Vietnam War. McCain spoke specifically about the danger of always playing defense. "To set up roadblocks after the bomb goes off is not the answer," he said. "We've got to get into prevention."

The irony is that the entire war had been initiated under Bush's "Preemptive Doctrine" of striking at nations that posed a threat rather than those that actually attacked America. The president had basically clung to the old football adage that the best defense is a good offense in attacking Iraq. But in the ground game, McCain and many others saw that the war was being conducted in a far less proactive manner.

The fact that McCain himself used Vietnam as a comparison was as harsh a criticism as one would hear from the right side of the aisle because Bush had bristled at the comparison between the two conflicts. The president instead compared Iraq with World War II Germany. After all, World War II was an American win and an effort that saw the entire country throw itself into the battle if only through paper drives and war bonds.

Bush routinely compared Saddam Hussein to Adolf Hitler and called Iraq part of the "Axis of Evil," which was more clever propaganda that tied Iraq, Iran, and North Korea to the evil empires behind World War II, Germany and Japan. Long before Murtha took his stand on the war, he saw clearly the difference between the two and, in a pragmatic way, explained what should have been obvious to everyone.

"We knew who the enemy was and why we were fighting in World War II," Murtha told a local reporter. "Hussein is a terrible man, but he is just not Hitler. We don't have a clear idea in the streets, that is, who the enemy is, and this war (Iraq) will never have the sort of nationwide support the Second World War did because of the questions about why we went in. We had faulty intelligence, some of it cherry-picked; that is, we were misled in some ways and we all know it. This is far more a Vietnam than a World War II, but that is really just a word game and something for the history books. It does not change what is happening now."

McCain's comments were a soft effort to coach the commander in chief into putting more boots on the ground and gear up more American military might. He was not alone, but even a small chorus of soft voices from his own side did little to inspire the president to do anything different at that point.

Senator Trent Lott, Republican of Mississippi, when asked if he favored any policy changes in Iraq responded, "We need to have a different mix of troops, is the key. We may need to move some troops around." Lott said more military police were needed, for instance. His comments were not to be taken as a criticism as he added, "Honestly, it's a little tougher than I thought it was going to be."

This is a classic example of how Republican leaders refused to criticize their president even when it was obvious that things were not going well. After all, Bush and company had said the United States would be treated as liberators, and saying now that it was "a little tougher" than expected was an understatement of tragically amusing proportions.

Lott provides a prime example of those who wanted a different approach in Iraq, but did not want to ruffle the president's feathers or create the appearance that they were not team players. Lott said his comments "should not be taken as a criticism," but he was still questioning the way things were being handled. Lott and other Republicans were so sensitive to criticizing the president that they abandoned the idea that they had any input. They could have offered advice to the president and taken strong public stands on issues, but they had become so frozen along party lines that many sacrificed conviction for party loyalty.

Lott, however, did not have a problem in leveling a more direct criticism at Iraq or, for that matter, leveling Iraq. "If we have to, we just mow the whole place down, see what happens. You're dealing with insane suicide bombers who are killing our people and we need to be very aggressive in taking them out," Lott said.

Lott's outrageous comments in endorsing the killing of millions of innocent civilians drew little reaction, whereas Murtha would soon make headlines when he referred to civilian casualties in Haditha as killings in "cold blood." Saying "mow the whole place down" suggested that the war fighters should not let the innocent live since sorting out the good guys from the bad guys was too difficult.

Lott's over-the-top tough talk could have been borne out of the frustration of wanting a more aggressive approach from Washington, but not having the political guts to say so to the man who could make that happen.

By December 2004, troop fatalities had reached 1,300. Slowly the public was becoming convinced that their leaders had gone off in the wrong direction, and many wondered if the cost was worth the outcome. Criticism started to increase from the Republican right, but was centered on Defense Secretary Rumsfeld.

At a local Chamber of Commerce meeting in Mississippi that December, Lott said, "I am not a fan of Secretary Rumsfeld. I don't think he listens to his uniformed officers." While he and others stopped short of calling for Rumsfeld's resignation at the time, he did suggest there should be a change in the position within the next year.

Republican Senators McCain and Chuck Hagel of Nebraska also stepped up their criticism of how the war was being conducted by Rumsfeld.

The American Enterprise Institute, a conservative think tank, rapped Rumsfeld. Unhappy with the direction of Iraq, Thomas Donnelly, a resident fellow at the AEI, criticized Rumsfeld for his preoccupation with transforming the military rather than winning the war "he helped to start."

Moderate Republican Senator Susan Collins of Maine lambasted the Pentagon for failing to provide adequate protective armor for the troops, an issue that Murtha had brought to light a year earlier.

For all the clamoring about Rumsfeld and how he was conducting the war, these leaders refused to call for change from the guy in the oval office. Any criticism of Rumsfeld should have been a criticism of President Bush.

Republicans actually would have needed to deal with two battle fronts if they would have spoken out against the war or even said it was being prosecuted poorly. First, questioning the war would be painted as unpatriotic or weak on terror, creating the risk of being lumped in with those left-wing Democrats, which would anger the Republican base. Second, it would be painted as un-Republican. Anything the president did was right because it was being done by their president.

Better to filter their frustration indirectly through Rumsfeld than appear to be breaking ranks with the president, who steadfastly refused to publicly accept that all was not well in Iraq and a major change in the game plan was needed.

The public attitude was altered by Murtha's actions. Angry Democrats turned up the heat. Some of them had lacked the backbone to be painted by the Bush spin team as un-American until Murtha was on the front line and drawing fire first. Other Democrats long opposed to the Iraq war did not have such fear but had been marginalized as left-wing doves who were effectively silenced by the the scant attention their words received. Their voices began to be heard.

Murtha's call for redeployment gave voice to Democrats frozen in fear of being labeled as un-American, cut-and-run cowards. It also gave voice to Republicans who now could be angry in public as they saw Iraq going south, especially if they attacked Rumsfeld or Murtha, not the president.

John McCain had long been upset with the direction of the war and was among the least shy about saying so. In fact, the case can be made he would eventually get his party's presidential nomination because he had the best case for not being Bush. He had called for a surge before Bush did, but he had done it in softer tones or by criticizing Rumsfeld or Murtha, instead of the man who was actually in charge.

McCain, in an op-ed in the *New York Post* on November 16, 2005, the day before Murtha called for redeployment, wrote, "At home, the American people wish to see us succeed in helping bring freedom and democracy to the Iraqi people, but express increased uncertainty about the way forward. Now is the last time we should send a message that withdrawing troops is more important than achieving success."

This thought comes as no surprise. Talk about timelines and leaving Iraq was always painted as weak and un-American, although given his long-held opinion on matters in Iraq, it is safe to say McCain was sincere and not just political with this language.

While addressing Senate amendments to designate a period of significant transition to full sovereignty, McCain wrote, "What it should have said is that America's first goal in Iraq is not to withdraw troops, but to win the war. All other policy decisions we make should support, and be subordinate to, the successful completion of our mission. If that means we can draw down our troop levels and win in Iraq in 2006, that would be a wonderful outcome. But if success requires an increase in American troop levels in 2006, then we must increase our numbers there."

McCain again talked about more troops, but softly couched it with a preface, saying that if we can win this thing with a troop draw-down, "that would be a wonderful outcome." His call for more troops is not even really a call for more troops, but a softly phrased "if success requires an increase", then we must increase our numbers.

Where McCain said the priority should not be to draw down the troops, but to win the war, political courage would have been to say that the president must send in 30,000 or more troops to make that happen. McCain and others could have been much bolder in laying their concerns on the White House steps instead of on Murtha's steps. But in bashing Murtha, they could subtly bash Bush without drawing political fire for bashing Bush.

Chapter 19

In Cold Blood

On November 19, 2005, the First Marine Regiment's Third Battalion was on deployment in Haditha, the sand-swept heart of Sunni-dominated Anbar Province, one of Iraq's hottest places in terms of temperature and danger. The battalion had lost a member just three days earlier when a bomb detonated under his vehicle. On this day, another unit member was killed and two were wounded by an improvised explosive device or IED. Before this day was over, twenty-four Iraqi civilians were dead, including children as young as one and three years old, a sixty-six-year-old woman and a seventy-six or seventy-seven-year-old man in a wheelchair who, by some accounts, was holding the Koran.

To some experts, photographs of the bullet wounds indicated that shots had been fired at close range directly into the heads and chests, execution style, not in a spray of shots that would have been fired from across the room by troops as they burst through a door and tried to clear a dim room. Although others argued that the evidence was not clear, no one disputed the fact that women and children had died from the bullets of U.S. Marines.

On May 17, 2006, when Jack Murtha accused Marines of killing innocent women and children "in cold blood," the critics were vicious and the debate was thunderous over whether Marines had slaughtered innocents in a blind rage or Iraqi propagandists had twisted the truth of an attack on the Marines and the circumstances of their response.

Many Marines were especially offended that a fellow Marine, Jack Murtha, would level such accusations before all of the evidence had been fully analyzed and the investigation had been concluded.

Murtha was accused of bashing the military. One commentator called him "a nightmare." Another said he and media outlets were "serving as al Jazeera satellite offices."

Ann Coulter, arguably the most vitriolic of Fox News commentators, called Murtha "the reason soldiers invented 'fragging.'"

"Fragging" is a term from the Vietnam War that meant to kill an unpopular member of one's own military unit. She was suggesting that someone should kill Murtha.

Many of the calls and faxes that flooded Murtha's office were equally outrageous, using profanity and saying such things as "Traitor! Death to All Traitors!"

Ironically, Murtha had called for an end of military actions just two days before this needless loss of life and subsequent international nightmare began.

On November 17, 2005, Jack Murtha called for redeployment to get the troops over the horizon and out of harm's way. He said U.S. forces had become targets caught in the middle of a civil war, attacks on U.S. forces were increasing dramatically, the forces were worn out from over-deployment, and the military and their families were carrying too much of the burden.

On November 19, 2005, two days later, a Marine died in Haditha, and fellow Marines killed innocent women and children. The timing is incredible. Most people never heard of the incidents until *Time* magazine ran a cover story on March 19, 2006. But two months later, when Jack Murtha accused Marines of being cold-blooded killers, pretty much the whole country knew something about it, although few people could digest much of it beyond the vague, vitriolic accusations.

Those who attacked Murtha relentlessly never listened to what he had said about the stress on the troops and his concern that, unless he spoke out, the incident would be covered up, resulting in another major loss in the battle for the hearts and minds of the Iraqis.

Murtha had called the news conference on May 17, 2006, to highlight the lack of progress in the Iraqi war in the six months since he had called for redeployment.

Noting that he visited the severely wounded at military hospitals almost every week, he said, "I ask, 'What happened to you?' And they say, 'I was looking for IEDs and I was blown up.

"That's their mission. That's a hell of a mission," he continued, anger obvious in the tone of his voice. "I mean, that's not what they should be doing, and that's what they're doing, and that's how they get killed, over and over again. Sixty-seven percent of the people killed in Iraq have been killed with IEDs."

He again described the sectarian violence as a civil war between 100,000 Shi'as fighting 20,000 Sunnis, adding that "our military is caught in between" as they try to maintain a 348-mile supply line from Kuwait to Baghdad that is constantly attacked and targeted with IEDs.

"Secretary Rumsfeld says progress in Iraq is evidenced by how many satellite dishes he sees on a rooftop," Murtha continued. "Now what's wrong with that? They only have 2.9 hours of electricity (per day). So if they have satellite dishes, they can't watch them twenty-one hours a day.

"This trivializes the situation that our Marines and many of our soldiers are facing every single day. Every convoy's attacked. Every convoy's attacked," he repeated, louder for effect. "IEDs exploding all around them. Being shot at every day. Watching their buddies die. Being unable to trust the Iraqis. They don't know who their friends are and who are the enemies."

Pressure. Stress. Murtha understood what these troops were facing, and he articulated it better than anybody. And in far too many cases, troops were not trained for the missions to which they were assigned.

In the end, Murtha concluded, "It's much worse than reported in *Time* magazine. There was no firefight. There was no IED that killed these innocent people. Our troops overreacted because of the pressure on them, and they killed innocent civilians in cold blood. And that's what the report is going to tell."

To be an effective soldier, one must be trained to let go of the natural hesitation to take a life. Likewise, a good war fighter does not do battle out of a sense of rage or hate. A situation is presented, and if extreme prejudice is the trained response, then it must be performed as trained. Anger, rage, remorse, sensitivity to the humanity of the enemy are barriers that must be drilled out of a man for combat so that he has no hesitation or overreaction, either of which can interfere with a war fighter accomplishing his mission. In this way, all killings in combat are cold-blooded. They need to be.

How does the military training to kill without remorse compare with the civilian standard of killing "in cold blood?"

Murtha's widow, Joyce, said she felt that he had regretted using the words "in cold blood."

"To me and to many people, that has a connotation of pre-planned or premeditated. He was saying they were not trained to handle it, and he was afraid the Marine Corps was going to cover it up. He said, 'You can't cover it up because the Iraqis know it and the Marine Corps knows it. If we covered it up, there would be no limit to it,'" Joyce said.

She added that, in talking about the fact that innocent women and children had been killed in their houses by Marines, this old Marine who truly loved the Marine Corps had often said, "Marines are better than that."

Most of his former staff and advisors agreed that he regretted using the words, "in cold blood."

"He tried to justify that so many times afterwards and there was just no way to justify it, and I think he knew it," one said.

But he steadfastly refused to apologize, convinced that his basic facts were right. Some who had looked at the evidence concluded that Marines had gone on a rampage and assassinated innocent Iraqis, including women and children, at point-blank range in what indisputably would have been cold blood. But even if that was an exaggeration, Marines had pointed guns directly at unarmed women and children. They had that instant to realize that pulling the trigger would be wrong..., but then pulled the trigger, anyway. To Murtha, that, too, was cold-blooded murder. Marines were better than that.

Murtha was also convinced that there was a cover-up and, unless he spoke out about it, he feared that the truth might never come out.

The original news release said, "A U.S. Marine and fifteen civilians were killed yesterday from the blast of a roadside bomb in Haditha. Immediately following the bombing, gunmen attacked the convoy with small arms fire. Iraqi army soldiers and Marines returned fire, killing eight insurgents and wounding another." Either by flaw or design, the release did not accurately depict the events of that day and thus at least raised the appearance of a cover-up.

Many facts here are not disputed. Kilo Company of the Third Battalion First Marines was assigned to protect a resupply convoy. An IED placed under the roadway was set off. It killed driver Lance Corporal Miguel Terrazas instantly. Lance Corporal James Crossan was blown from the passenger seat and trapped under the rear passenger tire. He would later receive a medical discharge based on his severe wounds. Private First Class Salvador Guzman was thrown from the back of the vehicle and, though both he and Crossan were helicoptered out for medical attention, he later recovered enough to return to active duty.

So the accounts that one had been killed did not fully describe what the members of Kilo Company witnessed that day. To them, three of their buddies were down, and this was just three days after another member of their unit had been killed.

Looking back, the Third Battalion had been deployed to Kuwait and took part in the Battle of Nasiriyah in the invasion of Iraq. They were re-deployed in mid-2004, and many members of Kilo Company won medals for their effort in taking the City of Fallujah after 150,000 residents had been evacuated to get innocent people out of harm's way. They were re-deployed in September 2005, but found themselves on a lesser mission: protecting convoys.

Lucian Read, a photographer embedded with Kilo Company in both Fallujah and Haditha, explained their morale in an interview with the PBS program *Frontline*.

"When you put them in a situation that they're not trained for, that they don't want to be in, that they don't particularly care about, it has no glory, has no honor, has no bravery. It's just about not getting killed every day. You're not going to get heroism out of them. You're going to get trying to save their own lives and save the lives of their buddies, and just sort of scrape through and get out. I think that's a lesson we should try to learn from this experience," Read said.

So early on the morning of November 19, 2005, an IED went off, one of their unit was instantly killed, another blown from the vehicle and seriously injured as he was trapped under a wheel, and a third was also blown from the vehicle and evacuated by helicopter with the second man.

Someone in the company reported small-arms fire coming from a particular house and the order was given to "clear that house." Staff Sergeant Frank D. Wuterich was in charge at the moment, and he later told a military judge, "I advised the team something like, 'Shoot first and ask questions later,' or 'Don't hesitate to shoot.' I can't remember my exact words, but I wanted them to understand that hesitation to shoot would only result in the four of us being killed."

Wuterich and the three other Marines burst into three houses in succession in pursuit of combatants. At the end of the day, the first house had seven dead, including the sixty-six year old woman and a four-year old. The second had eight dead, including a husband and wife, five of their children as young as age three, and a one-year-old child who had been staying with the family. The third house had four dead, all brothers ranging in age from twenty-seven to forty-one; in the news release, these brothers were among the eight considered to have been insurgents.

Also that day, Marines stopped a taxi. Witnesses said the four passengers and driver came out with their hands up to surrender. All five men were shot dead on the street and labeled as insurgents in the news release.

Eight Marines were later charged, four for their role in the killings and four officers for failing to properly investigate and report what had happened.

More than a half dozen Marines were given immunity for their testimony, leading some to ask: Who needs immunity if no one was guilty?

In addition, several relatives of the people who had been killed by the Marines were paid $38,000 as compensation by the military, money that some war critics described as "hush money."

Murtha had a different view. On *This Week with George Stephanopoulos*, two weeks after his news conference, he said he was convinced that not only had Marines wrongfully killed innocent civilians, but that their superiors were trying to cover it up. He said the decision to make compensation payments to Iraqis had to have been made by high-level commanders.

"That doesn't happen at the lowest level. That happens at the highest level before they make a decision to make payments to the families," Murtha said.

"There's no question about what happened.... The problem is: Who covered it up, why did they cover it up, and why did it take so long? We cannot allow something like this to fester. (The military has) got to put the blame where it goes," he said.

Murtha was drawing on his Vietnam experience here. As a Marine regiment intelligence officer, he had been told to exaggerate the number of Vietnamese killed because the public relations of the war was seen as critical to maintaining the support of the American public. He feared that history was repeating itself, and just as he had refused to falsify reports in Vietnam, he was not about to let the U.S. military begin a pattern of falsifying reports on casualties in Iraq.

Murtha was talking about these issues before there was much information in the media. Where did he get his information?

Murtha got his vivid impression of what he called the cold-blooded killings not from the media, not from some left-wing peace group, not from some Iraqi organization with questionable motives.

He got his information from the Commandant of the United States Marine Corps, General Michael Hagee.

The commandant recognized that when "the truth" came out, at least "the truth" as he knew it and conveyed it to Murtha, it would be downright ugly, the ugliest such incident in U.S. military history since the My Lai massacre in Vietnam some forty years earlier. In the My Lai incident, one soldier was convicted of slaughtering over five hundred villagers.

The commandant naturally was concerned that there would be a public outcry about how such atrocities had not only been carried out by Marines, but also kept quiet for so long. Based on the shortened careers of General Shinsecki, Army Secretary White, and others, the commandant would have known that he could not be the person who went public with a story that would make Bush and Rumsfeld look bad – not if he wanted to remain an active-duty general and head of the Marine Corps.

The silencing of voices, including the silencing of the voices of military leaders under Bush and Rumsfeld, is a huge subplot in the unfolding drama of the Iraq war here.

Gabrielle Carruth, the Murtha Defense Appropriations staffer, was there when Hagee briefed Murtha. She said Hagee never used the words "in cold blood." She said the commandant had said something like, "This is bad, Jack. I think these guys are in trouble.... These guys just went nuts. They had seen their buddies blown up just previously, and they went into this house for vengeance. Women and children were shot at point blank."

Carruth said there had been a few recent incidents that had been initially "misreported" by the military. The commandant and his aide "were sensitive to avoiding another similar episode, and were trying to head off" more controversy by briefing Murtha.

The commandant could easily have figured that, if he quietly conveyed the facts to his friend and trusted fellow Marine Jack Murtha, Murtha would step forward and be the voice of the military, that Murtha would let the world know that something awful had happened that needed to be addressed sooner rather than later.

If so, he surely did not count on Murtha using such politically charged words as "in cold blood" to describe a military action.

Carruth recalled a conversation with Murtha soon after the commandant's briefing. He kept telling her about his Vietnam experience and talking about the impact of killing innocent people. "We can't win the war like this. We become just like them," she recalled him saying.

Right after Murtha said that innocent people had been killed "in cold blood," Carruth pleaded with him, "People will not understand why you said that. They do not have your same experiences in war. It's too emotional. You have to explain what you meant.

"He never did explain it," she added. "He never apologized, but

I think in the end, he knew those words would hurt him more than anything. People don't know Jack Murtha, his love for the Marine Corps, his love for his country. He never meant it to come out that way, and that's what's so sad."

In assessing events that angered a host nation and ultimately divided the occupying nation, understandably there are several views of the circumstances. But in assessing the American political landscape and how war and civilian deaths are viewed, another incident in American history is telling.

In another conflict, far from Iraq, a military force was occupying a region. Some of the local population welcomed those soldiers, while others resented being occupied. Some wanted to kill those soldiers if given the chance. So even a critic of the military must acknowledge that these young men, put into a hostile environment, despite having at least some level of training, certainly knew that their lives were at risk.

Ultimately, the occupying force fired upon what would prove to be civilians. No one argues that innocents died. The argument is whether the war fighters who fired had committed murder. In fact, those men would be put on trial for murder. Given the common belief at the time, the conviction of these men seemed certain.

Facts, however, are elusive things. When the legal smoke had cleared, not a single soldier who had fired a shot that day was convicted of murder. This is a simplistic description of events, but on the whole accurate.

These events are not those of Haditha, but of a 1770 skirmish with British forces that had occupied Boston, Massachusetts, forever known as the Boston Massacre.

American colonists were gunned down in the street by British soldiers. Over two hundred years later, American textbooks still refer to the matter as a massacre, yet can it truly be defined as a massacre if none of the men who fired were convicted of murder?

American patriot and future President John Adams was the defense attorney for the British troops charged with murder. He never denied that innocents had died, stressing that the soldiers involved had been attacked and thus left with the right to defend themselves.

Certainly an occupying military force represents authority, and those who would attack that force should expect nothing less than extreme prejudice when that force responds. But who actually attacked or threatened the soldiers out of that crowd in Boston? Did the list of the dead correspond with a list of those who had committed actual acts of assault, or were they people who were just there in the crowd?

In such a crowded and intense scene, when confronted by an angry gang with some people who probably were real threats and others who were just angry and shouting, the soldiers at best would have an extremely difficult challenge in picking out which individuals were the real threats.

In Iraq, charges were dropped against all but one of the Marines involved in the Haditha incident, some after being granted immunity to testify, others when the military court was presented testimony that they had acted within the parameters of their military training. Their defense was that when troops are told to clear a house, this is what they do. It means they kill without remorse and as a means of survival. Again, one can contemplate where the military training to kill without remorse confronts the civilian standard of killing in cold blood.

A review of events in Haditha produces several points on which all can agree. A Marine died in a blast. Innocent Iraqis were shot to death. Marines killed them. No one can come to the conclusion that nothing went wrong at Haditha.

With no disrespect to any of the lives lost, American or Iraqi, in the broader sense of how this matter impacted the war effort, the events of Haditha were larger and darker than the actual list of the dead.

As the occupying nation, some feel the U.S. military acted within its power, even if that resulted in the unfortunate death of innocents. Those in Iraq wanted criminal charges brought against the Americans. Two hundred years from now, will Iraqi history books refer to this matter as a massacre just as Americans view the events in Boston in 1770?

Those British soldiers were not convicted of murder, although two were found to have committed manslaughter, had their hands branded, and were released. Yet even after the acquittal, Americans used the Boston Massacre as a rallying cry to strengthen the resolve of those who opposed the occupying force. Rightly or wrongly, many Iraqis view Haditha the way Americans two hundred years earlier viewed Boston.

Certainly Haditha had a devastating effect on the hearts and minds of those who were being occupied. The better history lesson was not My Lai, but Boston.

Defense attorneys for the Haditha Marines talked about the stress these men had been under, which is what Murtha was saying. They talked about how this group was a blunt force instrument that when told to clear a house did so aggressively. This is what Murtha was saying, too.

Had he simply stated that women and children had been wrongly killed, his handling of Haditha would not have created the same uproar.

In January 2012, as this book was going through final edits, Frank Wuterich was found guilty on only one count: negligent dereliction of duty. He was sentenced to three months confinement, but avoided doing time through a plea deal. Several charges of manslaughter were dropped.

The Iraqis reacted with outrage. "This is a joke, because according to Iraqi law, all those soldiers should be executed," the political advisor to the governor of Iraq's Anbar Province told CNN.

A military court found that the other Marines had acted within their training, and the sad but undeniable truth is that the killing of innocents happens, given the wrong circumstances. That was true in 1770 and true today. War is hell, and this is one of the reasons.

Two of the Marines filed suit against Murtha, claiming that he had damaged their reputation. Both suits curiously were filed during election years, which naturally grabbed headlines. Murtha and his backers saw the suits as politically motivated. Murtha refused to respond to an attorney's offers to withdraw the slander charges if he would apologize.

The attacks continued, saying that Murtha had convicted these soldiers in public before they had a trial.

In contrast, Abu Ghraib generated widespread public commentary long before any trials, but there was no outcry of "innocent until proven guilty" about those who were facing potential prison terms there. An American came forward with the prison photos, but if the same photos had been provided by an Iraqi, would America have handled Abu Ghraib the same way?

The military did institute changes in training soon after Haditha became a national issue. The Marine Corps and the Army both became more explicit in explaining the rules of engagement and the ethics of protecting civilians, and promised to enforce the rules on both.

Many Marines say privately that they find no excuse for how events unfolded in Haditha, that no matter what the stress or assignments, Marines are "the best of the best" and their training is such that women and children not involved in a firefight should not die at the hands of Marines.

The worst case scenario here is that Marines killed innocents as retribution, and others systematically covered for them. The best case scenario is that Marines were not trained for the situation in which they were placed, were unable to distinguish innocent women and children from attackers, and thus killed innocent people. Both are tragedies, but one is an atrocity. Many would agree that neither is what Americans should accept from their military or what any civilized country should accept as a natural by-product of war.

Murtha was guilty on two counts. First, he did not clearly articulate what he meant by "in cold blood." Second, he did not recognize the fury that his words would generate among some in the military and certainly from his critics, who would seize upon the words "in cold blood." His original thought was not about individual killers; it was about Marines in situations for which they were not properly trained, operating for long periods in repeated deployments under incredible stress. His point was that these war fighters faced overwhelming pressure and such tragedies are more likely to happen under such strain.

One historical note is that the British soldiers who stood trial for the Boston Massacre did so in the courts of the host nation. The Brits were tried in an American court. The Marines of Haditha were judged by their own military under an American Flag, not an Iraqi court.

The results quite possibly would have been different in an Iraqi court, which would not have looked at whether these men had acted within the scope of their training. An Iraqi court would have looked at this as America looked at the killings in Boston in 1770: a question of guilt or innocence.

Before long, the Iraqis insisted that Amiercan forces could not stay in Iraq without being subject to Iraqi laws. The White House would not accept those conditions, and U.S. troops were withdrawn completely in late 2011.

America can learn from its own history. Regardless of the truth, the perception of those being occupied is paramount. One cannot win hearts and minds in a nation whose women and children are killed brutally, and when human beings are pushed to extremes, chances are that they may overreact, especially if they have not received adequate training. This was Murtha's point.

Moments after his "in cold blood" statement, Murtha said, "Now, you can imagine the impact this is going to have on those troops for the rest of their lives and for the United States in our war and our effort in trying to win the hearts and minds."

Obviously his mind was on the big picture in Iraq, and his remarks here echoed what he had said back on December 14, 2004, remarks that deserve to be repeated here: "War is about killing. For those sent to fight an enemy, that killing will stay with them for the rest of their lives. It is in the faces of friends lost, in the shadows the soldiers feel on their souls for having killed. This is the nature of war."

Having operated "within the scope of their training" may offer little comfort in those quiet moments of those who were involved in Haditha.

Chapter 20

Swift Boaters and Basement Tapes

"**Hey, hey, ho,** ho, Jack Murtha's got to go! Hey, hey, ho, ho, Jack Murtha's got to go!"

The chants filled the Cambria County War Memorial Arena in Jack Murtha's home town, where a thousand people had come together for a "Boot Murtha" rally on October 2, 2006.

Larry Bailey, a retired Navy SEAL, helped organize the rally after he created and became president of "Veterans for the Truth" with support from the same folks who two years earlier had created "Swift Boat Veterans for Truth."

The Swift Boat group had derailed the presidential campaign of Senator John Kerry of Massachusetts by finding some veterans who had served with Kerry on a vessel called a Swift Boat that patrolled rivers in the Vietnam War. These veterans questioned Kerry's valor during the action for which he had received medals. The idea was to undermine an opponent by attacking his strongest assets, and the tactic became know as "swift boating."

Bailey made no secret of his intentions in 2006. In a small, earlier rally in Johnstown, he told the *Boston Globe*, "I called my buddies in the anti-Kerry movement from 2004. I will do my best to 'swift boat' John Murtha."

The Boot Murtha group distributed nasty anti-Murtha literature with a photo of Kerry testifying before Congress in 1971 about alleged U.S. atrocities committed in Vietnam. Plastered next to Kerry was a photograph that the *Globe* described as Murtha "scowling and wrinkled."

To comply with the law, this literature was clearly labeled "Paid for by the Iowa Presidential Watch PAC/Vets for the Truth – BootMurtha. com." The group was organized under the Iowa Presidential Watch 527 Political Action Committee, an independent PAC headed by Richard Schwarm. Schwarm had close ties to Karl Rove, the architect of much of the Bush agenda and a master of attack politics.

The idea that someone could beat Murtha was perhaps silly, but with Murtha's penchant for shooting from the hip and sometimes choosing the wrong word, Rove and the White House certainly were hot to take Murtha to task and hope he would make a big mistake or two. If nothing else, they would make him spend more time and money at home, which would give him less of both to spend in the political war over who would control Congress.

They recruited a petite woman with an engaging smile named Diana Irey, a Washington County commissioner from the opposite side of the 12th Congressional District. While she was well-known in one county, almost no one knew her around Johnstown. People who met her often commented on two things: that she was pretty and she wore a rock that was at least two full carats. That ring did not say "hockey mom" to folks in industrial Southwestern Pennsylvania.

Nonetheless, local Republicans were hyping her as a strong candidate who could win the western side of the district and unseat Murtha, given his controversial position on Iraq and the flap over his provocative description of the Haditha incident.

By most accounts, she was capable and had served her county well, even though she was the only Republican on a board of commissioners with two Democrats.

She was a shrewd political pick by the Rove machine: decent at her job, attractive, and a woman. Good at delivering a prepared line, she could spout all the anti-Murtha epithets she wanted and never worry about the congressman slamming back because she was a woman, and almost a foot-and-a-half shorter than Murtha. So any harsh attack would have looked like big ole', ill-tempered Murtha beating up on this poor, innocent lady.

As early as August that year, the Boot Murtha group was mailing flyers to members of the American Legion and other veterans' groups in the district using the swift-boat tactics that had helped to derail Kerry in 2004.

With all of the anger stirred up by Murtha's "in cold blood" remark, there were veterans even in Murtha's back yard eager to go after him. Two retired colonels from Johnstown became the face and voice of Boot Murtha, speaking wherever they could, writing letters to the editor and at least one op-ed, which compared Murtha with Benito Mussolini, the head of Italy who joined with Adolph Hitler and the Nazis to take on the free world in World War II.

When the swift boaters started planning a big rally for October 2, 2006, at Johnstown's War Memorial Arena, Murtha's friends heard about it almost instantly.

Their instant reaction: plan a bigger rally and stage it October 1.

The biggest name that the Boot Murtha gang could attract was David Beamer, whose son was famous for shouting "Let's Roll" on September 11, 2001, just before the passengers on United Airlines Flight 93 overtook the terrorist hijackers and crashed the plane into the field in Murtha's district. That rally, held indoors, attracted about a thousand people, according to media accounts.

The Murtha rally featured former Senator Max Cleland, a disabled Vietnam veteran who himself had been swift-boated, as the master of ceremonies. Speakers were former Chairman of the Joint Chiefs of Staff

General Hugh Shelton, former NATO commander General Wesley Clark, and former Senator John Kerrey of Nebraska, a winner of the Medal of Honor for his service in Vietnam, as well as Pennsylvania Governor Edward Rendell and some local veterans. Despite a day-long, drenching, cold rain, the outdoor event in Johnstown's Central Park attracted two thousand people, according to the official police estimate.

General Clark summed up the mission when he told the enthusiastic crowd, "This administration's leadership of the war has been incompetent, inept. We're not going to let any swift-boaters, shrimp-boaters, or anybody else take out Jack Murtha."

The duel of the rallies was clearly a win for Murtha, with several of the media accounts focusing on mothers who had lost sons in Iraq. "I've been called unpatriotic because of my opposition to the war. Murtha is one of my heroes," said Diane Santoriello, whose son, Brian, had been killed in combat in 2004.

Curiously, just an hour before the Murtha rally, Irey called a news conference about the sudden appearance of a long-lost video tape from the 1980 Abscam sting operation. Murtha was named an un-indicted co-conspirator while five members of Congress were convicted in the case, in which Federal Bureau of Investigation agents posed as representatives of Arab sheiks to offer bribes in exchange for help in becoming U.S. citizens.

The tape showed up mysteriously at the conservative *American Spectator* magazine after no one apparently had seen it in twenty-some years. Murtha knew the timing was not a coincidence. How deep into the Justice Department basement did Karl Rove have his boys dig to find that one? Certainly Rove was smart enough to keep his fingerprints from being directly on the tape, but Murtha was convinced that Rove had been behind it.

People interpreted Abscam in various ways, but the fact is that Murtha was never charged and was never even censored by

Congress. While Murtha does not look great on the tape, the video of his conversations with undercover agents showed him turning down an offer of a $50,000 bribe.

Decades later, political enemies tried to use the case to demonstrate that Murtha was corrupt. Video of a person not taking a bribe, even if he says he might talk about it later, is not proof of guilt. The tape political enemies used to discredit the man is a tape that prevented the man from being indicted.

And Murtha's supporters were always well schooled on pointing out that Murtha's motivation at the time was to attract a major investment in local businesses to create jobs when unemployment was at twenty-four percent.

The resurfacing of the tape in 2006 certainly did not come from Diana Irey's campaign, which in many ways was inept.

To introduce herself to the Greater Johnstown area as the Republican nominee in the 12th District, she staged a ribbon-cutting ceremony at a new campaign office. A small but enthusiastic crowd packed into the little office in Richland Township in suburban Johnstown on a sunny day in August 2006.

Irey slammed Murtha for his call for redeployment. "We don't need to redeploy our troops. We need to redeploy Jack Murtha," she proclaimed.

"Jack Murtha has disappointed us all. He's been gone too long and is out of touch," she said, slamming him for sharing "the values of liberal San Francisco."

Any member of Congress has critics. Even the most popular officeholders have those who really dislike them. But the idea of Jack Murtha as a San Francisco kind of guy? The idea never stuck because it was such a ridiculous claim, even to those who long disliked Murtha.

Over the years, some of his local critics felt he did not do enough for the region, that he did not bring in enough money, build enough highways, and create enough jobs. Ironically, his harshest critics from outside the region charged that he had brought in too much money and too many jobs through pork barrel.

But if all of Murtha's local critics had been put in a room to write all of the angry things they could say about the man, none of them who knew the man would have written that he had "the values of liberal San Francisco." If he was nothing else, Jack Murtha was staunchly pro-gun, pro-life, and pro-defense, not quite the platform that wins in San Francisco.

Irey, however, was not performing for the local media. She was performing for the national Republican base with a script from outside the region, which is where repeated attacks against Murtha were launched throughout the campaign. She was hoping to sway local voters, but her whole candidacy was centered on slamming Murtha on Iraq while painting him as out of touch at home. She called him un-American because he dared to oppose the war and bragged that her campaign had received donations from all fifty states, apparently oblivious to the fact that to the people of the 12th District, that rang of outsiders trying to impact their local area.

Irey's quip about San Francisco values was not her only faux pas that day.

On this warm and sunny afternoon with little if any wind, some in the media wondered why the ribbon-cutting and speeches were being held inside the small office. The office was cramped, but not because it was packed with a huge throng of supporters. The three dozen supporters were mostly squeezed into a hallway flanked by several offices within the new headquarters while a few others had been pushed to the sides of the room so the local media could get a clear view of the podium.

The cameras thus had a view of a candidate standing at a podium in what well could have been an empty room. A campaign sign hung awkwardly behind the podium on what was otherwise an empty wall – hardly magnificent political imagery.

This was not a mega media event with fifty press members and all the technical trappings of such an event. The wireless microphones of the four local television stations were simply placed on the podium before the speakers began. In the moments before Irey took to the podium, an aide came over, removed all the microphones and papers that had been left by the first speaker, and placed them in an adjoining room.

There was stunned silence from media who were covering the event. Surely she did not intend to have a press conference where her words could not be recorded?

As Irey spoke, one or two members of the media made their way around the crowd, no easy task given the cramped event, and asked the staffer why she had removed the microphones. She informed them that Irey had requested that she clear the podium because she did not want to have things that might interfere with her prepared notes.

When informed that she had removed the devices needed to record Irey's speech, she quickly put them back on the podium despite the puzzled look from the candidate, who continued to plow through her prepared text.

Clearly, while the rhetoric and press releases from Irey's campaign were coming from a state-of-the-art political machine, those running the ground game were clueless.

No connection to Karl Rove was apparent at that point, but some in the local media got the feeling that this campaign was more about the GOP taking shots at Murtha, not a real effort to fully support Irey, which suggested that the Republicans recognized she had little chance of really winning.

The sense that she was not fully supported got stronger with the campaign's response – or lack thereof – to a third faux pas that same day.

After the prepared speech, in a one-on-one interview to air on the local Fox affiliate, Irey had sort of a "Sarah Palin" moment.

The interview started on the local economy and what she would do that Murtha had not done; the loss of Murtha's seniority in the House if she were elected versus the benefit of having her in office; and how much support she was getting in Murtha's hometown of Johnstown.

She shared a story about how the City of Johnstown had embraced her because she was walking in a parade in Windber, when someone broke from the crowd and handed her a campaign check. Windber is not a neighborhood in Johnstown. While only a few miles from her suburban campaign office, Windber is twenty minutes from the city and located in a different county than Johnstown.

Then the interview turned to international politics, and Irey was pleased because she was fully prepared to talk "cut and run," "stay the course," and winning in Iraq.

At that time, President Bush was dealing with a very tense situation between Lebanon and Israel, so the reporter asked a broad question about the handling of the situation by Ehud Olmert. Three months earlier, many people may not have known that Olmert was the Prime Minister of Israel, but the situation had received wide media attention, so the reporter felt that a question on his performance, at that point, was a bit of a softball.

"Uh..., I think I'll take a pass on that one," Irey replied with the same puzzled look she had displayed at the podium when the microphones had been returned during her speech. She was then pressed about why she would take a pass and replied, "I just don't think I am going to answer that one at this time."

Irey was not only refusing to answer a pretty simple question about the Prime Minister of Israel, she was not going to explain her reasons for not answering. Her response left a distinct impression she had no idea what was going on in Israel.

The story was aired as a question-and-answer piece with a large portion of the conversation airing exactly as it happened: live without edit. The piece would speak for itself.

Several phone calls and e-mails were directed to the station immediately after the interview aired. Most notable was a message from Saul Glosser, a prominent member of the local Jewish community. He was amazed that a woman running for the United States Congress at such a time would be so clueless about Middle East events and Israel, in particular.

The next day, the Irey campaign people called from out of town wanting to view the piece. They offered no comment, they issued no statement, they just let it slip into the cracks and go unanswered, even as a story aired the next night with Glosser expressing his dismay.

Glosser basically said that even if a county commissioner had no need to know why Olmert was significant, she should at least be watching what was happening in the world right now in case she would accidentally win.

If this was really about getting Irey elected, the campaign managers would have taken some measure of damage control. They did not. They just kept screaming about Iraq and "cut and run."

The local media never made much of a splash about the fact that Irey's campaign was being run by John Brabender of Pittsburgh. Brabender is considered to be one of the best Republican campaign advisors in the Northeast, perhaps in the country. His top political client was Senator Rick Santorum, the arch-conservative who ultimately lost his re-election bid that year. No doubt, Brabender recognized that Irey was a long shot to beat Murtha, but money spent attacking Murtha served a dual purpose of defending Santorum.

Brabender's top client was so closely tied to Bush that anything that hurt the White House hurt Santorum. So Irey's campaign was directly or indirectly supporting Santorum's 2006 re-election bid, which was sure to be tougher because of Iraq and the snowball Murtha had started rolling.

Not surprisingly, Brabender did a better job handling Irey for the national stage than the local stage. Irey spoke to the National Press Club early in the campaign, getting coverage from the *Pittsburgh Post-Gazette* and the Associated Press, whose article ran all over the 12th District and, indeed, much of the state, which certainly did not hurt Santorum.

Several times during the campaign, Irey appeared on national shows on Fox News Channel, which absolutely fawned over the attractive, petite woman with the guts to take on the giant, Jack Murtha. Those appearances were promoted heavily on the internet, and Irey boasted that she had raised $45,000 within two days of an appearance on Fox.

If Irey had become a serious threat to Murtha, she was carrying her own baggage, which surely would have come into play.

In January 2005, the Associated Press published a story about a $300 million dollar deal awarded by the Iraqi Defense Ministry to a consortium that included Irey's husband, Robert, and his brother, William Irey. The Irey brothers had joined up with an arms dealer named Dale Stoffel. Stoffel's Iraqi patron was none other than Ahmed Chalabi, the former leader in exile, favorite of neo-conservatives, and alleged con man, who had provided bad intelligence about Saddam Hussein's weapons of mass destruction. With Chalabi's support, Stoffel and the Ireys won a bid to rebuild military equipment for the Iraqi armed forces and market military scrap metal from all over the war-ravaged country.

Stoffel wound up in a nasty financial dispute with the Iraqi Defense Ministry, which he accused of corruption. In December 2004, not long after Stoffel started making official complaints through Senator Santorum, unknown assailants murdered him and an American associate. According to the Associated Press, the contract awarded to Irey's consortium was obtained by hiring the same "powerful Washington lobbyists" who had represented Chalabi in his quest for American money and support.

Murtha supporters talked about the Irey-Stoffel connection almost constantly, but never used it in his campaign spots or speeches. If Diana Irey had become a serious threat, Murtha was ready to throw down the gloves, and her large diamond would have been connected to war money in a political ad. But such nasty ads sometimes backfire, and Murtha never needed to risk a frontal assault on Irey.

Depending on one's political persuasion, this messy murder over military contracts smacks of either corruption on the Irey side or typical political mudslinging by Murtha supporters. One thing was certain: it was not just a coincidence that Irey became Murtha's opponent. The Ireys and folks like Rove and Santorum swam in the same waters.

Diana Irey simply was not a strong enough candidate to run against arguably the most informed member of Congress on national defense, and the old tapes from the Justice Department basement were way too dusty to have much, if any, impact. Murtha won with sixty-one percent of the vote, and Irey did not even carry the precinct in which she lived.

But on election night, having parried every punch the Rove machine could throw, Murtha was quite anxious, not about the outcome of his own race, but about the outcome of a few dozen other House races where he had campaigned in trying to wrest control of Congress from the Republicans.

Chapter 21

Bringin' Down the House

More than 200 people packed the yard of David and Elaine Ahern's house in Hampton Falls, New Hampshire, to chow down on covered dishes, salads, and desserts that had been brought by their friends and fellow Democrats to share at the annual summer picnic of the Hamptontown Democratic Committee. This was double the number who usually came, but they came for a special guest: Congressman John P. Murtha.

By July 2006, Murtha was pretty much a household name between his call for redeployment, his provocative description of the Haditha incident, and his now-frequent appearances on television news shows.

"There were people in the military, people who had been in the military, people who had family in the military. There were people in tears. It was an overwhelming response," recalled Lenore Patton, Murtha's old friend from Indiana, Pennsylvania, who had moved to Hampton Falls after she and her husband, Gary, retired.

Murtha's rousing speech followed his usual themes. "They have to settle it themselves," he said of the Iraqis. "What makes you think it's going to get any better if we stay? Only they can fix it," he said, emphasizing that American forces were the target of both factions that were fighting a civil war within Iraq, and the presence of the troops was helping the insurgents find recruits.

The crowd loved it. They were not the usual crowd of the local loyal Democrats, but a mixed crowd with new faces who were inspired to come hear Murtha because he was the only national leader with the character and courage to speak with authority about the need to get out of Iraq.

"He went around with me and met every single person there personally, shook everyone's hand," Patton said. "I didn't know the one family; the father was a vet and the son was a Marine. There were just people who heard he was coming and came to meet him," she said, naming a couple she did know whose son was in Iraq.

At the time, four Democrats were vying for the Democratic nomination to take on incumbent Republican Jeb Bradley in New Hampshire's 1st District. Three of them came to the rally, including Carol Shea-Porter and front-runner Jim Craig, the state House Democratic leader.

Shea-Porter recalled, "At the time, nobody had any sense that there was a race in New Hampshire that could be won by a Democrat, so we were not on the radar screen, so to speak. This friend talked to Jack, explained my position, and he said he wanted to help. People came from everywhere to hear what he said about the Iraq war because he was so respected on military issues.... He basically drew people in, and spoke to people about me and how I was going to win. It meant a lot to me as somebody who was running a renegade campaign with no funding and no national attention."

After Shea-Porter won the primary, Murtha came for a fundraiser at a local home, Patton said, adding, "He spoke in her behalf. That also had a really good turnout. He was a strong supporter of her, spoke eloquently for her. People thought the endorsement was very helpful to her."

Shea-Porter went on to beat the incumbent with fifty-two percent of the vote.

That summer, Murtha went many places, none of them for vacations. He went to Florida, New York, California, Ohio, Connecticut, New York again, Colorado, Minnesota, California again..., mostly places where Democrats were in tough elections in swing districts.

He was committed to taking back the House for the Democrats in hopes that they could then force Bush to change course in Iraq, and he had stunned the political world when he announced that he would run for majority leader if the Democrats did, indeed, take control of the House.

He made a special effort to campaign for the thirty-three veterans who were running as Democrats, even in districts where those veterans had only an outside chance of winning.

In Colorado Springs, Colorado, home of the United States Air Force Academy, Republicans had more than a two-to-one voter registration majority. No Democrat had received more than forty percent of the vote there since the district was created in 1972.

But Murtha packed a few hundred people into the basement of a downtown Colorado Springs bar for a rally in support of Jay Fawcett, a retired Air Force officer running for the seat that was being vacated by the retirement of Congressman Joel Heffley.

Murtha told the crowd they needed someone with military experience who could look at what was happening "with a jaundiced eye." Referring to the folks leading the war back in the nation's capital, he added, "You just don't believe the civilians who never get off their fat backsides in their air-conditioned offices and say, 'Stay the course.'"

Ultimately, Fawcett received barely more than forty percent of the vote, but Murtha had a successful trip because he also campaigned in another Colorado race and, on his way back east, hit the stump in two Minnesota races, including an event for veteran Tim Walz, another Iraq war veteran who would soon hold a seat in Congress.

Murtha campaigned especially hard in his home state of

Pennsylvania, where no less than five Congressional seats offered potential to go from Republican to Democrat, or from "Red to Blue" in the parlance of the times. And he was especially excited about campaigns of two veterans who were running in tight races in the Keystone State.

Chris Carney was a lieutenant commander in the U.S. Naval Reserves campaigning in a Republican-leaning Northeastern Pennsylvania district where Don Sherwood was the incumbent.

In August, Murtha pounded his usual themes to rouse the crowd at a $250-per-ticket fundraiser in Clarks Summit, and received prolonged applause when he said Carney would get a seat on the powerful Appropriations Committee if he won.

But after his remarks, a reporter for the *Scranton Times-Tribune* asked about the lawsuit that that been filed just a day earlier by Staff Sergeant Frank Wuterich contending that Murtha had defamed him by calling the Marines involved in the Haditha incident "cold blooded murderers."

Murtha told the reporter that the killings were "a tragic incident" that "just breaks my heart," but said he stood by his comments. The lawsuit was an attempt "to distract from the fact that we need a change of direction," he said, adding, "You need to get the truth out. You can't cover it up. I'm not distracted by these kinds of things."

Despite the reference to the lawsuit, the overall media coverage for Carney was excellent and included reports on the area's television stations.

Early in the campaign, Carney got his picture in *Time* magazine in an article titled, "Iraq-War Vets: The Democrats' Newest Weapon." The article described a Carney rally that had drawn many Republicans who were angry with Bush and called it "Karl Rove's worst nightmare."

With Murtha attracting campaign contributions, media coverage, and solid crowds, and with incumbent Republican Don Sherwood soiled by reports of an affair, this race shaped up fairly early as a likely

Red-to-Blue pick-up for the Democrats.

Other races were tight down to the wire, such as Victoria Wulsin's challenge of Jean Schmidt in Ohio's 2nd District.

On a campaign trip there in mid-October, Murtha asked aide Patrick Alwine, "That's the one who said that stuff about me on the floor, right?"

Murtha knew damn well that Jean Schmidt was the one who had nearly created a free-for-all on the House floor when she proclaimed, "Cowards cut and run; Marines never do." It was just his somewhat odd sense of humor to let on like he did not know the name of "Mean Jean," as she had come to be known in political circles.

Wulsin had both a medical degree and a doctorate degree in epidemiology, and had been director of epidemiology for the Cincinnati Health Department before working for the U.S. Centers for Disease Control. She exuded confidence and was articulate. Her campaign was picking up steam in the early fall and was put on the Democrats' "emerging races" list as a heavily Republican district where the Democrats actually saw some possibilities.

"We went out there, and there was a huge rally. There was a big fundraiser, big money, and afterwards a big rally, and they packed this big hall," Alwine recalled.

The *Cincinnati Enquirer* covered the rally, reporting that more than two hundred people, including many military veterans, had jammed the International Brotherhood of Electrical Workers Union Hall in East Walnut Hills to hear Murtha "call for a 'return to civility' in a Democrat-controlled Congress."

"There were hundreds at the rally, lots of press, too. She put on a really good event; they set it up really well," Alwine said. "This gave us a really good feeling, but afterwards she lost. It wasn't like he was going out there to be vindictive, but he would have liked to have won that."

Murtha was disappointed. She had mounted a very strong

campaign and lost by only 2,517 votes out of 240,000 cast, which was the closest a Democrat had come in that suburban and rural district in forty-two years.

Despite that loss, this was destined to be a good year for the Democrats, and as election day neared, Murtha was getting more and more excited.

Oddly, the weekend before the election, Murtha had nothing scheduled. "We didn't have anything set up that weekend, and he wanted to go somewhere; he wanted to help out," Alwine said. "So he said, 'What can we do? Does Patrick Murphy need anything?'"

Patrick Murphy had served in Iraq in the 82nd Airport Division and was in a very tight race in suburban Philadelphia against Mike Fitzpatrick.

"It turns out that John McCain was coming in that weekend to campaign for his opponent, the incumbent Republican, and so at the last minute, Mr. Murtha went out there. All we did was a small rally, and then we did a veterans event, and there was tons of press there. Gwen Ifill (of the Jim Lehrer News Hour on PBS) was there, a lot of local media...," Alwine recalled.

"So it wasn't that big of an event, but it got Patrick Murphy more in front of the cameras. It got him in front of the nightly news, and the next thing in the *Philadelphia Inquirer*, instead of a big story about John McCain being in town, I think there was a picture of Patrick Murphy on the front page, and it changed the entire focus of the story. Instead of, 'Oh, McCain was in town,' it was about Patrick Murphy is challenging and the incumbent needs McCain to defend him. I really think that had a big impact in that race; not that Patrick Murphy really needed that to win, but I think that was very helpful to him."

The *Bucks County Courier Times* covered the event at the VFW in Croydon, Pennsylvania, and high in the story quoted Murtha telling the voters that the election was a chance for them to alter the balance of a Republican Congress that had "continually misled" Americans about Iraq, adding, "We're fighting for the soul of America and we're going to win that fight."

Murtha used that phrase, fighting for the soul of America, repeatedly in his campaigns for other candidates and in his own campaign that year. To Murtha, the fight was not only about changing course in Iraq; it was also a fight to elect people who would accept open debate on issues, to end the attack-and-destroy politics that used fear and false patriotism to stifle voice.

Election day, Murphy ended up with 50.3 percent of the vote, edging out Fitzpatrick by a mere 1,518 votes, one of four districts in Pennsylvania that Murtha helped to switch to Democrat. Chris Carney won with fifty-three percent of the vote. Joe Sestak, another veteran running as a Democrat, also benefited from Murtha's support, soundly defeating incumbent Republican Curt Weldon with fifty-six percent.

The Democrats had needed only fifteen seats to take control, but it was a big day for them. After several recounts in very close races, they gained thirty-one seats to control the House by a 223-to-202 vote margin. The Senate also went from Red to Blue that day.

Murtha was ecstatic. The morning after the election, he was in his office early, pouring over results, calling winners to congratulate them, reminding them that he was now a candidate for majority leader, but also savoring what this victory really meant. He had sent a message. He had sent a very big message to the White House, and to Rove, Rumsfeld, and company. There would be no more silencing of the voices in Washington. There would be real, open, and honest debate about the Iraq war and other issues. There would, Murtha hoped, finally be some accountability in Washington.

That accountability came quite fast. With polling showing that the Democrats were about to seize control, Donald Rumsfeld wrote a letter of resignation on November 6, 2006, the day before the election. The president saw the letter on election day, and the next day, November 8, he announced that Rumsfeld was history as defense secretary.

That was almost exactly one year after Jack Murtha put his political neck on the line, after trying so hard for so long to change how we conducted the war.

President Bush seemed to be loyal to a fault. Prior to Murtha's actions, there was not enough outside pressure from any direction to prompt such a change inside the Bush White House. Over the course of the election, even Republican leaders started to question, not the judgment of Rumsfeld, but rather the judgment of Bush in keeping Rumsfeld. Arguably this should have happened all along, but it did not happen until Murtha called for redeployment and took that call to the people through elections all across America.

Many Republicans ultimately blamed Bush for their fall from power, believing that they might have held on if he had fired Rumsfeld before the election. His resignation after the fact was too little, too late, as was the letter that Rumsfeld himself had written a day before the election.

"The situation in Iraq is evolving, and U.S forces have adjusted, over time, from major combat operations to counter terrorism, to counterinsurgency, to dealing with death squads and sectarian violence," the defense secretary wrote. "In my view, it is time for a major adjustment. Clearly, what U.S forces are currently doing in Iraq is not working well enough or fast enough. Following is a range of options."

Rumsfeld listed seventeen options above the line or most desirable, to be done in concert with each other. They included:
- "Begin modest withdrawals of U.S. and coalition forces so Iraqis know they have to pull up their socks, step up, and take responsibility for their country.
- "Withdraw U.S. forces from vulnerable positions - cities, patrolling etc. - and move U.S. forces to a Quick Reaction

Force (QRF) status, operating from within Iraq and Kuwait, to be available when Iraqi security forces need assistance.
- "Position substantial U.S. forces near the Iranian and Syrian borders to reduce infiltration and, importantly, review Iranian influence on the Iraqi Government."

Rumsfeld proposed doing exactly what Murtha had called for in November 2005: redeploy and keep troops over the horizon for fast deployment when needed. Murtha could have written this memo himself.

Yet no one called Rumsfeld "cut and run." No one called Rumsfeld a "coward." No one called Rumsfeld a "traitor" who should be "fragged." Of course, Rumsfeld was called many things by his detractors, but again, one must question who was giving and who was taking orders at the White House for those several years leading up to this election debacle of the Republicans.

Rumsfeld's memo listed five "below the line" or less attractive options. Top on his list of unattractive options was "continue on the current path."

"Stay the course" had been a rally cry for the president and his allies up and down the right wing, including Donald Rumsfeld. Now, as he was set to leave, Rumsfeld said staying the course tops the list of the less attractive options on how to handle Iraq. The term went from its intended message of strength to a term identified with futility and weakness.

"Stay the course" was removed from the White House vernacular because even they finally recognized that this was not a course on which one should stay. Murtha knew it. Rumsfeld ultimately knew it. It seems everyone knew it except the people who were in charge. But no one gave it voice. No one dared say all the nation had gotten was more dead, more debt, and less esteem in the view of the world.

After the election, the president ignored Rumsfeld's above- and below-the-line options, and supported a surge in troops. Murtha first opposed the surge, then acknowledged that the surge was working and had created a window of opportunity for what he said needed to happen all along: Iraq determining the fate of Iraq.

He remained skeptical that the surge would work, but it had happened and he was dealing with the cards on the table when he said it was working. Unlike so many others, he was not playing a word game. He was not looking for political cover. He was looking for a way to save one more soldier's life, spend one less tax dollar, not waste one more moment of time in Iraq based on the current situation.

While some criticized Murtha because he voted for the war, then was against it, then was against the surge, then said it was working, his actions were intellectually consistent. In August 2003, after returning from a tour of the Iraqi theater, he urged Bush to work with other countries to bring in international troops and to ramp-up training of Iraq's military as two steps that would put more boots on the ground. The idea then was to win the necessary military battle, secure the peace and, before losing the hearts and minds of the Iraqi people, establish a better standard of living in a free society so the Iraqis would not allow a return to such chaos.

But with inadequate troop levels and increasing hostility toward the American troops, the violence got worse and worse until, in 2006, the surge created a window of opportunity, a window that Murtha felt should have occurred much sooner and at a radically lower cost in American blood and treasure.

Part of what gave Murtha's words so much weight when he called for redeployment was his history and his consistency. Murtha was no dove, and even his call for redeployment was not a matter of him "going soft." He had stood shoulder-to-shoulder with Bush I in the first Persian Gulf War, not only because he believed in the cause, but also because he believed in the man in charge and how that man was handling everything: talking to allies, talking to Congress, listening to suggestions....

Many of Murtha's critics have said that Murtha of 2005 contradicted Murtha of 1991. But as he emphasized repeatedly, Bush I built a true frame for burden-sharing with other nations and leaned on experienced senators and congressman for guidance. Murtha met with the senior Bush eleven times within a few months of the first Gulf War. That President Bush listened.

George W. Bush did not listen, and instead of eleven meetings in less than five months, took seven months to get a staffer to reply to Murtha's original letter urging Bush to bring in allies, ramp up Iraq's military, and build the energy and other infrastructure that would create jobs and hope for the regular Iraqis. This President Bush listened to none of it.

The problem was not a different Murtha, but a different Bush.

Murtha had stood shoulder-to-shoulder with the senior Bush. He stood nose-to-nose with the junior. Junior never blinked, but neither did he realize that he had perched himself on a house of cards. Murtha worked methodically, district by district, to knock out those cards until the House fell along with the Senate.

Rumsfeld was history, Bush's cards were scattered across the table, and Murtha was not done yet.

Chapter 22

Civility and Results

The letter was really quite simple: just two sentences. It was delivered to all Democratic members of the House, and said:

"If we prevail as I hope and know we will, and return to the majority this next Congress, I have decided to run for the open seat of the Majority Leader.

"I would appreciate your consideration and vote, and look forward to speaking to you personally about my decision."

The letter was signed, "Respectfully, John P. Murtha."

Dated June 9, 2006, just three weeks after creating a national ruckus over his "cold blood" assessment of the Haditha incident, Murtha created another ruckus in Washington, D.C., by announcing his campaign for the second highest position in the U.S. House of Representatives.

Curiously, his letter said he would run for "the open seat of Majority Leader."

Steny Hoyer, the Maryland Congressman who at that time was the Democrats' minority whip, had the second-highest position on their side of the House aisle. Everyone in Congress, every political pundit and analyst, every outsider interested in anything political, had assumed that Nancy Pelosi of California would move up from minority leader to speaker and that Hoyer would move up from whip to majority leader, creating a vacancy somewhere further down the chain of command.

Murtha stunned them all by announcing that he planned to jump in front of Hoyer, who then might have opted to simply move from minority whip to majority whip, but that would have been a step back from number two to number three in the hierarchy.

That day, ABC News quoted an unnamed person "close to the deliberations" as saying, "Murtha has always been a darling of the more conservative members of the caucus, but his recent leadership of the anti-war movement has won him wide praise among more liberal members, as well."

The *Washington Post* said Murtha had "startled his political colleagues," and Reuters news service said Murtha's announcement "appeared to take his party and Capitol Hill by surprise."

No kidding.

Only a few of Murtha's closest political allies and folks such as his wife, Joyce, knew what he intended to do.

Minority Leader Nancy Pelosi did not even know. Pelosi had become minority leader largely because Jack Murtha had engineered her win over Hoyer for minority whip in 2001. Murtha liked Pelosi because, although she was more liberal than him, she was the daughter of the former mayor of Baltimore and had a broad and deep understanding of politics in the trenches. From her family roots in working-class Baltimore, she was somewhat of a "street corner guy" who would have fit in with Tip O'Neill.

Pelosi considered Murtha a close advisor, consulting him not only on the war and foreign affairs, but also as a moderate on other issues within the Democratic caucus.

Pelosi, in an interview for this book, called his decision "a bit of a surprise," adding, "We hadn't talked about it. Jack came and said, 'I want to run for leader.' I had the highest regard for Jack. He had my support and I agreed that he'd have a bigger platform (on the war), that this war was just an enormous mistake."

Asked if he had at least floated the idea to get her thoughts, she said, "He said he was running unless I told him not to (run), and I never told anybody to run or not to run: they had to decide on their own."

Murtha's announcement went only to House Democrats, not to the national media, but the media knew instantly. Hoyer immediately released a statement through his spokesperson, Stacey Bernards, putting the national campaign for Congress ahead of the leader race:

"Mr. Hoyer has worked extraordinarily hard to unify the caucus and take back the House for Democrats, and that is his first focus. As a result of that unity, he's confident that we will be successful in November, and intends to run for majority leader."

Pundits, politicians, and media questioned the timing of Murtha's announcement because it would fracture the Democrats and potentially keep them fractured during the critical months from June through the general elections in November.

"This is a huge distraction," a senior House Democratic aide told CNN, adding that Democrats in the House were "really angry and confused that Jack Murtha would disrupt the focus of the caucus from taking back the House."

On June 13, just four days after suddenly announcing his campaign, Murtha decided to "suspend" his campaign until after the election.

One reason Murtha's first announcement came as such a shock was because many people felt he would have more clout and influence if he remained on the House Defense Appropriations Subcommittee. There, he would be elevated from ranking member, the top committee member from the minority party, to chairman, the guy who really sets the agenda and calls the shots as the head of the committee.

In the national budget, if entitlements such as Social Security and Medicare are not considered, the defense budget roughly equals everything else: all other discretionary spending on education, housing, transportation, national parks, etc. So chairman of Defense Appropriations is a mighty powerful position, and Murtha knew better than anyone how to wield that power by helping members of Congress get projects for their district – or not get projects for their district.

On October 3, 2006, Murtha told the *New York Times*, "You need to get things done, so you give them the votes to get the things done. There is no question that some projects come out of it (defense appropriations) for our members, and that is not a bad thing. Deal-making is what Congress is all about."

Before he decided to run, Murtha had quietly asked some of his closest staffers and advisors what they thought about the idea.

His chief of staff, John Hugya, felt Murtha would have broader influence on the nation's direction as majority leader. But most told him they felt he would have much more influence as defense chairman and expressed concern that, as a party leader, he would at times need to defend positions taken by the party nationally that would be unpopular in socially conservative Southwestern Pennsylvania. Some reminded him that just a few years earlier, House Speaker Tom Foley had been defeated for re-election in his home district in Washington State, even though that state was much more liberal than Murtha's part of Pennsylvania. That was the first time since 1862 that a speaker of the House lost for re-election, and it was in large part because local voters did not agree with some of the party's national positions.

So why did Murtha decide to run? Interviews with a half-dozen of the people closest to him produced nearly a half-dozen widely different reasons. Some talked about the big picture: to have more impact on the war debate, to balance the party, or to reform how Congress did business.

Others suggested far more personal reasons. One had the impression that his wife liked the idea and subtly "pushed" him, although Joyce Murtha emphatically said that was not the case.

Another advisor said Murtha had been motivated to run because he had a strong dislike for Steny Hoyer. Virtually all of Murtha's friends and advisors said, whatever his prime reasons, Hoyer was at least an underlying factor.

Murtha certainly talked about reforming the way the House operated, which was listed by some close associates as the primary reason he sought the position.

Congressman Bob Brady of Philadelphia, one of Murtha's top lieutenants, said Murtha wanted to put some structure into the House so that members would know when they would have votes and when they could plan events back in their districts. Congress typically is in session Tuesdays through Thursdays so that members can get home to their districts for Friday, weekend, and Monday events or meetings. But quite often, Brady said, "On a Thursday, they keep us all weekend.... There were times when I set up events in the district and then I couldn't go because we find out a day or two ahead we have to be in session. He just wanted some structure to the house."

David Morrison, who was staff director for the Defense Appropriations Subcommittee, agreed largely with Brady's assessment.

"He felt he knew how to run the House as well as anybody. He had learned at the foot of the master, Tip O'Neill," Morrison said, referring to Murtha's mentor, the former House speaker from Massachusetts. "He knew it would be a sacrifice (to become majority leader), but he was sick of all the procedural stuff, the lack of the use of the rules, the strong-arm use of the rules. He was disenchanted that the House would come in Tuesday evening and be gone by Thursday afternoon. There was little, if any, collaboration. The people (members) didn't know each other."

Imagine that. The members of Congress who make the policy of the country, debate the issues, and very often get things done only when they can work together to compromise, spend so little meaningful time in Washington that they don't even know each other. Profound. And typical of Murtha, nobody else was even thinking about this issue, let alone articulating it.

In essence, Murtha was saying, "We need to talk" as members of Congress.

In a 2005 interview with Robert V. Remini, a professor of history emeritus at the University of Illinois in Chicago, for Remini's book, *The House: The History of the House of Representatives*, Murtha recalled how things had been done during O'Neill's tenure as speaker.

"In those days, you got along, there was comity. Tip played golf with (Minority Leader Bob) Michel and, you know, there was all kinds of things that went on. Today, you have some individuals that deal with them; like I get along fine with (Congressman Tom) DeLay (Republican of Texas) and so forth. I get along with him, but it's not the same. It's business dealings rather than any kind of personal dealings at all, and it's too bad because it's hurting the process."

Murtha often was asked how Congress had changed over his tenure of more than thirty years. His answer repeatedly was that, when he arrived in the mid-1970s, members on the left got up and made their speeches, members on the right got up and made their speeches, and in the end of the day, the moderates from both parties reached a compromise that never fully pleased everyone, but moved the nation forward.

He often said that the worst thing that had happened during his tenure in Congress was the polarization, in which each party tries to strong-arm all of its members to vote its party line. He preached constantly that members need the ability to vote their districts.

Murtha told historian Remini, "I always tell members when they come, you know, 'Stick to your guns. Don't pay attention to the damned (party) leadership. I mean, you do what you think is right. You represent a district, damn it; you represent that district. That's the first responsibility you have.' And the ones that do that stay here."

In 1994, when the Republicans took control of Congress, Newt Gingrich got a lot of credit for his "Contract with America." Murtha said bunk. The Republicans won because the Democrats had strong-armed several of their members from moderate or conservative districts to vote for gun control and health care. The cardinal rule in politics, always advocated by Murtha and O'Neill, was that all politics is local. Gun control is a national issue that has been made local all over the nation through the grass-roots connections of the National Rifle Association. Murtha, by the way, was a card-carrying "Life Member" of the NRA and a proud recipient of its "Kentucky Rifle."

Murtha blamed Gingrich for the change in tone in Washington. "I think it changed with Gingrich," he told Remini. "And he knew he had to blow the place up in order to win. He never thought he'd win. None of us thought he'd win. We didn't think we'd lose more than eighteen seats that year, and I was shocked when we lost fifty-two. I remember sitting there, the biggest victory I ever had (at home) and I'm looking at these guys falling by the wayside. And it came about because of (President) Clinton's mishandling of the medical bill and gun control."

Murtha said at least fifteen Democratic House seats were lost that year strictly because of gun control.

Murtha argued against pressing for party-line voting on many politically divisive issues. Perhaps nobody in Congress was known more for working in a bipartisan way, especially on Defense Appropriations. Murtha prided himself in getting the House defense-spending bill passed with just a few "no" votes.

Morrison said, "He felt there was no discipline, and he felt that he could bridge the gap" between the Republicans and Democrats, adding, "He wanted the House to be in session Monday through Friday and done by five o'clock every day. He wanted committees in the morning and floor action in the afternoon. He hated the fact that you never knew what time you'd be done."

Pelosi alluded to that structure in a general reflection about Murtha when she mentioned his widow: "One of the things we all knew was Joyce ruled. He wanted an earlier end of the day to be home with Joyce. Their bond, his pride in his children was a source of strength."

But when asked why he had decided to run, Pelosi recalled, "He and some other members decided he should do so. It was based on his position on Iraq. He thought in a leadership position he would have a higher platform to speak about the war. I supported him and supported that agenda for him. I was... I don't want to say I was surprised, but I said, 'Do you really want to do this? You love what you do and you have so much power as Defense chairman. You'd have to give up your chair.' But he felt the message about Iraq was so important to the country."

Joyce Murtha said he had been asked from time to time if he would run for speaker or majority leader, and he turned it down every time. "He felt he could have more impact staying where he was, as chairman of Defense Appropriations. One day we were talking, and he said he wasn't interested in majority leader, and I said, 'Well, it would help Nancy (Pelosi),'" she recalled. "A few days later, he announced he was running. He did it because he felt that Nancy needed him.... There was the perception that she's far too liberal.'"

Congressman Mike Doyle of Pittsburgh, the other close Murtha lieutenant, noted that Steny Hoyer already provided balance as a "new Democrat, the businessman's Democrat."

"Jack was more of the blue-collar Democrat. Who's representing the Western Pennsylvania type of Democrats, the socially conservative Democrats? Those Democrats were not represented. But there was something else going on there (between Murtha and Steny Hoyer)," Doyle said.

While almost everyone close to Murtha knew that he had clashed with Hoyer, none seemed to know exactly what had transpired. Some said their differences went way back, but only a few could trace their differences back to the contemplated coup against O'Neill when Murtha was an O'Neill lieutenant.

O'Neill had become speaker in 1977. Hoyer first got elected to Congress in 1978. Hoyer hooked up with then-Congressman Richard A. Gephardt of Missouri in 1982. They were plotting to oust O'Neill, when Murtha identified the members of the group and O'Neill summoned Gephardt before the plan was fully developed, forcing Gephardt to back off and pursue less ambitious goals, such as committee assignments and development of caucus positions.

The bad blood between Murtha and Hoyer became almost legend over time. Murtha played an instrumental role in helping Pelosi beat Hoyer for minority whip in 2001, a fierce insiders' battle that Pelosi won by only twenty-three votes. Hoyer got back into the House leadership a year later when Gephardt decided to leave Congress. Media often noted the contrast in style and constituencies between Pelosi, the liberal, and Hoyer, the pro-business moderate who, all observers agreed, was a prolific fundraiser for his party.

Media also loved to paint the contrast between the slender, "smooth operator" Hoyer and the burly, gruff Murtha during their fight for majority leader.

While Murtha suspended his campaign for majority leader in June 2006, he started hearing that Hoyer was still working on colleagues and leaning on any candidates who might soon, if elected, be faced with the choice between the two men.

Murtha recognized that he needed to work for votes, too, and quietly did some of his own campaigning, but he and Hoyer both focused far more energy on winning back the House for the Democrats as both men clearly understood that neither could win if their party did not win.

That November, when the nation had voted, and both the House and Senate had flipped from Republican to Democratic control, Hoyer wasted no time in taking off the gloves.

The Abscam tape, which after decades had resurfaced during Murtha's local election, made a cameo appearance in the leader campaign, with Murtha's friends and supporters in Congress needing to explain how Murtha had turned down the bribe offered by undercover FBI agents.

The media quoted watchdog groups such as Taxpayers for Common Sense, Democracy 21, and Citizens for Responsibility and Ethics in Washington, which accused Murtha of winning elections back home through earmarks to local businesses, raising money through a "pay to play" system in which lobbyists who contributed got earmarks for their clients, and having cozy relationships with former staffers and a brother who worked for a lobbying firm.

He was furious when his brother, Kit, took a job as a lobbyist, even though Kit lobbied in Harrisburg, not in Washington. When confronted by Jack Murtha, Kit Murtha shot back, "Hey, I need to make a living, too."

When Pelosi endorsed Murtha for leader, the president of Citizens for Responsibility and Ethics in Washington said, "How can Americans believe that the Democrats will return integrity to the House when Speaker Pelosi has endorsed an ethically challenged member for a leadership position? Representative Murtha is the wrong choice for this job."

Murtha adamantly refused to apologize for earmarks, citing numerous examples of how programs he had supported had saved lives, limbs, and money for the taxpayers. He was never charged for wrong-doing and later, in 2008, he was cleared in an ethics investigation of his fundraising tactics.

But in 2006, Murtha took a bad situation and made it worse when he did what he was becoming famous for doing: he made a flip remark to media that truly damaged his chances to beat Hoyer.

He said all the talk about ethics was "total crap."

Murtha went on *Hardball* to defend himself, telling Chris Matthews, "It is total crap that we have to deal with an issue like this (ethics) when we've got a war going on, and we got all these other issues."

Murtha said he was again being "swift-boated," emphasizing that Hoyer had continued to support "staying the course" in Iraq while talking about how he would change Congress.

Murtha also generated a letter to his Democratic colleagues, which would have made him a huge hero among the millions of Americans who have become disenchanted with the rancor that now defines Washington politics. Much of that letter, which also ran as an op-ed in a few local newspapers, follows:

> I hear people say more and more frequently that they are fed up with both sides and feel there should be more than two major parties. I believe this is because Americans expect that Republicans and Democrats will work together, not dig in their heels and refuse to work toward compromises when it is clearly urgent that we move forward and get something done.
>
> I think the American people are optimistic that their message has been received by both Democrats and Republicans in Washington and that the new Democratic leadership they've elected will not claim a "mandate" exclusive of the minority party, but that it will sincerely work to end the gridlock as well as the partisan rhetoric. The public wants us to put aside the rancor....
>
> Talk is cheap, which is why, up until Iraq forced me to, I didn't do a lot of it. But empty rhetoric is expensive. It has cost America three years in a failed war and nearly three thousand lives lost, and will cost us a trillion dollars by the

time we can extricate ourselves from it.

Empty rhetoric has cost us years of lost time in finding a solution to our dependence on foreign oil, at a price tag that is nearly impossible to guess, but surely in the hundreds of billions of dollars.

And it cost us the loss of an institutional understanding in this body (Congress) that your word is your word, that you mean what you say and say what you mean, and that there is a line of honesty, civility, statesmanship and basic decency and respect for your fellow American that you will not cross. That the political end does not justify assassinating one's character or willfully misrepresenting or sugar-coating the facts. And that when you say you're going to do something, you don't just talk about it to give the impression you're doing something: you do it.

That's what it will take to restore the credibility of this institution in the eyes of the American people. And that is priceless. And it is what I intend to help to bring back to this institution: civility; credibility; respect for each other and the offices we hold; and, most importantly, hard work, compromise and results.

Murtha acknowledged that this would be difficult at times, but insisted, "We must set a new standard for leadership in this Congress because Americans are watching and we must lead by example. That is the tone I hope to set as majority leader in the U.S. House."

Perhaps no one in Congress read Murtha's letter.

On November 16, 2006, just one day shy of a year after his call for re-deployment, Murtha went down to a dismal defeat by a vote of 109 to 86. He graciously agreed to come out before the national media, stand behind Pelosi, Hoyer, and others in the new majority leadership, and, despite what most would describe as a scowl, say humble things about how the battle was over and Democrats were uniting for the good of the country.

Hoyer was also gracious, saying, "In my opinion, it was not that somebody was rejected today, it was that a team that had been successful was asked to continue to do that job on behalf of the American people."

In the end, some of the people closest to Murtha said that, in his heart, he did not want to be majority leader.

"Jack never really wanted to be majority leader," Joyce said. "He would have been uncomfortable in that role. But he realized that making that announcement and carrying it through would help the Democrats. Later, I asked him if he wasn't glad he lost. He said, 'Absolutely! I would have been miserable in that position, and I would have had to give up my chairmanship of the Defense Subcommittee, where I can do the most good.'"

He never campaigned for himself the way he had campaigned for Pelosi, Congressman John Larson of Connecticut, or others who had gotten into the leadership with Murtha's help. One close associate said, "It was frustrating. Jack had a hard time asking for things for himself. He did so much for everybody else, but.... People would tell him, 'I'm with you Jack,' or 'You're my guy Jack,' but until they say, "I'll vote for you...."

Another, asking not to be identified because of the sensitivity, frankly said that Murtha had offended and alienated some members of Congress over the years. "He was certainly respected and admired, but at same time, he was sometimes gruff and had no patience for people. I've seen him in action on the (House) floor where he ripped (members) apart.... The results were not surprising to me. The power of helping people on the defense bill is one thing, but it's not everything."

Both the media and those close to him said he had been hurt most by the ethics issues, especially when he called ethics "total crap," and by the perception that he was "an old style politician."

The day after Murtha lost, a column appeared that articulated a tack Murtha might have used in fighting back. John Nichols, in his "Online Beat" column for the *Nation* magazine, referred to the address of many lobbying firms when he wrote, "Of course, House Democrats made a mistake in choosing the slick favorite of Washington special interests, Steny Hoyer, over shambling populist John Murtha to serve as House majority leader. In one of the more ridiculous exercises of journalistic irresponsibility by a Washington press corps that is distinguished by nothing so much as its ineptness when it comes to offering useful perspective to the American people, Murtha was dismissed as an ethically-challenged mess of a man while Hoyer, the candidate of K Street, was presented as the tidier Democrat."

The column called Hoyer "the embodiment of everything that is wrong with the insider Democrats of Washington."

Murtha's staff wanted to write an op-ed for newspapers and post excerpts from that column on his web site. Murtha said no, perhaps because he was often criticized for the campaign support he received from people in the defense industry and their lobbyists.

But Murtha also knew that posting that column would not have been the civil thing to do. It was time for Congress to stop with the rancor, get down to work, and produce some results.

Chapter 23

Race and Rock Ridge

On April 20, 2008, with only two days remaining in the tight primary campaign, 1,500 people packed the gymnasium at Greater Johnstown High School to hear Senator Hillary Rodham Clinton pledge to fight for the middle class.

"I'm offering leadership that you and your families can count on," Clinton proclaimed to the enthusiastic crowd.

She was flanked by Pennsylvania Governor Ed Rendell and Congressman John P. Murtha, who had just introduced her as "the next president of the United States."

Although Murtha would prove to be wrong on that prediction, he had become a strong supporter of Clinton, whom he felt would do more for the working-class folks who called Southwestern Pennsylvania home. Murtha had worked with her husband when Bill Clinton was president, as well as many of Hillary Clinton's current advisors who previously had worked for President Clinton. So Murtha also knew that he would have easy access to the White House if she won.

While in town, she sat down with the editorial board of the local newspaper, the *Johnstown Tribune-Democrat*, and told them Murtha had been "extremely helpful, especially on military and national defense matters."

"I hope that Congressman Murtha's very strong support sends a clear message," she said.

On Iraq, Clinton echoed Murtha in saying, "There is no military solution. The future of Iraq is up to the Iraqis." She said she agreed with Murtha that U.S. troops should be withdrawn, pledging to begin bringing them home within two months of taking office.

Some people had spoken against the war from the beginning, but Hillary was not among them. Earlier, she had backed the resolution to go to war and continued to oppose withdrawal without clearly defining her position until late in the campaign.

The fact that Murtha endorsed Clinton, not Barack Obama, says something about his tendency to form an overall view and not react in a knee-jerk fashion on any single issue. Of course, she had come around on Iraq, so the three of them did not differ that much by the time of the Pennsylvania primary. But earlier, Murtha had expressed frustration that she was not taking his advice and continued to support the war. He said he would stay neutral in the presidential race, but finally, barely a month before the state's primary, he endorsed Clinton.

Being slow to change her position as the war became increasingly unpopular, she lost the front-runner position for the Democratic nomination and was open to charges of waffling, especially by those who still supported the war. Although Obama was now the clear front-runner nationally, with endorsements from Murtha and Governor Rendell, Clinton led in the Pennsylvania polls until late in the campaign.

Obama was dynamic and young, and his message of hope and change struck a chord that reverberated especially with younger voters. With a big lead from the earlier primaries and caucuses, when Obama beat Clinton in the working-class state of Pennsylvania, her campaign was basically over.

Murtha later told a local reporter he felt that if Clinton had followed his lead when he called for redeployment on November 17, 2005, things might have been different for her presidential hopes.

"She is a fine leader and great politician, but most people had come to agree with what I was saying," he said. "Either we were misled or followed bad information; it doesn't matter. We were fighting a war that had been discredited, and the way we were fighting it was getting us nowhere. Now I think if she had said she was misled or even regretted the vote, the gain for her would have been bigger than any jump Obama would have gotten out of her admission. The primary ended so close, I think that would have been enough for her to get over the top."

The Iraq war played a role in the Republican primaries, too.

Only six House Republicans had voted against the war resolution in 2002. One of them ran for president, but his campaign never got traction. Congressman Ron Paul of Texas had voted "no" and railed against the war at every turn. Part populist, part libertarian, Paul was dismissed by his own party. Less than a month after Murtha's call for redeployment, he welcomed the new debate when he spoke on the House floor on December 7, 2005.

"The recent debate over Iraq shows the parties are now looking for someone to blame for the mess we're in. It's a high stakes political game," he said before apparently referring to Murtha:

"The argument in Washington is over tactics, quality of intelligence, war management, and diplomacy, except for the few who admit that tragic mistakes were made and now sincerely want to establish a new course for Iraq. Thank goodness for those who are willing to reassess and admit to these mistakes. Those of us who have opposed the war all along welcome them to the cause of peace."

Noting that sixty-three percent of Americans now disapproved of the handling of the war, and fifty-two percent said it was time to bring the troops home, Paul turned to a highly suspect excuse for remaining in Iraq:

"We hear constantly that we must continue the fight in Iraq, and possibly in Iran and Syria, because, 'It's better to fight the terrorists over there than here.' Merely repeating this justification, if it is based on a major analytical error, cannot make it so. All evidence shows that our presence in Iraq, Saudi Arabia, and other Muslim countries benefits al Qaeda in its recruiting efforts, especially in its search for suicide terrorists.... It is a serious error to conclude that 'fighting them over there' keeps them from fighting us 'over here,' or that we're winning the war against terrorism. As long as our occupation continues, and American forces continue killing Muslims, the incentive to attack us will grow. It shouldn't be hard to understand that the responsibility for violence in Iraq, even violence between Iraqis, is blamed on our occupation. It is more accurate to say, 'The longer we fight them over there, the longer we will be threatened over here.'"

Paul concluded, "False patriotism is used to embarrass the good-hearted into succumbing to the wishes of the financial and other special interests who agitate for war. War reflects the weakness of a civilization that refuses to offer peace as an alternative.... A policy that endorses peace over war, trade over sanctions, courtesy over arrogance, and liberty over coercion is in the tradition of the American Constitution and American idealism. It deserves consideration."

In the final presidential debate between Obama and McCain, one of McCain's shining moments came when he told Obama that he was not George Bush, that if Obama wanted to run against George Bush, he should have run four years ago. It was a good line, but in retrospect, if the best way to get elected was to not be George Bush, then Ron Paul was the best Republican candidate when the primaries started, especially in terms of Iraq, which was driving the election at the time.

Paul's internet fundraising success was a big clue that Iraq could not be ignored. Paul was the only Republican presidential candidate against the war, and when he raised nearly six million dollars in a single day and four million dollars on another day over the internet, people noticed.

Ron Paul never became a serious Republican contender, but this kind of grass roots cash meant there were a lot of everyday folks who liked what he said. Paul had much more to say than just get out of Iraq, but his "no" to war did attract many people.

In the end, without knowing why, Republicans did choose the guy they thought was the least like George Bush, although the traditional conservative base found it a hard swallow.

Before Murtha, Ron Paul's words were more easily dismissed. Once debate took flight, however, such views were seen as more statesman-like. Those who earlier had railed against the war were now taken more seriously.

McCain had not railed against the war, but had done the next best thing in saying the war was right, but was being handled poorly. Murtha enabled him to ramp up his criticism without appearing to be slamming the president, which could have left him on the sidelines with Ron Paul.

Paul's line that "false patriotism is being used to embarrass the good hearted" captures the essence of what went wrong in America. Those who disagreed on the war itself or how to handle the war were afraid to argue with the White House, which had wrapped itself in the American Flag and painted its position as patriotic. Any other position by definition was unpatriotic.

Murtha gave people the courage to speak, regardless of whether they wanted us to get out or wanted us to go all in.

In the dying days of his presidential campaign, McCain pushed hard on the idea that he was not George Bush. Many political commentators said he should have done that sooner, arguably long before he was officially a candidate. McCain or any other Republican who wanted the White House could have confronted Bush, as Murtha had – if not by calling for redeployment, then by urging a new wave of warriors, a surge, which was actually Murtha's first plea.

When Bush finally decided to increase troop levels in 2007, the improvement in Iraq was simply too little, too late for McCain's political aspirations. By then, the American people had come to agree with Murtha that it was time to get out.

Ironically, while Obama handily beat McCain, Murtha found himself in a dogfight.

Lieutenant Colonel Bill Russell, who had never lived in Pennsylvania's 12th District, chose Johnstown as his new home so he could run for the Republican nomination for Congress.

Russell at first was removed from the ballot when some prominent business leaders, understanding the value of Murtha's power, challenged his nomination petition. Russell failed to get enough legitimate signatures and was removed from the primary ballot but, with some supportive locals, organized a write-in campaign in the primary to win the nomination to challenge Murtha in the general election.

The local leaders who helped knock Russell off the ballot were a bipartisan group, hardly a surprise since Murtha had always received strong Republican support in the district. He was pro-life, pro-gun, and strong on the military. When the district was reconfigured in 2002 and he faced another Democrat in the primary, an organized effort was made to get Republicans to switch their registration to Democrat. Murtha won easily.

Russell's message was more of the same Haditha material used by Diana Irey, although he wore a shirt that had a star on the heart for a quasi-military look and labeled his campaign the Russell Brigade. Murtha did not take the challenge seriously at first, and most likely would not have needed to at all, if not for his own words.

The knock on Russell was that he was not from the 12th District. Murtha's people claimed he had been handpicked by Karl Rove to challenge Murtha, perhaps just to keep beating on the man who had challenged the president's Iraq war. There were questions about whether Russell actually moved to Johnstown. His wife and kids did not move there with him at first. He still owned his home in Virginia, and his business was in Virginia.

To Murtha supporters, the only thing Russell did in Johnstown was run against Jack Murtha and buy gas for the drive home. Murtha often referred to him as a carpetbagger, and the running joke was that when Russell had to buy groceries, he needed a GPS to get home from the market.

Russell said he had chosen the region as his home after a lifetime of military service, that his wife and kids eventually did move to the area, and that he had the receipt for the private school that his kids attended.

In the grand scheme of things, the geography was a small point. Obviously he had come to run against Murtha, and the rules allowed him to do so if he had lived in the state long enough prior to the election.

As the campaign unfolded, some veterans remained angry at Murtha for his Haditha comments, which they felt had turned Iraqis against the United States and were prejudicial. So he lost a slice of his political base, but he had lost those voters two years ago against Irey.

One difference in 2008 was that Russell was able to raise money. He raised far more money than Murtha had anticipated by targeting right-wing radio and television programs to get many small donations from across the country.

However, what made this a race was, well, race. In an interview with the *Pittsburgh Post-Gazette* about Obama's chances of winning Pennsylvania, Murtha said, "There's no question Western Pennsylvania is a racist area," although he still thought Obama would win.

Many in the area were offended, and the national media seized on the words because this was Jack Murtha who, thanks to his call for redeployment, was now a national figure. *Saturday Night Live* lampooned him in a skit with its Joe Biden character making repeated offensive comments.

Russell suddenly had some traction, and a poll published in the *Pittsburgh Tribune-Review* showed Murtha leading by a mere three percentage points, which was within the margin of error. That brought an influx of cash from the right wing, who were frothing at the mouth over the potential to take out the unsinkable Jack Murtha.

Despite the flap, consider the context. Political guru Jim Carville was running a U.S. Senate campaign several years earlier in which he reviewed extensive polling data about the attitudes of Pennsylvanians. Carville described the state as "Philadelphia and Pittsburgh with Alabama in between" as a way of noting the drastic difference in attitudes between the urban populations of the big cities and the rural population in "the T" between the cities. When Carville said people in "the T" were Alabama, he was not saying that they ate grits and cheered for the Crimson Tide. Although political analysts and media have tossed around Carville's description for years, no one had the courage to say publicly what exactly that meant. Nobody, that is, except Murtha.

The Bradley effect was also a hot topic. Tom Bradley, the Los Angeles mayor who ran for California Governor, was ahead in the polls, but when people actually were protected by the privacy of the voting booth, some of them just could not bring themselves to vote for a black man. In 2008, media and pundits were debating how the Bradley effect would play out in Pennsylvania. The McCain campaign was betting on the Bradley effect by pumping millions of dollars into Pennsylvania for its last stand, despite trailing in the polls by double digits. Was the McCain campaign in effect calling the state racist?

Murtha made his comment about racism about two days after a rally in Johnstown for Republican vice presidential candidate Sarah Palin. A man came to the rally with a stuffed monkey with an Obama sticker on its head and people around him cheered and laughed. The embarrassing episode immediately hit You-Tube.

The morning after Murtha called the area racist, concerned about the fallout, he asked a few supporters how they thought he should handle it. One advisor recommended that he say nothing about his comment but instead turn the issue on Palin by giving the media the You-Tube link and saying, "When the person with the monkey doll and everyone who's cheering him come out and apologize for their racist behavior, then I'll apologize, too."

Instead, Murtha immediately issued an apology and told media he had meant to say the area was "redneck." Oops. Talk about making a bad situation worse. Even many avid, long-time Murtha supporters began to question if he was getting too old and "losing it."

But Murtha immediately raised a lot of money and focused his message on jobs. He also mobilized a major army: locals who understood his clout, people from other areas who backed his war policy, and political friends who brought in their friends. For instance, Congressman Brady bused in people from Philadelphia. They literally look the campaign to the streets with an army of volunteers.

Murtha won with fifty-eight percent of the vote and Obama won Pennsylvania, but McCain actually carried a small margin of victory within the 12th District.

Overall, the Bradley effect seemed to have been marginal, and perhaps a more enlightened version of the Bradley effect was what might be called "Rock Ridge Syndrome."

Rock Ridge is the old western town in the outrageous, satirical Mel Brooks movie *Blazing Saddles*. A corrupt government official looking to chase residents away and buy land for a railroad picks a black man as sheriff. Sheriff Bart embraces his new job and actually thinks he can win over the town's people. In an early scene, Bart tips his hat to an elderly woman who promptly says, "Up yours" followed by the politically incorrect "N" word. Later, after the sheriff had rid the town of a huge and nearly unstoppable bad guy named Mongo, that same little old lady arrives at the back window of the sheriff's office with an apple pie and apologies for her earlier "Up yours." Bart graciously accepts, closes the window blind, and smiles, thinking he has started to win over the very white Rock Ridge. A second tap on the window, and the little old lady looks humbly at Sheriff Bart and says, "Of course, you'll have the good taste not to mention that we spoke."

That is the Rock Ridge Syndrome. Instead of people wanting to not appear racist and then voting in a racist way, some people did not want to publicly support Obama, but voted for him privately.

After Murtha's comment on racism, many locals whispered, "Murtha should not have said that. He is right, but he should not have said it." Most people in the region knew Murtha was not talking about everyone, and they knew, too, that he was right about racism existing.

Most people who were upset were upset because the poorly chosen words made the entire region look bad.

Russell seized on the moment. He received a huge influx of campaign cash and pounded the airways relentlessly with television commercials that replayed Murtha's comment about racism several times in a row. He continued to criticize Murtha on Haditha.

Then he made his own stumble. In an interview with the *Altoona Mirror*, Russell said people in Johnstown were not qualified for the jobs at the National Drug Intelligence Center, which Murtha was instrumental in bringing there. This did not create a huge firestorm, but it did highlight an issue that eventually would help Murtha whip Russell in the election.

All the talk about Haditha, Russell's real home, or race mattered little when the real deal here for many years had been jobs. Some PAC money was dumped into local radio slamming Murtha for pork-barrel projects, but an outsider's pork is a local's bacon. Locals understood that getting rid of Murtha meant surrendering influence for the area, and meant jobs and money that would have come home then would go elsewhere.

Murtha always knew that all politics is local. He barely addressed the race issue once he fired up his campaign and focused on the jobs issue.

His strength among his constituents gave him solid ground to stand on when challenging the president's handling of the war. He figured soldiers like Russell would be sent after him politically, but he knew he needed to alter the course of Iraq and was confident that his district had his back.

After the election, Russell never called to congratulate Murtha, refusing to make any sort of concession. He said he was going to run again because he felt Murtha was "vulnerable."

Two years later, when Murtha died, Russell was deserted by the Republican Party, which endorsed another candidate to replace Murtha. Ultimately, Murtha's former district director, Mark Critz, was elected to succeed him.

Perhaps the biggest irony of Russell's campaign against Murtha was his slogan, "Join the Russell Brigade." The slogan had a vaguely familiar ring to many people, but very few knew that it had come from 1862, when Robert Milton Russell was a Colonel in the Confederate Army leading the South at Shiloh, Tennessee, the deadliest battle in American history at the time. On the battle's first day, the South nearly crushed General Grant's northern forces, but the tide turned on the second day. If the "Russell Brigade" and the South would have won at Shiloh, being a racist might still be legal.

That point never became part of the 2008 campaign. But the campaign signs for the man attacking Murtha for his comment on racists actually were celebrating a cog in the military machine of the

Confederate States that fought to preserve a man's right to own other men.

The inescapable irony: in a year when the United States would elect its first black president, a Pennsylvania congressman who had made the mistake of acknowledging racism existed was challenged by a white guy from Virginia, whose campaign slogan referred to a battle to save slavery and divide the United States of America.

Chapter 24

The Soul of America

On February 6, 2010, as he lay comatose in a hospital in Arlington, Virginia, John Patrick Murtha Jr. became the longest-serving member of Congress from Pennsylvania in the nation's history, with thirty-six years. He died two days later.

The next day, as his widow, Joyce, contemplated the funeral arrangements, the phone rang. President Barack Obama offered his condolences. Jack Murtha was a great man and he would be missed, the president told her. Joyce had not even hung up the phone when there was a knock at the door. The garbage men picking up the trash felt compelled to stop and express their condolences. Jack Murtha was a great man and he would be missed. Murtha's sudden and untimely death, caused by complications from gall bladder surgery, touched all sorts of people from all walks of life, from all socioeconomic strata.

On February 16, Murtha was laid to rest in the city that he had long called home, Johnstown, Pennsylvania.

A blizzard had hit Johnstown during the two days of public viewing, creating challenges for the many members of Congress, dignitaries, friends, and even total strangers who felt compelled to come and pay their respects. The day of the funeral was one of the coldest days of that winter, with howling winds and blowing snow accentuating the cold emptiness felt by those who watched as the casket, draped in an American Flag, was carried into the church while Marines stood at attention, saluting.

Murtha was buried with full honors from the Marine Corps. Fifteen members of the Pennsylvania Congressional delegation served as honorary pall bearers. More than fifty members of Congress came from all over the country: Democrats Charlie Rangel of New York, Gene Taylor of Mississippi, Norm Dicks of Washington State, Patrick Kennedy of Rhode Island, and Silvestre Reyes of Texas. Some Republicans came, too, most notably Bill Young of Florida, the ranking member of the Defense Appropriations Subcommittee.

Former President Bill Clinton attended the funeral and, even though he did not speak during the service, his presence spoke volumes about the respect with which Murtha was held.

The funeral service had only three featured eulogists, a simple but elegant service befitting the style of Joyce Murtha. The Murthas' daughter, Donna Murtha, offered personal reflections on how much he had loved watching the birds and deer in the back yard, and how he worked to outwit the squirrels and keep them from getting into his bird feeder. Marine Corps Commandant James Conway recalled comments from Murtha's fitness reports during Vietnam, which said he was "forceful and energetic," and he was "at his best when in the field with his Marines."

In her eulogy, Speaker Nancy Pelosi talked about how Murtha had always welcomed new members, offered them advice, and talked about the great institution that is the United States Congress.

"Patriot. Champion. Hero. Giant. Jack Murtha: we will never see his like again." With those words, Pelosi ended her remarks.

After the service, U.S. Senator Robert P. Casey Jr. of Pennsylvania reflected on how Murtha had worked with his father back when the elder Casey was Pennsylvania governor. "They were both fighters for the people who sometimes don't have a voice," he said.

Pelosi, in an interview for this book, said Murtha had bridged two eras. "He was tied to the past with Tip O'Neill and tied to the future with the guidance he's given to new members of Congress.... He combined old school with new school, the spirit of bipartisanship he brought. He had served in a time when that was the way things had happened here, and he was able to carry it on because of the friendships he had" with both Democrats and Republicans, she said.

Murtha's old friend, Chris Matthews, summed up Murtha's legacy in simple terms:

"The statutes don't make government work. They're nice statutes but they don't do anything. They guide you, but they're just there. It's the living people that make democracy and our government work."

Jack Murtha was one of those rare individuals who knew how to make democracy work. He was one man who made a difference.

He was intense, and that intensity at times caused him to erupt, building his reputation as being gruff. But he had a passion for people: for the people of his district, especially the workers and those struggling to find work; for older people who struggled with failing health and fixed incomes; for the people with cancer, heart disease, diabetes, brain injury, and other ailments that received research funding through the earmarks for which he was so routinely criticized; for the people who served in the military, who were indeed like extended family to him.

He was a voracious reader and often, when he really liked a book, he bought a case or more to pass out as gifts.

Murtha in many ways was a simple man. Hot dogs and macaroni and cheese were among his favorite meals. He almost totally avoided alcohol, and although his team debated whether he knew that the Irish coffees he enjoyed during flight re-fueling at Shannon Air Base contained Irish whiskey, Joyce said, "Oh, he knew!" He loved nature, a reflection of his summers in the woods in West Virginia and the influence of his mother, whose abuse had prompted an altercation between the teenaged Murtha and his father, who then deserted the family again.

Perhaps those secrets of that past were what had made him an intensely private man. But he was not private about his love for his country and his love for people in the military, who made such sacrifices to keep this country free. And he was not private about his love for the institution of Congress.

Those who have lived through the ugliness of politics over the last twenty years or so have, no doubt, made up their minds about Jack Murtha. Some love him, some hate him. This book was never intended to change anyone's mind.

Politics has always had fits of anger, but it seems in the past when campaigns stopped, governing began, and political debate gave way to discussion and compromise. That is certainly the way it worked back when Jack Murtha came to Congress. In the years leading up to Murtha's stand on November 17, 2005, the campaigns never stopped, which means that in many ways the governing never began. Somewhere along the way, many of our nation's leaders have gotten caught up in political gamesmanship, and the game too often is played at all times on all issues and apparently at all costs.

Murtha's call for redeployment was a watershed moment for our nation, and not because he was right about Iraq. It was a defining moment because he willingly took political fire and public scorn over his use of voice and because he inspired so many others to speak as well. Some spoke for, some against, but all spoke out loud, all with value, all no longer afraid of being branded as unpatriotic for speaking out.

When Murtha was presented the Profile in Courage Award in 2006, the late Senator Edward Kennedy of Massachusetts recalled how Murtha had been accused of surrendering to the terrorists and endorsing the policies of Michael Moore and the extreme left.

"It was a familiar response from an administration with a pathological aversion to thoughtful criticism – or any criticism for that matter – of its policy on Iraq," Kennedy said.

At first, many waged war on the messenger and, even now, many people remain more focused on destroying the man and his reputation than on arguing against his points.

Soon after his death, Navy Secretary Ray Mabus announced that the next amphibious transport dock ship would be named the USS *John P. Murtha* (LPD-26) in his honor, and three Facebook sites sprung up opposing that decision. In December 2011, the *New York Times* found documents about the Haditha incident and other classified information were being burned by a junkyard attendant, and reported that those documents "confirmed much of what happened in Haditha." That report brought out news commentary that mentioned Murtha, which brought out the attack squad – nearly two years after Murtha's death – to once again slam the man in an op-ed column in the Johnstown newspaper.

While perhaps some may never change, perhaps, on the whole, our nation has changed, and hopefully for the better.

Which patriot first said out loud that America should be its own nation? Who was the first American to give voice to the notion that slavery was wrong, or women should vote, or children should not work eighteen-hour days in dangerous factories? Who gave voice to the idea that there are things we should not do to our environment or things that a man cannot do to a woman just because she is his wife?

The history books will give credit to certain individuals who led movements and changed America for the better. But surely the first time someone said America should be a free and sovereign land was not a politician on a stump in front of a crowd. The first time someone spoke of such freedom, it was one friend to another and then another. When the idea had taken hold, some brave soul had to face the threat of retribution and climb upon that stump and boldly declare what so many had said privately to see if there were even more who felt that way, yet did not have the courage to give voice to the dangerous new idea.

Jack Murtha did not invent the idea that, as a nation, we had mishandled the war in Iraq. He was hearing it from military leaders who were not allowed to speak out. In his own district, as in the rest of the nation, the idea was fomenting in talk between mothers, between brother and sister, father and son, neighbors and friends, students and mill workers. But the idea needed someone to climb up on the stump. In some cases, people felt the administration was wrong to begin with; in others, right in their action, but wrong in the execution. But the nasty tone with which people were branded as unpatriotic cowards had made cowards of all. The constant state of campaigning, rather than the traditional break for governing, had created a stifling silence.

Many of our leaders in Washington still hold to those rules of engagement that had silenced America from 2001 through 2005: attack, attack, and keep on attacking anyone who disagrees.

When campaigning for control of Congress in 2006, Murtha often said, "We're fighting for the soul of America." Many people took that as a comment on the war, but it was more of comment about the tone of America's political discourse.

With Murtha's passing and the war in Iraq turned over to the Iraqis, we as a nation are far from fixed.

But more and more people are speaking out against the nasty tone of politics, the ruthless branding of people, the bumper-sticker approach to looking at complex issues, and the thoughtless, relentless, attack-and-destroy attitude toward all those who oppose our ideas. This will, of course, encourage more voices, some agreeing, some disagreeing on any particular issue, but most well-intentioned and recognizing the need to return civility to our national debates. Free and open debate is arguably the most fundamental pillar of our democracy, which is our strength as a nation.

One does not need to like Jack Murtha to agree that his voice, while perhaps not speaking for us all, provides a beacon for us all. Murtha helped, not by his opinion on Iraq, but by his willingness to speak that opinion despite the attacks, which, in turn, empowered others to do the same.

Murtha warned Bush and Cheney that our commercial airlines could be used as weapons against us months before 9/11. His voice was not heard. He warned that we had greatly miscalculated the challenge we faced in Iraq once the battle was underway and that we needed more troops years before a surge actually happened. His voice was not heard.

He warned that conditions in Iraq had made our military the targets of both sides in the civil war, that repeated tours in Iraq were wearing out our military equipment and our military people, and that bad things could happen when those in uniform were pushed beyond their training and endurance.

Eventually, this patriot had no choice but to speak out publicly and face the nastiness and name-calling. Only someone who had been such a hawk and who worked so diligently behind the scenes; who had the political capital of a decorated war veteran; who had the backing of a district that saw the value of his work for them; who had supported past presidents of the opposite party in military actions; who never once said, "I told you so," despite his warnings that our airplanes would be used against us on American soil. Only such a person could have climbed up on the stump, spoke the truth, and faced the consequences in such a hate-driven time in American politics.

Murtha was viciously attacked, needed to defend himself, and yet stood up repeatedly, despite the ongoing personal and political attacks, to make his case in a heated political time. That context enabled many to claim that he had become just another politician and was not a statesman. But in taking such a stand, Murtha defined statesmanship.

Imagine if the day had never come when America changed course in Iraq, that the day had never come when meaningful debate on such a monumentally important issue was allowed in American politics. Imagine if the nation had remained frozen in a perpetual state of "false patriotism" and thus unable to ever challenge the decisions of a tiny few who held the highest positions of power. Imagine that the day had never come when someone said in public what so many had begun to say in private.

The Americans who came to love Jack Murtha only because he opposed the political leaders they hated are missing the point, too. Murtha's actions were not driven by the politics of hate. He altered the course of our nation for the better, despite knowing he would face such hate. He was driven by a lifetime of experience, years of frustration over sound advice ignored, and a sincere belief that there was a better way. Murtha did all this with what has always been America's most powerful weapon of change, voice.

Despite his many critics, it turned out there were indeed many more who agreed with Murtha and that his words were, in fact, trumpeting the voice of the masses. That is where the power comes from for the guy on the stump: his voice is echoing their voices.

One wonders how it was that we were all so afraid to speak? One wonders, have we as a nation learned anything, or will false patriotism and partisanship again leave us as a nation without a voice, as a nation that cannot talk at the next critical time in our history?

Jack Murtha tried desperately to get both sides of the aisle to come together and talk. He quietly made this case for years in Congress, both in his words and in his actions in working with Republicans. He argued this case first quietly and then publicly for eight years in the administration of George W. Bush. He argued this case to his fellow Democrats in his 2007 race for majority leader, which was largely about returning civility to the institution of Congress. He was a man who understood that statutes are not what make democracy work, people do. And that nothing works if people do not talk and treat each other with respect.

Jack Murtha embodied the mantra that had been given to him by his great-grandmother: One man can make a difference.

Jack Murtha clearly made a mark on world history: in changing our course in Iraq; in bringing down the Soviet Union by funding Stinger missiles and similar actions behind the scenes dealing with other international conflicts; in the appropriations he directed into supporting our military and veterans; in appropriations he directed into research on head injuries, pain management, cancer, and other ailments; and in his mentoring of and everyday dealings with other members of Congress and other national leaders.

Murtha also tried to make a difference in telling America and her political leaders that we need to return civility to our national discourse, that, in essence, "we need to talk."

In the end, Murtha's life presents an inescapable irony. This gruff old Marine was the only man tough enough to remain standing after taking all of the nastiness that Karl Rove and Company could heap on him. Yet this gruff old Marine, this tough son of a bitch, had a simple message: let's be civil and talk through our differences.

Perhaps in the end, this gruff old Marine's call for civility may be just too "old school" to be heard in the shrill and partisan "new school" of today's attack-and-destroy political arena. For the soul of America, let's hope not.

CPSIA information can be obtained at www.ICGtesting.com
Printed in the USA
BVOW032132290712

296460BV00001B/2/P